Experimental Ethics

Experimental Ethics

Toward an Empirical Moral Philosophy

Edited by

Christoph Luetge
Technische Universität München, Germany

Hannes Rusch
Justus Liebig University Giessen &Technische Universität München, Germany

and

Matthias Uhl
Technische Universität München, Germany

First published 2014 by
PALGRAVE MACMILLAN

Palgrave Macmillan in the UK is an imprint of Macmillan Publishers Limited,
registered in England, company number 785998, of Houndmills, Basingstoke,
Hampshire RG21 6XS.

Palgrave Macmillan in the US is a division of St Martin's Press LLC,
175 Fifth Avenue, New York, NY 10010.

Palgrave Macmillan is the global academic imprint of the above companies
and has companies and representatives throughout the world.

Palgrave® and Macmillan® are registered trademarks in the United States,
the United Kingdom, Europe and other countries

ISBN: 978–1–137–40979–9

This book is printed on paper suitable for recycling and made from fully
managed and sustained forest sources. Logging, pulping and manufacturing
processes are expected to conform to the environmental regulations of the
country of origin.

A catalogue record for this book is available from the British Library.

Library of Congress Cataloging-in-Publication Data

Luetge, Christoph.
    Experimental ethics : toward an empirical moral philosophy / Christoph
Luetge, Technische Universitat, Munchen, Germany, Hannes Rusch, Justus-
Liebig University, Giessen, Germany, Matthias Uhl, Technische Universitat,
Munchen, Germany.
    pages cm
    ISBN 978–1–137–40979–9
    1. Ethics – Research. I. Title.

BJ66.L88 2014
170—dc23   2014022092

Contents

List of Figures

List of Tables

Notes on Contributors

Fernando Aguiar: Research Fellow at the Institute for Advanced Social Studies (IESA-CSIC), Córdoba, Spain.

Kwame Anthony Appiah: Professor of Philosophy and Law, New York University, NY, USA.

Martin Bruder: Research Fellow, Department of Psychology/Zukunftskolleg, University of Konstanz.

Andreas Bunge: PhD Student, Philosophy, University of Nottingham, UK.

Brendan Caldwell: Research Assistant, Kenan Institute for Ethics, Duke University, Durham, NC, USA.

Daryl Cameron: Assistant Professor, Psychology Department, University of Iowa, USA.

Niklas Dworazik: Research Associate, Developmental and Cultural Psychology, University of Osnabrück.

Ulrich Frey: Postdoctoral Researcher, Philosophy, University of Giessen.

Antonio Gaitán: Lecturer, Philosophy, Universidad Carlos III, Madrid, Spain.

Alexander Lenger: Postdoctoral Researcher, Sociology, University of Freiburg i.B.

Christoph Luetge: Full Professor and Chair of Business Ethics, Technische Universität München.

Nikil Mukerji: Postdoctoral Researcher, Philosophy, LMU Munich.

Julian F. Müller: Research Associate, Business Ethics, TU München.

Ezio Di Nucci: Assistant Professor of Philosophy, University of Duisburg-Essen.

Blanca Rodríguez-López: Senior Lecturer, Philosophy, Universidad Complutense, Madrid, Spain.

Jacob Rosenthal: Supplementary Professor, Philosophy, University of Konstanz.

Hannes Rusch: Postdoctoral Researcher, Behavioral Economics & Business Ethics, JLU Giessen & TU München.

Jana Schaich Borg: Postdoctoral Research Associate, Psychiatry, Kenan Institute for Ethics, Duke University, Durham, NC, USA.

Eric Schwitzgebel: Professor of Philosophy, University of California, Riverside, CA, USA.

Walter Sinnott-Armstrong: Professor of Philosophy, Kenan Institute for Ethics, Duke University, Durham, NC, USA.

Alexander Skulmowski: Research Associate, E-Learning and New Media, TU Chemnitz.

Nina Strohminger: Postdoctoral Fellow, Kenan Institute for Ethics, Duke University, Durham, NC, USA.

Attila Tanyi: Lecturer, Department of Philosophy, University of Liverpool, and Research Fellow, Zukunftskolleg, University of Konstanz.

Matthias Uhl: Postdoctoral Researcher, Business Ethics, TU München.

Verena Wagner: Postdoctoral Researcher, Philosophy, University of Konstanz.

Stephan Wolf: Lecturer and Research Associate, Environmental Economics, University of Freiburg i.B.

1

Introduction: Toward an Empirical Moral Philosophy

Christoph Luetge, Matthias Uhl, and Hannes Rusch

Academic philosophy has experienced a major upheaval in the last decade. Venturous young philosophers, psychologists, and economists have begun to challenge the traditional stance that philosophy is an undertaking best pursued from the safety and calm of an arm-chair. Instead, they took the gloves off and tried to bring philosophical questions to the experimental laboratory.

To date, more than 500 works have been written which fall into the category of 'Experimental Philosophy' – see, for example, philpapers.org. Not all of them present actual experimental results, though. The very beginning of Experimental Philosophy was accompanied by a fierce debate about its general purpose, its methodology, and, most importantly, its significance for philosophical theorizing. And this debate is far from being settled.

With this volume we intend to set the stage for the development of a consistent theoretical framework for one of the branches of Experimental Philosophy: the empirical study of human moral reasoning, that is, Experimental Ethics.

To this end we invited contributions from philosophers, psychologists and cognitive scientists, economists, and sociologists active in this lively and growing field of research. We are convinced that their elaborate and substantiated works which constitute the main part of this volume will enable its readers to immerse themselves into Experimental Ethics' history, its current topics, its methodology, and the criticism it is subject to. We organized the volume accordingly:

Part I ('An Experimental Moral Philosophy?') provides a general introduction to Experimental Ethics and its recent history. Starting with K.A. Appiah's 2007 APA presidential address in which he outlines the general scope of Experimental Philosophy, C. Luetge then presents an overview of the chances, current problems, and potential limitations of Experimental Ethics. His chapter is followed by N. Dworazik's and H. Rusch's sketch of the history of empirical research on human moral reasoning.

Part II ('Applied Experimental Ethics: Case Studies') offers a sample of contemporary studies in Experimental Ethics. In his chapter, E. Schwitzgebel presents a review of his latest empirical efforts in tackling the question whether the study of moral philosophy is able to provoke changes in actual behavior using data on professional moral philosophers, that is, ethicists. The chapter by E. Di Nucci focus on one of the most prominent tools in recent experimental moral philosophy, the trolley cases, adding valuable insights to this strand of research. S. Wolf and A. Lenger and U. Frey, finally, present and discuss the results of their original studies on the democratic choice of distributive rules and value assignment in environmental ethics.

Part III ('On Methodology') is devoted to systematic discussions of methodological aspects of Experimental Ethics' tool-box. N. Strohminger et al. present a comprehensive review of recent work on the problem of eliciting implicit morality. Their review represents a promising step forward in overcoming the deficits of mere self-reports, which are the current gold-standard in Experimental Philosophy. In a similar vein, combining the available expertise from philosophy and cognitive science, M. Bruder and A. Tanyi propose a new set of methods for studying philosophically relevant intuitions. A. Bunge and A. Skulmowski, for their part, try to disentangle the pragmatic and the descriptive parts of research in Experimental Ethics and propose respective methodological improvements. Building on work in experimental economics, F. Aguiar et al., finally, devise experimental procedures for bringing Rawls' famous idea of 'reflective equilibrium' to the laboratory.

Part IV ('Critical Reflections'), then, takes a step back and presents critical discussions of experimental approaches to ethics. In his chapter, J. Rosenthal critically assesses the relevance of survey results for philosophical theorizing. N. Mukerji analyses the weaknesses of three common lines of argumentation against the relevance of empirical results for philosophical reasoning by invoking that all three make use of empirical assumptions themselves.

Part V ('Future Perspectives') concludes the volume with perspectives on possible coming developments of Experimental Ethics. Freely taking the idea of experimenting to a higher level, J.F. Müller devises the ambitious idea of large scale social experiments in political philosophy. Comparing the recent history of psychology and economics to

current developments in philosophy, H. Rusch, then, provides a historically informed view on the prospects of Experimental Philosophy itself.
Finally, we qualitatively summarize our contributors' personal views on
the current state of Experimental Ethics, which we asked them to report
in a brief and informal opinion poll.

As Experimental Ethics is still in its infancy, our readers should not
expect this volume to be able to deliver a systematic, didactically refined
textbook on the subject, though. Rather, we understand this book as
a snapshot of the current state of affairs in the empirically informed
philosophical study of human moral reasoning and decision making.
Readers will find that some of our authors hold opposing opinions. The
strongest of such tensions can probably be found between the chapters
by J. Rosenthal and N. Mukerji. However, we explicitly welcome these
contrasts as they exemplify the many challenges Experimental Ethics
still has to overcome.

All contributors of this volume agree, nevertheless, that an experimental approach to research questions traditionally deemed purely
philosophical was overdue. It is particularly the focus of this volume,
namely, the study of moral intuitions, justification, and decision making
as well as metaethical stances, that seems to provide fertile ground
for probing the capacity of empirical research in philosophy without
directly deriving norms from facts, to be sure.

We would like to stress one point in particular: In our view, because
of the natural relevance that research on decision making and actual
behavior have in its study, ethics should be regarded as a genuinely interdisciplinary enterprise. While traditional philosophers have contrived
a wealth of theories on how we could and should ethically evaluate
human behavior, Experimental Ethics has now successfully started to
investigate how close their descriptions of moral practices come to
what we actually do when we judge an action as 'right' or 'wrong',
how these judgments relate to our actions, and how both processes are
influenced by individual, situational, and cultural factors. It is plainly
mistaken, we think, to claim that ethics as a research program can be
pursued using only one single method – be it philosophical arm-chair
reflection or experimental work in the laboratory. Instead, we suggest
understanding Experimental Ethics as an interface of *all* methods appli-
cable in the study of moral reasoning and action. These include, but
are not limited to, philosophical theorizing, deontic logic, game theory,
surveys of moral attitudes, vignette studies, choice and behavioral
experiments including incentivized economic games, and, not least,
field and archive studies. Every method that promises new insights into

the proximate mechanisms and ultimate functions of human morality should be welcomed – notwithstanding the due critical reflection on each single method's scope and limitations.

With this volume, we hope, this endeavor is brought a small step further.

Acknowledgements

Some of our contributors took part in our 2012 workshop: 'The Scope and Limits of Experimental Ethics' at Konstanz University. We thank all participants of this workshop for lively and fruitful discussions. Furthermore, we would like to thank Palgrave Macmillan for very professional support, Wally Eichler for excellent administrative assistance, Peter Löscher for financial support, and Simone Schweizer for her help in editing the manuscripts.

Part I
Experimental Moral Philosophy?

2
Experimental Philosophy

Kwame Anthony Appiah

2.1

Some three score years ago, the Norwegian philosopher Arne Naess found himself dissatisfied with 'what are called "theories of truth" in philosophical literature'.[1] 'The discussion has already lasted some 2500 years', he wrote. 'The number of participants amounts to a thousand, and the number of articles and books devoted to the discussion is much greater.' In this great ocean of words, he went on, the philosophers had often made bold statements about what 'the man in the street' or 'Das Volk' or 'la conscience humaine' made of truth or Wahrheit or vérité. And Naess had a few simple questions about these claims (Naess, 1938, pp. 12–15): 'How do the philosophers know these things? What is the source of their knowledge? What have they done to arrive at it? ... their writings', he complained, 'contain almost nothing of this matter'.[2] And so Naess began the research that resulted in the publication in 1938 of his first book in English: *'Truth' as Conceived by Those Who Are Not Professional Philosophers*.

Naess's tone is one of irritated astonishment. 'Even superficial questioning of non-philosophers would make it almost impossible for anyone to believe that the philosophers writing about the opinion of ordinary people actually ask others than themselves. ... Have the philosophers any interest in writing on a subject capable of empirical treatment without knowing anything about it?' He proposed to do better. His study began by recovering what he called the 'verbal reactions', (Naess, 1938, pp. 17–18) both oral and written, of non-philosophers of varying 'degrees of philosophical virginity', (Naess, 1938, p. 45) to a series of questionnaires designed to elicit their views as to the 'common characteristics' of the things that were true. The subjects he called *ps*, the common characteristics c.c.s., and he referred to himself throughout as l (for Leader). Thousands of hours and 250 ps later, l was able to report on the 'fundamental formulations' in his subjects' answers to the question-naires about the c.c.s.

There are scores of distinct formulations ranging from (1) 'agreement with reality' to (98) 'that one is ready to defend the statement, to direct one's behavior according to it'. l patiently examines whether there are statistical correlations among these choices and the age, sex, class, or educational level of the ps (Naess, 1938, pp. 42–45). l also reproduces brief excerpts of some of his oral examinations, of which the first begins (Naess, 1938, p. 32):

l: What is the c.c. of that which is true?
p: –silence–
l: Have those things anything in common?
p: That is not certain.
l: Is it quite incidental, when you in some situations use the word 'true'?
p: It is probably founded on something or other.

It would be a serious project to establish what, among the portentous behaviorism of the talk of 'verbal reactions', the solemn abbrevia-tions of every technical term, the mock indignation of l's comments, and the splendid silliness of the interviews, would get the average Norwegian to crack a smile. I myself, as a sample of one, would report that the monograph is hilarious. It is worth re-examination – I am very grateful to Larry Hardin for drawing it to my attention – for this reason alone.

But Naess was making a serious point. It really is an interesting ques-tion how we should decide what ordinary people think 'truth' means. And it turns out that just asking them produces a vast and indigest-ible mess. What you have to do, as Naess showed, is to sort, interpret, and analyze what people say, and then reflect. Towards the end of the book Naess proposes a name for this enterprise (Naess, 1938, p. 161): 'The diversity and consistency of amateur theories of truth, point to the possibility of an "experimental philosophy".'

Naess went on to a distinguished philosophical career, writing about skepticism, applied semantics, and the history of philosophy; but his most influential contribution, as philosophers of the environment will be aware, was the invention of the notion of deep ecology, and he was a leader among Norway's environmental activists at a time when their ranks were thinner. (Aestheticians and others with an interest in music will surely know him as the uncle of Arne Naess Jr., who was for fifteen years the husband of Diana Ross.) But I'd like to talk today about the prospects of his suggestion – which was largely ignored outside Oslo – that it was time to take up experimental philosophy.

2.2

Or should I say: take it up again? Because it's a fair question to ask whether experimental philosophy is a matter of innovation or of restoration. In philosophy, perhaps more than any other discipline, we say what we are by telling stories about what we were: hence Naess's pointed reference to a 2500 year-old lineage. But most philosophers look back in ways that are quite unhistorical. We pick and choose among those who carried the label in the past without taking much notice of the people around them who also bore it, people whose work would not belong in our current stories of what we do. And we even pick and choose among the works of those we acknowledge as ancestors, as well. Newton and Locke were both called 'philosophers' in the English of their day, but we don't claim Newton; even though, in saying 'hypotheses non fingo', he was apparently announcing himself to be an anti-realist about gravitational theory. And we don't take much notice of many of Locke's contributions to the work of the Royal Society, either; even though he would no doubt have been simply puzzled by someone who said this was not philosophy.

There are reasons why we proceed this way, of course. Our contemporary ideas about what makes a question or an answer philosophically interesting are at work in these processes of editing out of the past the stories we choose to tell. Now, you might think that we could explain what philosophy is without telling these stories: that we could say what it is for a question to be philosophical, independently of these stories, and then explain that, in looking back, we are looking for past answers to the philosophical questions, and claiming as ancestors those whose answers were interesting or otherwise valuable contributions. I myself doubt that this sort of approach will do – I doubt the prospects of defining a trans-historical essence for philosophy and looking for the history of that essential subject back through the millennia. Disciplinary identities, so it seems to me, are like many other what you might call historical identities: to decide who is entitled to the label today you need a story about who had it yesterday; and whoever has it tomorrow will be continuing – with modifications – the projects of whoever has it today.

Ernest Renan, the great French historian and nationalist, made a similar point about *national* identities in his lecture *'Qu'est-ce qu'une nation?'* some 125 years ago. 'Forgetting', he wrote, 'and I would even say historical error, is an essential element in the creation of a nation, and that is why the progress of historical studies is often a danger for the nation itself' (Renan, 1882a, chapter 1, para. 7). What he meant was that the stories of the past that served the modern national identity needed to leave out certain things that had actually happened in order that they could hold the nation together. Perhaps something like this is true of our discipline as well; but we can hope that philosophers, unlike the French, can construct stories that do their work without falsifying the past. What we cannot hope for, certainly, is an unedited past, a story that forgets nothing. And in the editing we will be guided, willy-nilly, by our sense not only of where we are but also of where we need to go. As Renan also said: 'The Spartan song: "We are what you were; we will be what you are" is in its simplicity the abridged hymn of every country' (Renan, 1882b, chapter 3, para 1).

This is, mutatis mutandis, a truth about disciplines as well. The crafting of a disciplinary history matters, in part, because disciplinary identities are also contested (as I do not have to remind the members of the Eastern Division). In editing the past – even the very recent past – you foreground some contemporary questions and diminish the claim of others. Kant or Hegel? Frege or Husserl? Russell or Heidegger? Kripke or Derrida? But most pressingly, we seek, in our ancestry, the contour of an overarching identity that will distinguish us from our neighbors.

2.3

Consider, for example, just one of those neighbors: psychology. It's often said that psychology has a short history and a long past. Might the opposite be true of philosophy, taken as an endeavor that sits apart from the realms of empirical research? In a 1668 treatise called *Observations upon Experimental Philosophy*, Margaret Cavendish urged that 'the experimental part of philosophy' was not to be 'preferred before the speculative,' for 'most experiments have their rise from the speculative' (Cavendish, 2001, p. 44, p. 49).

Still, it's significant that, in those days, few of our canonical forebears confined themselves to the realm of unsullied abstraction. Descartes spent plenty of time with his hands inside freshly slaughtered cows, and his physiological findings were scarcely marginal to his thought; indeed, without the pineal – as the Danish anatomist Nicholas Steno pointed out in 1669 – Descartes has no story of how mind and body are functionally integrated (Descartes, 1988, p. 331). By the next century, the growing prestige of experimentation was apparent everywhere. The encyclopedist D'Alembert praised Locke for reducing metaphysics to what it should be: *la physique expérimentale de l'âme* – the experimental science of the spirit.[3] And Hume subtitled his great *Treatise of Human Nature*, as we do not sufficiently often recall, *Being an Attempt to Introduce the Experimental Method of Reasoning into Moral Subjects.*

Some have seen the epistemological preoccupations of modern philosophy presaged in the work of Thomas Reid, whose 'common sense' school looks like a forerunner to the past century's ordinary language philosophy. But Reid himself was emphatic in his suspicion of mere conjecture. Every real discovery, he says, is arrived at by 'patient observation, by accurate experiments, or by conclusions drawn by strict reasoning from observation and experiments, and such discoveries have always tended to refute, but not to confirm, the theories and hypotheses which ingenious men had invented' (Reid, 1822, pp. 367–368). And Kant, to whom we owe the analytic-synthetic distinction, worked avidly on both sides of the putative divide; Herder revered him mainly for his lectures in geography.

The point is not just that the canonical philosophers belong as much to the history of what we now call psychology as to the genealogy of philosophy. It's that you would have had a hard time explaining to them that this part of their work was *echt* philosophy and *that* part of their work was not. Trying to separate their 'metaphysical' from their psychological claims is, I fear, rather like trying to peel a raspberry.

And though we typically suppose that psychology calved off from philosophy, you can make a case that it was the other way around. The psychology labs at Harvard are in William James Hall because its inhabitants rightly think of James (who migrated from Harvard's physiology department to its philosophy department in 1881) as one of their ancestors, just as we contemporary philosophers claim him for ourselves. His colleague Josiah Royce was elected president of the American Psychological Association in 1902, and president of the American Philosophical Association in 1903. The common germline is visible in the history of our professional journals as well. When the philosophical quarterly *Mind* was founded in 1878, and for a couple of decades afterward, much of it was devoted to articles we would now consider to be psychology. Even in the years following the rise of experimental psychology, a habit of intimacy was presumed. *The Journal of Philosophy* was founded, in 1904, as *The Journal of Philosophy, Psychology,* and *Scientific Methods*.

Modern philosophy has its origins in a sort of self-exile: the powerful swerve away from psychologism that began in the latter half of the 19th century – here the touchstones are Bolzano, Frege, Husserl – and that culminated in the golden age of conceptual analysis... *and* also, I should add, of phenomenology. We know that experimentalists and pure speculators coexisted in the Harvard philosophy department until the mid-1930s, and, give or take a few years; you find a similar pattern at other universities. I was educated at Cambridge University, where the degree in philosophy had not long ago before been called the Moral Sciences Tripos, and experimental psychology was still one of the fields in which you could choose to be examined for that degree. To see when what we would recognize as philosophy departments came into existence, look to see when psychology departments came into existence.

Indeed, we should be hard-pressed to establish to everyone's satisfaction that we noble philosophers, and not those knavish psychologists, are the legitimate heirs to what mainly went under the name philosophy in previous eras. These slippery movements of group designations are familiar to all historians, not to mention any sports fan who has watched the Jets, who used to be the Titans, play the Titans, who used to be the Oilers.

2.4

So, as Renan might have asked: *Qu'est-ce qu'un philosophe?* In the heyday of analytic philosophy – the decades before and after the Second World War – the answer went like this. Philosophy is now what the best philosophy has always been: conceptual analysis. The claim about what philosophy had always been at its best was underwritten by some reference to Plato's *Theaetetus*, say, or Descartes' *Meditations*, each construed as attempts at analysis of the concept of 'knowledge'. From there you would proceed by identifying conceptual analysis with exploring meanings. Since meanings are what speakers know in understanding their language, any speaker of a language knows already, without looking beyond her own linguistic competence, what she needs to know to do the analysis. Philosophical claims – knowledge is justified true belief, say – are true (*if* true) in virtue of the meanings of the words they contain. This way of doing philosophy presupposed, obviously, theories about concept possession and knowledge of language.

'Conceptual analysis' was the examination not of just any old concepts but of the important ones; most of these were familiar from the earlier history of philosophy. They were to be explored in an essentially a priori way. The older conceptual analysts would have agreed with Timothy Williamson, when he said in his presidential address to the Aristotelian Society a few years ago, 'If anything can be pursued in an armchair, philosophy can' (Williamson, 2005, p. 123). You considered, then, not how things *are* but how we think about them, more or less *however* they are; and the only access you really had to how we *think* was to notice some of the patterns in what we do and don't *say*.

Though the 'we' here was meant to be all those who had a native-speaker's grasp of the language, the actual conversations were naturally discussions among philosophers. W. H. Auden once wrote (Auden, 1972, p. 25):

> Oxbridge philosophers, to be cursory,
> Are products of a middle-class nursery:
> Their arguments are anent
> What Nanny really meant.

Now, Auden, like many poets, had a wonderful ear for other people's language; so what he had in mind, I suspect, was the *sound* of philosophers at Oxford, when he was Professor of Poetry there from 1956 to 1961. And, though comic verse does not aspire to be either accurate or fair, he had a point. 'Suppose I did say "the cat is on the mat" when it is not the case that I believe that the cat is on the mat, what should we say?' asked J. L. Austin, one of Auden's leading philosophical contemporaries in the Oxford of those years, in his 1955 William James lectures at Harvard (Austin, 1962, p. 50). 'What is to be said of the statement,' he went on, 'that "John's children are all bald" if made when John has no children?' (I don't know about you, but that gets my nanny to a T.) For Austin, 'What is to be said?' was not an invitation to collect data about how a given population of persons might make sense of these statements. The answer was supposed to be obvious. What a person knows in knowing her language is what every competent speaker *should* say in a certain situation; and so, being competent myself, I know what every competent speaker *would* say. That is why it wouldn't matter if we found someone who *didn't* say it: it would just show she wasn't competent.

Philosophy gained an institutional aerie all to itself just about the time the theory of meaning on which it was based was being subjected to sustained assault by leading exponents of the analytic tradition itself; most influentially in the work of W. V. O. Quine, who persuaded many people that the idea of an analytic truth, the idea that a sentence could be true in virtue solely of the meanings of the words it contained, was mistaken. Belief in analyticity was, Quine famously argued, one of the 'dogmas of empiricism'; epistemology, in his view, 'simply falls into place as a chapter of psychology and hence of natural science' (Quine, 1969, pp. 82–83).

Anti-psychologism, which had enabled philosophers to hive themselves off from experimental science, is now just one position in philosophy among others. The separation of philosophy from the empirical succeeded as an institutional project, but faltered as an intellectual one. Michael Dummett has written that certain errors of Frege and Husserl 'have left philosophy open to a renewed incursion from psychology, under the banner of "cognitive science". The strategies of defense employed by Husserl and Frege will no longer serve: the invaders can be repelled only by correcting the failings of the positive theories of those two pioneers' (Dummett, 1991, p. 287). Dummett's bellicose rhetoric, even if tongue-in-cheek, suggests a genuine measure of unease, but no such strategy for repelling the marauders has gained widespread acceptance. Indeed, *anti*-anti-psychologism is now perfectly conventional. Philosophy, after Quine, was in the peculiar position of having surrounded itself with a moat – only to have drained it of water.

2.5

Now, in bringing the empirical entanglements of canonical philosophers back into view, I am doing just what Renan suggested we do with national identities. I am crafting a genealogy that supports a conception of the subject to which I am sympathetic. In deciding what story to tell of philosophy's past, those who were convinced of the importance of the distance between, say, philosophy and psychology, picked their way through the past accordingly. The recent return to these shores of the epithet 'experimental philosophy' is – as one tendency in our profession might put it – a return of the repressed.

There are all kinds of ways in which experimentation has been brought to bear in our discipline. For decades, of course, philosophers of mind have been working closely with their peers in psychology and psycholinguistics and computer science; there has been an effort to ground the philosophy of language, too, in more naturalistic theories of the mind (an effort to which my first two books belong). Philosophers who work on consciousness can tell you all about Capgras Syndrome and research in various forms of neurologically induced agnosia.

The relevance of empirical research tends to be more hotly contested in the obviously normative reaches of moral theory. But here, too, the 'renewed incursions' have been hard to miss. Over the past decade, for instance, there's been a debate between virtue ethicists and critics armed with findings from social psychology – in particular, empirical evidence for what's called 'situationism'. These critics draw on decades of research suggesting that much of what people do is best explained not by traits of character but by systematic human tendencies to respond to features of their situations that nobody previously thought to be crucial at all (Doris, 2002; Ross and Nisbett, 1991).

Situationists think that someone who is, say, reliably honest in one kind of situation will often be reliably dishonest in another. Back in 1972, experimental psychologists had found that, if you dropped your papers outside a phone booth in a shopping mall, you were far more likely to be helped by someone who had just had the good fortune of finding a dime waiting for them in the return slot. A year later, John Darley and Daniel Batson discovered – this is probably the most famous of these experiments – that Princeton seminary students, even those who had just been reflecting on the Gospel account of the Good Samaritan, were much less likely to stop to help someone 'slumped in a doorway, apparently in some sort of distress', if they'd been told that they were late for an appointment. More recently, experiments showed that you were more likely to get change for a dollar outside a fragrant bakery shop than standing near a 'neutral smelling dry-goods store' (Isen and Levin, 1972, pp. 384–388; Darley and Batson, 1973, pp. 100–108; Matthews and Cannon, 1975, pp. 571–577; Baron and Thomley, 1994, pp. 766–784).

Many of these effects are extremely powerful: huge differences in behavior flow from differences in circumstances that seem of little or no normative consequence. Putting the dime in the slot in that shopping mall raised the proportion of those who helped pick up the papers from 1 out of 25 to 6 out of 7; that is, from almost no one to almost everyone. Seminarians in a hurry are six times less likely to stop like a Good Samaritan.[4] Knowing what I've just told you, you should surely be a little less confident that 'she's helpful' is a good explanation next time someone stops to assist you in picking up your papers, especially if you're outside a bakery!

Philosophers inspired by situationists have argued that this reality is at odds with the conception of human character that underlies virtue ethics. For when virtue ethicists ask us to be virtuous, they typically mean that we should have, or cultivate, persistent, multitrack dispositions to, say, act compassionately, or honestly. Their situationist critics object that we're simply not built that way – that character, as the virtue ethicists conceive it, is about as real as phlogiston. Crudely put: If there's no such thing as character, then the project of a character ethics – a morality centered on virtues – is a waste of time.

2.6

But can mere facts about how we *are* disqualify an account of how we *ought* to be? Perhaps nobody is fully virtuous; still, virtue ethics is hardly alone in assigning a role to elusive ideals. Our models of rationality are also shot through with such norms. They tell us not how we do reason but how we ought to reason; and you don't need to be a Kahneman or a Tversky to know that we don't do it how we ought to (Kahneman and Tversky, 1973, pp. 237–251). If you have been following debates about the role of ideals in cognitive psychology, you might think that the answer is to treat claims about virtues as moral heuristics. One eloquent advocate of modern virtue ethics, Rosalind Hursthouse, encourages this approach – even though it is decisively not her own – when she insists that a virtue ethics is just as helpful as, say, utilitarianism, in offering guidance as to what we should do in particular cases: quite simply, we should do what a virtuous person would do (Hursthouse, 1999; Hursthouse, 2003).

But there are many difficulties, I think, for a heuristics of virtue (Appiah, 2008, chapter 4). Here is one: Virtues are not merely instrumental. Virtue ethics wants us to aim at *becoming* a good person, not just at maximizing the chance that we will do what a good person would do. (As the 19th-century logician Archbishop Richard Whately once observed, honesty may be the best policy, but this is not a maxim that guides an honest person.)

By contrast, cognitive heuristics are, so to speak, twice dipped in means-end rationality. First, the right outcome is defined by what someone possessed of infinite cognitive resources would do. Second, means-end rationality is used to determine how people with limited cognitive resources can maximize their chances of doing what's right according to the first test. When we try to concoct a heuristic of virtue, we must start, analogously, by defining the right outcome as what someone ideally virtuous would do. Since we're not ideally virtuous, the heuristics model should next introduce means-end rationality to maximize your chance of doing what's right by the first test.

The trouble is, of course, that virtue ethics requires that we aim at the good for reasons that aren't reducible to means-end rationality. With the cognitive heuristic, what matters is the outcome: but if virtue ethics tells you that outcomes aren't the only thing that matters, then you cannot assess heuristics by means-end rationality – by looking at the probability that they will produce certain outcomes.

That doesn't leave virtue ethics without argumentative recourse – far from it. But the confrontation with social psychology has forced virtue ethicists to clarify the contours of their account – to make claims and concessions about which psychological claims are and are not necessary for their view; and, quite significantly, many of them have made arguments about what the psychological evidence actually shows about human nature. From our metaphilosophical perspective, what matters is not so much whether the situationists' claims are right as whether they are relevant. In that sense, there may be victory even in defeat.

2.7

In recent years, however, philosophers have done more than draw upon research by experimentalists in other disciplines. The recent currency of the phrase 'experimental philosophy' often refers to research that, in the mold of Arne Naess, has actually been conducted by philosophers...often, as with Naess, on nonphilosophers. Much of this work is in a continuation of the project of conceptual analysis.[5] If conceptual analysis is the analysis of 'our' concepts, then shouldn't one see how 'we' – or representative samples of us – actually mobilize concepts in our talk? So one strain of this work seeks to elicit and tabulate intuitions people have about various scenarios.

The use of such scenarios, or thought experiments, is a hallmark of philosophy. Yet the newer philosophical experimentalists seem to have noticed that many thought experiments in philosophy were, so to speak, at a double remove from reality. Not only were the scenarios unrealized, the claims about how we would respond to those scenarios were also simply asserted, rather than demonstrated.

Recall Hume's Missing Shade of Blue argument. If a man had never encountered a particular shade of blue, and is now presented with a sequence of deepening shades, absent that one, will he notice the gap and be able to imagine the unseen shade? Hume, the great empiricist, writes, 'I believe there are few but will be of opinion that he can.' That has been the usual protocol. We conjure a scenario, and then announce that, in such case, 'it would be natural to say' X, Y, or Z. (In the empirical spirit, I should report that, when I typed the phrase 'it would be natural to say' into Google's Book Search, it happily returned, as its top search results, passages by Gilbert Ryle, Peter Strawson, Max Black, and Bertrand Russell.)

Most thought experiments are unrealized for good reasons. With the stroke of a pen, Frank Jackson can summon up in imagination Mary, the scientist raised in a world without color. *Actually* raising such a scientist, however, would be arduous, time consuming, and costly... and likely to get bogged down in human subjects review committees. Any attempt to reproduce Judith Jarvis Thompson's thought experiment about the comatose violinist would run into protests from the musician's union. Yet the other part – finding out what people would think when contemplating such scenarios – can be expeditiously and inexpensively done. So why not remove at least some of the thought from our thought experiments?

2.8

This approach is well exemplified by the work of Joshua Knobe (2003), who, in his best-known study, asked subjects to consider two scenarios. In the first, the chairman of a company is asked to approve a new program that will increase profits and also help the environment. 'I don't care at all about helping the environment', the chairman replies. 'I just want to make as much profit as I can. Let's start the new program.' So the program is launched, and the environment is helped. The second story is identical – except that the program will *hurt* the environment. Once again, the chairman is indifferent to the environment, and the program is launched in order to increase profits, with the expected results.

Rather than surmising what 'it would be natural to say', Knobe totted up the responses of actual subjects, and found that when the program helped the environment, only 23 percent agreed that the chairman had 'helped the environment intentionally'. When the program harmed the environment, though, 82 percent agreed that the chairman had 'harmed the environment intentionally'. And a similar pattern recurred when various other scenarios were tested.

As Cavendish told us, most experiments have their rise from the speculative, and Knobe's research is part of a larger exploration of how judgments about responsibility, intentional action, and causation can be affected by moral or, anyway, evaluative considerations. In his original view, then, our intuitions about intention aren't incoherent; rather, they track with our ascriptions of praise and blame. Similar judgments shape our intuitions about causation, he finds. If a mishap is the combined result of more than one factor, one of which is a misdeed, most subjects say that the misdeed, not another necessary factor, was the 'cause'. In fact, that very dynamic is visible in the way the question about the chairman was framed: it supposed that the chairman 'harmed' the environment, as opposed to, say, allowed the environment to be harmed. (We don't automatically suppose that people have performed, or even caused, the foreseeable consequences of their actions.)

In this line of studies, a seeming anomaly in our folk concept of intentional action is identified and defended. In other studies, Knobe and collaborators are not so generous toward the anomalies they find. One has to do with intuitions about determinism and moral responsibility, and aims to shed light on the dispute between compatibilists and incompatibilists. In that study, subjects were asked to imagine a fully deterministic universe, in which everything that happens is completely caused by whatever happened before. They're told about Mark, who arranges, in this universe, to cheat on his taxes, as he has done many times before. Is Mark fully morally responsible for cheating on his taxes? Most people said no. But the responses changed when the scenarios involved were, as they put it, 'high affect' cases: for example, when people were told about Bill, who, as he often has done in the past, stalks and rapes a stranger. In that case, most subjects thought that he *was* fully morally responsible for his misconduct. Now, the investigators here – Josh Knobe and Shaun Nichols – are persuaded by psychological research that patients who are incapable of affective responses don't act like people who engage in cool moral assessment; rather, they act like people who don't see the point of moral assessment. Our philosophers hold that affect is part of our competence in making judgments about responsibility. But they also believe that it can lead to performance errors. When strong emotion converts us to compatibilism, we have been led into error.

2.9

Are the compatibilists really driven by emotion? You might use a brain scan to make sure. Consider Josh Greene's work in moral psychology, where he and his colleagues have studied the fMRI images of people thinking through those celebrated trolley-car experiments. Why do people think it's OK to reroute a runaway trolley car from a track where five pedestrians will be killed to a track where just one will be killed – but not OK to stop the trolley by pushing a large man hovering innocently nearby onto the track? Greene thinks it's related to the fact that when subjects contemplate pushing the large man, the parts of the brain that 'light up' – the medial frontal gyrus, the posterior cingulate gyrus, and the angular gyrus – are regions associated with emotion (Greene et al., 2001, pp. 2105–2108). If, like Greene, your sympathies are broadly consequentialist, and, so to speak, revisionary, you'd conclude that our reluctance to support tipping the large man arises from morally irrelevant considerations – how 'up close and personal' the action is, as Greene puts it.[6] Emotions have overridden cool judgment, and here are the pictures to prove it.

Especially given the glamour of neurological imaging, though, we might want to bear in mind that slides and surveys are not arguments. For what inferences would you make if you started with the premise that pushing the large man onto the tracks below was wrong? Then those brain scans, assuming they show what they're supposed to show, would be marvelous evidence for the moral authority of affect: our emotions are more exquisitely attuned to the moral features of a situation than are our crude powers of calculation, you would say. In just this way, it's open to compatibilists to laud the superior analysis elicited by the more emotionally fraught case – the rapist – and to find performance error in people's permissive views about the tax cheat. Neither questionnaires nor brain scans are likely to settle debates between deontologists and consequentialists, or compatibilists and incompatibilists. And, of course, they are not offered to that end.

For here, as with the debate with the situationists, the confrontation with evidence can help theorists clarify what claims they are and are not committed to. Indeed, the argument over the usefulness of experimental philosophy itself can be illuminating – that is to say, useful. In the old days of conceptual analysis, it could sometimes seem as if the philosopher was a kind of fancy lexicographer, sorting out the definitions of various grand words. But that paradigm suggests lurking trouble, for within lexicography itself there has always been a tug between normative and descriptive – or, as you might say, empirical – impulses.

Suppose – if you'll tolerate a thought experiment about thought experiments – the APA decided to hire Zogby International to poll test those thought experiments we love so well: scenarios about the Experience Machine; Twin Earth; Mary the Color Scientist; Thompson's comatose violinist; Williams's body-swaps. What could the survey results tell us that we don't already know?

Well, we might learn that, in some instances, what philosophers supposed 'would be natural to say' wasn't what non-philosophers found it natural to say. Some of our intuitions might be less popular than we assumed. Some of our intuitions might turn out to be culturally specific. When Eduoard Machery and colleagues posed a famous thought experiment of Kripke's to students, they found that those from Hong Kong had quite a different pattern of response than those from New Jersey. But my guess is that in most cases the results would shore up the basic intuition it was meant to pump; and that, where it did not, philosophers, too, have already been left divided. What we're not going to end up with is some sort of metaphysics by plebiscite; we wouldn't want to. For most of us don't believe the truth is simply what most of us believe.

2.10

In a friendly review in the *Journal of Philosophy* of Arne Naess's monograph with which I began, Ernest Nagel remarked (Nagel, 1939, p. 79):

> Since most philosophers will not be prepared to undertake the sort of 'dirty work' to which Dr. Naess invites them, he will no doubt remain an outcast from the philosophic community and will have to find what solace he can in being a 'mere' scientist.

Well, it took half a century, Professor Nagel, but I think your hypothesis has been disconfirmed. Many of today's experimental philosophers, as we've seen, like Naess, think it is important to elicit the intuitions of non-philosophers: in general, we want our theories to be about intention, not some guild-specific variant, shmintention, as it were; we want to be describing Truth, not something else we guild members have come to honor with that name.

It's common to analogize folk psychology with folk physics. But, of course, professional physicists can happily leave folk physics far behind as they tinker with their Calabi-Yau Manifolds and Gromov-Witten invariants. By contrast, moral psychology, however reflective, can't be dissociated from our moral sentiments, because it's basic to how we make sense of one another and ourselves. In a deliberately awkward formulation of Bernard Williams's, moral thought and experience 'must primarily involve grasping the world in such a way that one can, as a particular human being, live in it' (Williams, 1981, p. 52).

That's where philosophy and natural philosophy part company. Chemists don't read Humphrey Davy, and physicists don't read Aristotle. So why do philosophers still read, quarrel with, or defend, figures from centuries ago? A couple of thousand years later, we're still kicking around versions of a question from *Euthyphro*: Is an action good because the gods love it, or do the gods love it because it's good? You could say – it has been said – that science is the 'successful' part of philosophy, 'philosophy' the remains. But there's a reason that we're having the same debates: it's that these are stories about *us*. The other methods of inquiry, when they came of age, left the family and lighted out on their own. Philosophy, bound to make sense of a distinctively human realm of meaning, can't sever its ties to ordinary human intelligibility – to the language we use every day to make sense of ourselves and others.

2.11

The new experimental philosophy, I hope I've made clear, poses no threat to philosophical analysis. It offers stimulus, challenge, interest, and not just new sources of funding. Indeed, if anything shadows the prospects of experimental philosophy, it is, I think, that our notion of experiment, of the empirical, may be too conservative, too narrow. In the social sciences – not least in economics – we have lately heard a great deal about 'natural experiments', the offerings of history. (Two of the last three John Bates Clarke medalists in economics have specialized in natural experiments.) If our former colleagues in the other moral sciences find nourishment in natural experiments, perhaps we should not be so neglectful of this resource. I want to suggest, in closing, that one of the many things that philosophers might usefully do, as philosophers, is to attend to such natural experiments – to examine the moral history of our species.

Consider how the practice of dueling came to be regarded as an exercise not in honor but in ignominy; how foot-binding, after a millennium, came to be discarded as a barbarism; how slavery went from being considered part of the natural order to being an unpardonable offense. Would moral philosophers go wrong to take an interest in how these arguments were actually waged and won? There is, after all, an ancient adage that history is philosophy taken from examples. It is usually attributed to the Augustan historian of the Roman republic, Dionysius of Halicarnassus – after Herodotus, the most famous historian to have been born in that Ionian city. So it was a long-ago historian who invited us philosophers to the party.

Surely we have good reason to accept the invitation: we can absorb a certain amount of historical richness without relinquishing the rigor we rightly prize. Some of the most exciting work in the philosophy of science, after all, has arisen from theorists who have a detailed interest in the actual work of actual scientists. Moral theorists are inclined to suppose, reasonably enough, that issues involving specific judgments about specific customs involve too great a level of specificity, and that our distinctive contribution, as philosophers, is to attend to more fundamental issues.

So it's worth remembering, yet again, that the arguments of those we like to consider our disciplinary ancestors have often depended on stories about the actual doings of actual people. It's worth recalling Hume's famous footnote in his *Enquiry Concerning Human Understanding* in which he denounced the tendency of writers 'on *moral, political, or physical* subjects, to distinguish between *reason* and *experience*, and to suppose, that these species of argumentation are entirely different from each other' (Hume, 1902, p. 43). Hume's *History Of England* – five volumes of empirical information, elegantly organized – has rightly been seen as expressing ideas about morality and politics and psychology. For him, it was an extension of the project of a work like the *Enquiry Concerning Human Understanding*. For him, history was too important to relegate entirely to the historians. Ernest Nagel talked, wryly, in that review of Naess about 'dirty work'; bringing philosophy to the realm of the natural experiment is still dirtier. But, if I may paraphrase Chesterton and generalize outrageously, this approach has not recently been tried and found wanting; it has been found difficult and left untried.

So I am a pluralist on many levels: the wild eclecticism of our profession delights me. Insofar as method is concerned I have only this modest pluralist suggestion: that we would do well to sustain a variety of traditions of reflection on questions that matter to us. Unless you already know all the answers, I say, you don't even know for sure which questions are worth asking.

Is it worth asking, for instance, how shifts in our moral judgments, changes in our basic values, take place? What would happen if a few more of our contemporary ethicists turned their subtle anatomizing intelligence – as Hume or Montesquieu once did – to the thick, untidy realm of our moral history? John Stuart Mill famously talked about 'experiments in living', and our species has engaged in a great many of such experiments, sometimes disastrously. We, like our ancestors, are all subjects in a vast ongoing natural experiment, ps without an l; we feel our way through life in a world, a planet, whose fragility Arne Naess was among the first to recognize. There are arguments to be made, truths to be defended or discovered. Our own experiments in living – the changes in moral perceptions we ourselves have lived through – provide a trove of information that will fit on no questionnaire. Experimental philosophy of this sort might indeed be dirty work. But doesn't someone have to do it?

Notes

1. Presidential Address delivered before the 104th Annual Eastern Division Meeting of The American Philosophical Association in Baltimore, Maryland, on December 29, 2007. Reprinted with permission of the APA. Original source: Appiah, K. A. (2008) 'Experimental Philosophy', *Proceedings and Addresses of the American Philosophical Association*, 82, pp. 7–22.
2. The French passage is on p. 164. (The original book has the author's name as Ness; but he is best known under the spelling Naess.)
3. The fifth edition of the *Dictionnaire de l'Académie Française* (1798) defines 'âme' as 'Ce qui est le principe de la vie dans tous les êtres vivans'. 'Physique' is defined as 'Science qui a pour objet les choses naturelles'.
4. And people are about one tenth as likely to help someone behind a curtain who has had what sounds like an accident, if there's someone else standing by who does nothing (Latane and Rodin, 1969, pp. 189–202).
5. One impetus to this experimental turn is the fact that, since the 1970s, it has been common among philosophers to refer to our concepts of intention, belief, desire, and so on under the rubric 'folk psychology'. And, once we did so, it raised the possibility of error – or, anyway, the possibility of the possibility of error, since many denied, on conceptual grounds, that there was such a possibility.
6. Greene maintains that people should 'develop a healthy distrust of moral common sense', and that 'our social instincts were not designed for the modern world' (Greene, 2007).

References

Appiah, K. A. (2008) *Experiments in Ethics* (Cambridge: Harvard University Press).
Auden, W. H. (1972) *Academic Graffiti* (New York: Random House).
Austin, J. L. (1962) *How to Do Things with Words* (Oxford: Clarendon Press).
Baron, R. A. and J. Thomley (1994) 'A Whiff of Reality: Positive Affect as a Potential Mediator of the Effects of Pleasant Fragrances on Task Performance and Helping', *Environment and Behavior*, 26, 6, pp. 766–784.
Cavendish, M. (2001) *Observations Upon Experimental Philosophy*, edited by Eileen O'Neil (Cambridge: Cambridge University Press).
Darley, J. M. and C. D. Batson (1973) '"From Jerusalem to Jericho": A Study of Situational and Dispositional Variables in Helping Behavior', *Journal of Personality and Social Psychology*, 27, 1, pp. 100–108.
Descartes, R. (1988) 'The Passions of the Soul', *Selected Philosophical Writings*, trans. by J. Cottingham, R. Stoothoff and D. Murdoch (Cambridge: Cambridge University Press).
Dictionnaire de l'Académie Française (1798) available online from the Project for American and French Research on the Treasury of the French Language (ARTFL) *Dictionnaires d'autrefois* site: http://portail.atilf.fr/dictionnaires/onelook.htm.
Doris, J. (2002) *Lack of Character* (Cambridge: Cambridge University Press).
Dummett, M. (1991) *Frege and Other Philosophers* (Oxford: Oxford University Press).
Greene, J. D. (2007) http://scholar.harvard.edu/joshuagreene/content/research-5.

Greene, J. D., R. B. Sommerville, L. E. Nystrom, J. M. Darley and J. D. Cohen (2001) 'An fMRI Investigation of Emotional Engagement in Moral Judgment', *Science*, 293, 5537, pp. 2105–2108.

Hume, D. (1902) *An Enquiry Concerning Human Understanding*, A. Selby-Bigge 2nd edn (Oxford: Clarendon Press).

Hursthouse, R. (1999) *On Virtue Ethics* (Oxford: Oxford University Press).

Hursthouse, R. (2003) 'Virtue Ethics', *The Stanford Encyclopedia of Philosophy* (Fall 2003 Edition), edited by Edward N. Zalta, http://plato.stanford.edu/archives/fall2003/entries/ethics-virtue/.

Isen, A. M. and P. F. Levin (1972) 'The Effect of Feeling Good on Helping: Cookies and Kindness', *Journal of Personality and Social Psychology*, 21, 3, pp. 384–388.

Kahneman, D. and A. Tversky (1973) 'On the Psychology of Prediction', *Psychological Review*, 80, pp. 237–257.

Knobe, J. (2003) "Intentional Action and Side Effects in Ordinary Language". *Analysis*, 63, pp. 190–193

Latane, B. and J. Rodin (1969) 'A Lady in Distress: Inhibiting Effects of Friends and Strangers on Bystander Intervention', *Journal of Experimental Social Psychology*, 5, as cited in Doris.

Matthews, K. E. and L. K. Cannon (1975) 'Environmental Noise Level as a Determinant of Helping Behavior', *Journal of Personality and Social Psychology*, 32, 4, pp.571–577.

Naess, A. (1938) *'Truth' as Conceived by Those Who Are Not Professional Philosophers* (Oslo: I Kommisjon Hos Jacob Dybward).

Quine, W. V. O. (1969) 'Epistemology Naturalized', *Ontological Relativity and Other Essays* (New York: Columbia University Press), pp. 69–90.

Reid, T. (1822) *Essays on the Intellectual Powers of Man*, Essay I., iii, 'Of Hypothesis', *The Works of Thomas Reid*, Vol. I (New York: Published by N. Bangs and T. Mason, for the Methodist Episcopal Church, J. and J. Harper, Printers) pp. 367–368.

Renan, E. (1882a) *Chapitre 1,* Qu'est-ce qu'une nation?, http://bmlisieux.com/archives/nation02.htm.

Renan, E. (1882b) *Chapitre 3,* Qu'est-ce qu'une nation?, http://bmlisieux.com/archives/nation04.htm.

Nagel, E. (1939) "'Truth' as Conceived by Those Who Are Not Professional Philosophers" by Arne Naess', *The Journal of Philosophy*, 36, 3, pp. 78–80.

Ross, L. and R. E. Nisbett (1991) *The Person and the Situation* (Philadelphia: Temple University Press).

Williams, B. (1981) *Moral Luck* (Cambridge: Cambridge University Press).

Williamson, T. (2005) 'Armchair Philosophy, Metaphysical Modality and Counterfactual Thinking' (Presidential Address), *Proceedings of the Aristotelian Society*, 105, 1, p. 123.

3
Chances, Problems, and Limits of Experimental Ethics

Christoph Luetge

Throughout its age-old tradition, philosophy has continuously been presented with new challenges. The latest one in this series comes from the experimental disciplines and their methodology: experimental philosophy has, during the last 10 to 15 years, increasingly gained reputation, and it has certainly been a controversial issue. Within this movement, the field of ethics deserves more attention. This article aims to give not a complete overview of, but at least an introduction to, the newly rising field of 'Experimental Ethics', the chances it offers, the problems for discussion, and the criticism to be expected.

I will start out by briefly summarizing the development of experimental philosophy (Section 3.1) before turning to Experimental Ethics (Section 3.2). Some of its precursors will be discussed in Section 3.3. Section 3.4 is concerned with the future opportunities that this new approach might hold. Section 3.5 points to (possible) key research problems, while Section 3.6 outlines some of its (possible) practical implications. The final section focuses on the critical comments to be expected before I draw a conclusion.

3.1 Experimental philosophy

The starting points and the development of experimental philosophy have been discussed at length elsewhere. Experimental philosophy started as a critique of the frequent appeal of philosophers, moral philosophers, and others to intuition. Experimental philosophers often draw near caricatures of an 'armchair philosophy' approach that supposedly relies more on the intuitions within a particular philosopher's head than on more general or widespread intuitions of a society or population (see, e.g., Knobe, 2007). Experimental philosophy aims at finding out about the intuitions of 'ordinary people' concerning hypothetical cases of philosophical interest. Its proponents have found interesting effects like the 'Knobe effect' (Knobe, 2003) and have come up with at least sometimes quite intriguing insights into the moral judgments of ordinary people. The exact scope of relevance to philosophy in general is under debate and will most probably continue to be so.

Here, however, experimental philosophy is faced with the same responses as other philosophical endeavors that made use of methods from other disciplines: experimental philosophy is closely linked with cognitive science and moral psychology. It is certainly fair to say that, currently, experimental philosophy is growing into a full research program.

In terms of the relevant subfields of philosophy, the experimental approach has invaded quite a number of them, such as philosophy of mind (Schultz, Cokely, and Feltz, 2011; Huebner, Bruno, and Sarkissian, 2010), epistemology (Buckwalter, 2010; May et al., 2010), questions of free will (Nichols, 2006; Weigel, 2012; Feltz and Cokely, 2009), metaphysics (such as the problem of causation, Cf. Knobe, 2009; Alicke and Rose, 2012), and not least moral philosophy (Kahane, 2013; Knobe, 2005; Paxton Ungar, and Greene, 2012; Inbar et al., 2009; Strohminger et al., 2014). This I will now turn to.

3.2 Experimental ethics

While in the past years, as laid out, many experimental philosophers have mainly focused on questions of theoretical philosophy, the domain of practical philosophy seems to me the most promising field for an experimental approach. In particular, practical philosophy has connections with other disciplines, such as psychology and economics, which have been employing experimental methods for a long time (see Rusch, 2014). Within these disciplines, research questions often reach into moral and ethical dimensions such as questions of moral motivation or justice. It would therefore seem to be much more natural to look for successful applications of the experimental approach within practical philosophy, in particular within the field of ethics.

Indeed, there is at least one prominent philosopher who has been calling for a similar or related approach to ethics. In his book *Experiments in Ethics* (Appiah, 2008), Kwame Appiah has accused many recent paradigms of ethics of neglecting possible collaborations with other – and above all, experimental – disciplines. Appiah reminds us that many great philosophers of the past also did research in other disciplines, like Descartes, Leibniz, or Kant. While this is not totally unknown, it is interesting to see that Appiah's accusations are mostly levelled against contemporary Analytic Ethics (and not primarily against traditional non-Analytic approaches), which according to him is too much concerned with speech analysis and thought experiments that have no perspective on social and economic phenomena. Appiah argues that ethics should instead turn much more toward the empirical disciplines and concern itself more with experiments. To be sure, Appiah does not claim to have conducted such experimental research himself, but at least he prepares the ground within ethics for such a development.

3.3   Philosophical precursors

Despite being, as we claim in this book, a new enterprise, Experimental Ethics is not without precursors. While the term itself has not been explicitly used in the past, conceptions of ethics have indeed made use of methods and results from the empirical (though not necessarily experimental) disciplines (also see Dworazik and Rusch, 2014). Two such conceptions will be mentioned here: first, an ethics on a naturalistic basis, and second, business ethics with economic means.

3.3.1   Ethics on a naturalistic basis

The concept of naturalism in ethics has often been regarded with rather skeptical eyes, as the term 'ethical naturalism' has been used by G. E. Moore and others for an approach that tries to derive, falsely, norms from facts (the so-called 'naturalistic fallacy'). This is, however, not at all what we have in mind when talking about naturalism in ethics.

First and foremost, we do not employ the term 'ethical naturalism' for the conception advocated here, but rather, in a weaker sense, we speak of an *ethics on a naturalistic basis*.

Second, we do not claim to derive norms from facts, and we acknowledge that there always has to be some set of basic norms with which to start. Bertrand Russell once remarked, in a different context: 'from blank doubt, no argument can begin' (Russell, 1952, chapter 14). From blank facts, we cannot hope to derive norms or normative arguments – and we do not claim to be able to do this. What we do claim, however, is that empirical facts as well as experimental findings can help in reducing greatly the set of feasible (or implementable) norms.

Third, we employ a concept of naturalism that does not deal exclusively with findings of the natural sciences but includes the social sciences and economics as well (Cf. Kitcher, 1993 and others). The common core is the rejection of a 'prima philosophia', of a type of 'armchair' philosophy that does not take the empirical sciences seriously and tries to rely purely on argumentation, discourse, and non-empirical reasoning. While this is certainly indispensable, even a discipline like philosophy cannot (and should not) ignore the progress made by the empirical sciences. Some philosophical enterprises like neurophilosophy (Churchland, 1989) or evolutionary epistemology (Campbell, 1974) have already taken this into account, regarding the empirical disciplines (at least partly) as a model for philosophy. Among the theoretical resources used so far are: evolutionary biology, game theory, (institutional) economics, moral psychology, and others. And here, we would like to take it a step further by adding the experimental dimension.

3.3.2 Business ethics with economic means

The second approach to be discussed here is known mostly in the field of business ethics. While many approaches to business ethics rely chiefly on philosophical arguments and theories, there is at least one prominent conception that centrally (and not only additionally) employs methods and results from economics: order ethics. The approach of *order ethics* ('Ordnungsethik') rests on foundations from institutional and constitutional economics as well as game theory and has been under discussion for roughly 25 years now (Cf. recently Luetge, 2014; Luetge and Mukerji, forthcoming). One of its central tenets is that an ethics of the economy and of business operations must take the logic of the economy seriously – and in particular its ethical logic. The main mechanisms of the economy, such as competition, have ethical value and hold ethical lessons in themselves. For example, in many cases and situations, competition is beneficial for all parties involved, though the individual actors (like companies or managers) are not ethically motivated or altruistic at all.

Moreover, order ethics maintains that ethical categories can be reinterpreted in terms of economics (Cf. Luetge and Mukerji, forthcoming): Duty, for example, can be reconstructed as an encouragement for long-term (and not just financial) investment and for long-term commitment. The concept of phronesis can be seen as wise economic and ethical balancing. These and other examples show that economics and ethics can be two sides of the same coin.

Both approaches can be considered as philosophical precursors of the conception advocated here. Experimental Ethics, in this view, is a consistent and 'logical' continuation and extension of these and related approaches.

3.4   Chances: why Experimental Ethics?

A fundamental question to be asked right at the start is the question of justification: Why would there be a need for a project like Experimental Ethics at all? Or, to put it differently: In what ways might Experimental Ethics do better than traditional ethics? Without a good answer to this question, it will be hard to convince the scientific community of the value of the experimental approach.

One suitable starting point would be to state one or more deficits in traditional ethical argumentation. Order ethics has done the same within business ethics, by pointing to deficits in the argumentation of those business ethicists who simplistically called for more moral motivation and appealed to the conscience of individuals in order to change what were deficits in incentives and in the order framework.

Similarly, it should be possible to find deficits in traditional ethics in a more general sense. Underestimating the role of empirical, in particular experimental, knowledge is definitely a candidate. Another one could be the failure to experimentally, in a controlled way, research the ways in which moral motivation can decline when the incentives or the framing of a situation changes. Certainly, this is a research program with open questions for the moment.

The following list is not meant to be anywhere near exhaustive, but contains my suggestions for further proceeding with Experimental Ethics:

First, it will not be enough to merely argue against an 'enemy' like armchair philosophy. Even if it is certainly a valid concern, it also means, in many regards, arguing against a dummy, as even traditional philosophers do get out of their armchairs at times and discuss findings of the natural and social sciences. So Experimental Ethics should be more specific and more constructive when criticizing other approaches.

Second, while theoretical issues will eventually be on the agenda too, Experimental Ethics should not start with a huge theoretical debate. Rather, it would be more fruitful to show in application just what this approach can do and what interesting findings there are.

Third, as mentioned above, the presumed deficits within traditional ethics should be spelt out. What deficits are there in traditional ethical argumentation? Where and how can Experimental Ethics help resolve these deficits or at least improve the situation? How can specific results improve these deficits in specific ways?

Fourth, the relation of Experimental Ethics to other experimental disciplines like experimental economics, psychology, and biology must be clarified. In what ways is experimental research in ethics different from experimental research in psychology or economics? What does it add?

Fifth, one (not the least) important task of Experimental Ethics could be to bring together the relevant results from different disciplines – something that is rarely done in ethics.

Sixth, a particularly fruitful area for applying Experimental Ethics could be the different subfields of applied ethics. Medical ethics, bioethics, or business ethics (if it is to be called a subfield of applied ethics, Cf. Luetge and Mukerji, forthcoming) would be suitable candidates for such an approach.

3.5 Problems: what could be key research problems of experimental ethics?

A key question for a new research field is how to generate and establish sufficiently original and sustainable research questions. From a more general perspective, some of the ethical problems relevant to Experimental Ethics could be the following:

3.5.1 Value assignments and moral intuitions

What ethical value do people assign to different actions, consequences, outcomes, and so on? What are common or shared moral intuitions on certain actions, situations, or even people? In what ways do these value assignments shift when people are faced with changing incentives, with changing rules of the game, or with changing actions of their cooperating (or non-cooperating) partners? Moreover: Are moral intuitions unequally distributed among a population, are they stable under all conditions, and can they be changed in principle, by allowing participants in experiments to experience certain (positive or negative) behavior? Can the concept of a reflective equilibrium (John Rawls) be reproduced or at least approximately validated in experiments?

3.5.2 Moral motivation: what motivates people to act in ethical or unethical ways?

This is certainly a more traditional question of ethics, but one that Experimental Ethics can take on from a fresh perspective. Schwitzgebel (2009), for example, on the basis of data on missing books from library shelves, argues that knowing ethical principles does not automatically induce people to act in more ethical ways – as ethicists do not seem to steal fewer books than others (also see Schwitzgebel, 2014). Likewise, within order ethics, it has for a long time been argued that in prisoner's dilemma situations, neither more ethical knowledge nor more appeals to ethical behavior can improve the situation for the participants. Rather, it is only changes in the incentives (in the order framework) that can lead to improvements in ethical ways, allowing – and not punishing – morally motivated people.

3.5.3 'Ought implies can': what can we realistically expect of people in ethical terms, if they are put in dilemma situations constrained by social and economic incentives?

Here again, situations like the prisoner's dilemma are central. In those situations, we cannot realistically expect the participants to ignore or sidestep the rules of the game on their own, because that would, eventually, leave them dramatically worse off. We cannot expect them to do something that the situation does not allow for. And if we do not expect people to sidestep realities – as, for example, we do not need to forbid people to jump 20m high – there are other realities, which can be validated in experimental settings, that similarly narrow down the range of ethically feasible and implementable ways of action.

3.5.4   Trade-offs: what kind of ethical trade-offs do people take, and under what conditions?

Even in many traditional approaches to ethics, it has been acknowledged by now that trade-offs in ethical matters take place and should not be condemned in principle. Here, the Experimental Ethics approach could help in collecting more knowledge with regard to those trade-offs present in general as well as in more special (and domain-specific) scenarios.

To be sure, these are only some tentative and nowhere near exhaustive questions, some of which are already being explored. All of them are, to my mind, worth being researched further. Certainly, this will not be feasible without the help of other experimental disciplines, in particular experimental and behavioral economics, experimental and behavioral psychology, as well as biological and cognitive sciences. There will always, however, be a moral or ethical dimension added to questions and research in the field of Experimental Ethics: while experimental economists and psychologists certainly, at times, do border on ethical questions, experimenting ethicists will regard this domain invariably as central to their work.

For the moment, this might suffice as a *prima facie* demarcation, which will of course need to be spelled out in detail as the development of our field progresses.

3.6   Practical implications of Experimental Ethics?

Having outlined some research questions of Experimental Ethics, I will try to give at least some general ideas about what implications this type of research might have. Certainly, it would be too much to ask from an emerging field to come up with all possible practical implications right at the start, particularly in the case of a *philosophical* subfield. However, as experimental economics and psychology have been around for a while, we might draw some (hypothetical) consequences from the analogy to their work:

I have stated before that economics is an important resource for business ethics, and the same holds for experimental economics. Likewise, there are consequences for suggestions of institutional reform which business ethics develops. For example, following Kahneman (2011) and others, we should beware of certain biases and mental traps when making such suggestions. To name but a few, there exist biases toward the present (the 'here' and the 'now') and against the future, toward greater security and against additional gains, weaknesses at estimating time horizons, framing effects, and more. People are willing to sanction offenders and free riders – provided the costs of punishing are not too high. People also tend to overlook the large role that chance plays in many situations and settings, as well as to overgeneralize and judge too much from single cases.

Therefore, when designing institutions, we have to take these biases into account. And likewise in everyday practice, Kahneman suggests a number of strategies, like not excluding options too early, or widening one's look considerably before deciding.

Looking at the development of experimental economics should also hold another lesson for Experimental Ethics: one should not get stuck, as experimental economics seemed for a while, in a particular research direction: For quite some time, their protagonists were mainly busy trying to falsify the concept of the economic actor and show that there is a much greater deal of moral motivation present in people than neoclassical economics believes. While this was certainly a valid and (at least in terms of publications) successful approach, quite a number of studies in recent years have shown that moral motivation can also erode and decline significantly (Gürerk, Irlenbusch, and Rockenbach, 2006; Binmore, 2010; Andreoni, 1988) and that moral motivation is just one part of a larger story. So, for Experimental Ethics, this means: widen your scope of analysis, and do not try to draw direct practical implications too soon. At the Experimental Ethics Lab (EEL) of the Technical

University of Munich, which I established in 2011, we are trying to do exactly that. First results of our work can be found in the present volume as well as in numerous articles like Levati, Uhl, and Zultan, 2014; Rusch and Luetge, in prep.; and Luetge and Rusch, 2013.

3.7   Criticism to be expected

In order to be prepared for future counterarguments against Experimental Ethics, it might be useful to compile a list of possible types of criticism to be encountered. Critiques will most probably fall into two parts: first, there will be general critiques levelled against the experimental approach in general. Second, one should also expect special critiques of using the experimental approach in ethics in particular.

Among the general critiques, there are those statements to be expected that implicitly assume that experiments within the social sciences and economics are in themselves flawed, because supposedly they do not deal with the 'real social world'. Sociologists from different camps have been particularly keen on criticizing experimental approaches in this way. However, during the last 15 to 20 years, the reputation of experiments within the social sciences has dramatically risen, and critics are on the retreat. Still, the best way to counter those criticisms would be to point to successful experimental approaches in other disciplines and show how futile it is to accuse experimental social sciences of being too idealistic or oriented toward theoretical modelling: in the end, all sciences necessarily have to abstract from reality and use theoretical models.

Thus, among the critiques concerned with ethics in particular, there are several standard counterarguments to be expected:[1]

'Experimental Ethics is committing the naturalistic fallacy.'

The short answer is that we do not at all try to derive norms from facts. Rather, all work here falls within the 'ought implies can' perspective: empirical constraints on implementable ethical judgments are being identified.

'The two concepts "experiments" and "ethics" are reminiscent of questionable projects like the Milgram experiment and suggest using human beings as guinea-pigs.'

This would definitely be a misunderstanding. Certainly, human beings are involved as experimental subjects. But this has been standard practice in the experimental social sciences for decades and is frequently under close scrutiny by ethics committees and the like. (Though in general, our experiments are not as invasive as the Milgram experiment anyway.)

'What does this have to do with ethics?'

This criticism is sometimes raised from a traditional philosophical perspective. Very briefly, one could respond by pointing to the obviously ethical nature of the concepts employed, the questions asked, and the research problems focused on. To deny that this is relevant to ethics would mean, in consequence, relegating ethics to a purely non-empirical 'armchair' discipline which only the keenest traditionalists would find desirable.

'You are doing nothing different from anthropology.'

This point should be taken seriously: No, Experimental Ethics should not look exclusively at *individual* actors and their judgments. Rather, the situational framework, the situational constraints, and their incentives should play a significant role in the experiments conducted as well.

3.8 Conclusion

Finally, a general point should be made against those who believe that a scientific discipline must be conducted in one way and one way only: Philosophy has more leeway than other disciplines – and this should be used as an advantage for Experimental Ethics. I suggest regarding philosophy as an 'interface of sciences' that brings different disciplines and their different methodological approaches together. And the thematic scope of the philosophical zoo is sufficiently wide to allow for the addition of a new inhabitant: Experimental Ethics.

Note

1. Similar criticisms have been raised against order ethics, Cf. Luetge and Mukerji, forthcoming.

References

Alicke, M. and D. Rose (2012) 'Culpable Control and Deviant Causal Chains', *Personality and Social Psychology Compass*, 6, 10, pp. 723–735.
Andreoni, J. (1988) 'Why Free Ride? Strategies and Learning in Public Goods Experiments', *Journal of Public Economics*, 37, pp. 291–304.

Appiah, K. A. (2008) *Experiments in Ethics* (Cambridge: Harvard University Press).

Binmore, K. (2010) 'Social Norms or Social Preferences?', *Mind and Society*, 9, pp. 139–158.

Buckwalter, W. (2010) 'Knowledge Isn't Closed on Saturday: A Study in Ordinary Language', *Review of Philosophy and Psychology*, 1, 3, pp. 395–406.

Campbell, D. T. (1974) 'Evolutionary Epistemology', in P. A. Schlipp (ed.), *The Philosophy of Karl Popper*, Vol. I, pp. 413–459, Illinois: La Salle.

Churchland, P. (1989) *Neurophilosophy – Toward a Unified Science of the Mind/Brain* (Cambridge: Bradford Book).

Dworazik, N. and H. Rusch (2014) 'A Brief History of Experimental Ethics', in this volume.

Feltz, A. and E. T. Cokely (2009) 'Do Judgments About Freedom and Responsibility Depend on Who You Are? Personality Differences in Intuitions About Compatibilism and Incompatibilism', *Consciousness and Cognition*, 18, 1, pp. 342–350.

Gürerk, Ö., B. Irlenbusch, and B. Rockenbach (2006) 'The Competitive Advantage of Sanctioning Institutions', *Science*, 312, p. 108.

Huebner, B., M. Bruno and H. Sarkissian (2010) 'What Does the Nation of China Think About Phenomenal States?', *Review of Philosophy and Psychology*, 1, 2, p. 225–243.

Inbar, Y., D. A. Pizarro, J. Knobe, and P. Bloom (2009) 'Disgust Sensitivity Predicts Intuitive Disapproval of Gays', *Emotion*, 9, 3, pp. 435–443.

Kahane, G. (2013) 'The Armchair and the Trolley: An Argument for Experimental Ethics', *Philosophical Studies*, 162, 2, pp. 421–445.

Kahneman, D. (2011) *Thinking, Fast and Slow* (New York: Farrar, Straus and Giroux).

Kitcher, P. (1993) *The Advancement of Science: Science without Legend, Objectivity without Illusions* (Oxford: Oxford University Press).

Knobe, J. (2003) 'Intentional Action and Side Effects in Ordinary Language', *Analysis*, 63, pp. 190–193.

Knobe, J. (2005) 'Ordinary Ethical Reasoning and the Ideal of "Being Yourself"', *Philosophical Psychology*, 18, 3, pp. 327–340.

Knobe, J. (2007) 'Experimental Philosophy and Philosophical Significance', *Philosophical Explorations*, 10, 2, pp. 119–121.

Knobe, J. (2009) 'Folk Judgments of Causation', *Studies in History and Philosophy of Science Part A*, 40, 2, pp. 238–242.

Knobe, J. and S. Nichols (eds) (2008) *Experimental Philosophy* (New York: Oxford University Press).

Levati, M. V., M. Uhl, and R. Zultan (2014) 'Imperfect Recall and Time Inconsistencies: An Experimental Test of the Absentminded Driver "Paradox"', *International Journal of Game Theory*, 43, pp. 65–88.

Luetge, C. (2014) *Order Ethics or Moral Surplus What Holds a Society Together?* (Lanham, MD: Lexington).

Luetge, C. and N. Mukerji (eds) (forthcoming) *Order Ethics: An Ethical Framework for the Social Market Economy* (Heidelberg/New York: Springer).

Luetge, C. and H. Rusch (2013) 'The Systematic Place of Morals in Markets: Comment on Armin Falk & Nora Szech "Morals and Markets"', *Science*, 341, 6147, p. 714.

May, J., W. Sinnott-Armstrong, J. G. Hull, and A. Zimmerman (2010) 'Practical Interests, Relevant Alternatives, and Knowledge Attributions: An Empirical Study', *Review of Philosophy and Psychology*, 1, 2, pp. 265–273.

Nichols, S. (2006) 'Folk Intuitions on Free Will', *Journal of Cognition and Culture*, 6, pp. 57–86

Paxton, J. M., L. Ungar, and J. D. Greene (2012) 'Reflection and Reasoning in Moral Judgment', *Cognitive Science*, 36, 1, pp. 163–177.

Rusch, H. (2014) 'Philosophy as the Behaviorist Views It?', in this volume.

Rusch, H. and C. Luetge (in preparation) 'Spillovers from Coordination to Cooperation: Positive Evidence for the Interdependence Hypothesis from the Lab', under review.

Russell, B. (1952) *The Problems of Philosophy* (Oxford: Oxford University Press).

Schultz, E., E. T. Cokely, and A. Feltz (2011) 'Persistent Bias in Expert Judgments About Free Will and Moral Responsibility: A Test of the Expertise Defense', *Consciousness and Cognition*, 20, 4, pp. 1722–1731.

Schwitzgebel, E. (2009) 'Do Ethicists Steal More Books?', *Philosophical Psychology*, 22, pp. 711–725.

Schwitzgebel, E. (2014) 'The Moral Behavior of Ethicists and the Role of the Philosopher', in this volume.

Strohminger et al. (2014) 'Implicit moral attitudes', in this volume.

Weigel, C. (2012) 'Experimental Evidence for Free Will Revisionism', *Philosophical Explorations*, 16, 1, pp. 31–43.

4
A Brief History of Experimental Ethics

Niklas Dworazik and Hannes Rusch

The recent years have seen a continual rise of interest in the empirical study of questions traditionally located in moral philosophy, that is, studies in Experimental Ethics. Figure 4.1 shows the respective trends of publication numbers listed in the most prominent online repository for philosophical research, philpapers.org, for the last three decades.

Experimental Philosophy, however, is not an exclusively philosophical endeavor (Knobe and Nichols, 2008). Rather, neuroscientists, cognitive psychologists, biologists, and economists, among others, have been struggling with traditionally philosophical concepts for quite some time now, concepts like free will (Libet et al., 1983), moral judgment (Kohlberg

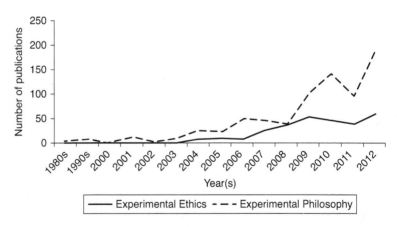

Figure 4.1 Number of publications listed on philpapers.org by year; separate lines for Experimental Ethics (dashed line) and Experimental Philosophy (excluding Experimental Ethics; solid line); data was collected from philpapers.org in March 2014.

and Kramer, 1969; Piaget, 1952; 1997), or rationality (Cosmides and Tooby, 1994).

In this chapter we briefly outline the history of one branch within Experimental Philosophy: the empirical study of ethics. In order to do so, we will have to cross disciplinary borders to quite some extent. After a short review of early scientific approaches within this area of research, we briefly characterize four current topics of Experimental Ethics which are intensively investigated: moral relativism, individual and cross-cultural differences in moral judgment, and interactions of moral evaluation with other philosophical concepts. We conclude with a short historically informed comment on the demarcation problem of Experimental Ethics.

4.1 The beginnings: moral psychology

There can be no doubt that morality is a human universal. Yet, it is highly variable in its characteristics and adapted to particular historical and cultural environments. It is incorrect, in our opinion, to claim that moral philosophy, that is, the study of the various conceivable systems of moral rules and their justification, is historically detached from the study of the very concrete determinants of human social interaction. One of the greatest moral philosophers of all time, Immanuel Kant, for example, presented a naïvely biologistic account of the moral capabilities of non-European 'savages' in his 1775 lecture on human races ('Von den verschiedenen Racen der Menschen'). While the study of implicit and explicit racism in Kant's work is a completely different matter, we think this example suffices to demonstrate that interest in the biological and socio-ecological influences on human moral judgment is no new phenomenon at all.

Accordingly, soon after psychology had branched off from philosophy and become an independent scientific discipline, psychologists began to tackle the question of how human capabilities for moral judgment develop in the individual with their new methodology, that is, controlled experimental and observational studies. For many years, however, moral psychology referred to moral, or rather socio-cognitive, development in a very narrow sense. This branch within psychology has its beginnings in the late 1930s with Jean Piaget and Lawrence Kohlberg.

4.1.1 Piaget's stage theory and Kohlberg's improvements

Piaget's influence on experimental psychology can hardly be overestimated, although his particular influence in moral psychology subsided recently. Piaget's interest in morals was inspired by the Kantian idea of a universal, generalizable, and obligatory morality, which Piaget thought to be highly dependent on peer interaction (Piaget, 1997). He conducted various experiments and observational studies, which indicated that children advance through different socio-cognitive and moral stages during their ontogeny. At the age of five years, for instance, Piaget observed children reasoning about moral concerns and adapting rules from authorities without taking into account those rules' justification. In contrast, 10-year olds represent moral norms as social agreements between persons. At this age, children know that others' thoughts about morality can be diverse and are able to take into account changing context variables like motivation, intention, and abilities (Piaget, 1952).

Although Piaget's work was seminal for developmental psychology, his moral stage model was relatively vague. One of his own disciples, Lawrence Kohlberg, extended this model to a more consistent and structured stage model of cognitive moral judgment (Kohlberg and Kramer, 1969). Like Piaget, Kohlberg attempted to show that morality is a staged developmental competency which advances from more egocentric authority-dependent reasoning to more socially oriented and authority-independent reasoning during ontogeny (Gräfenhain and Wiegmann, 2013). In addition to Piaget's methods, Kohlberg was the first to systematically conduct studies using moral dilemmas and can therefore also be considered a methodological forerunner of the recent work in Experimental Ethics. Even more so, according to Kohlberg and his colleagues, moral psychology must begin with specific metaethical assumptions that define a moral judgment (Kohlberg, Levine, and Hewer, 1983). While being known as psychologists, Piaget and Kohlberg thus already crossed the disciplinary border to philosophy.

4.1.2   Nucci's and Turiel's domain theory

Kohlberg's and Piaget's rather rationalistic approach, claiming that moral judgment always requires conscious moral reasoning, became the target of much criticism later on. In particular, the idea of fixed developmental stages fell into disrepute. Therefore, Larry Nucci and Elliot Turiel tried to improve Piaget's and Kohlberg's methods by conducting standardized stimulus-driven interviews with school and preschool children. An element of these interviews was to judge real-life scenarios illustrated by pictures or vignettes. They attempted to show that, from early childhood on, children tend to differentiate between conventional and moral judgments (e.g., hitting someone or lying to someone vs. chewing gum in the classroom or addressing teachers by their first name; Nucci and Nucci, 1982). Moreover, they suggested that these judgments are processed in domain-specific cognitive structures which develop during every child's socio-cognitive ontogeny (Gräfenhain and Wiegmann, 2013), that is, in their view, the capacity for moral judgment is acquired in early life when children interact with each other and anticipate their own actions' consequences on the rights and well-being of others (Gräfenhain and Wiegmann, 2013). Thus, morals can be understood as general agreements within a social group and therefore depend on common knowledge within this specific group. As a result, moral judgments may be highly context dependent and may vary across different social groups (Nucci and Turiel, 1978). The distinction between conventions and morals highlighted by Nucci and Turiel, however, has been challenged by recent research. According to their critics, Nucci's and Turiel's results may have been evoked by a limited set of stimuli typical only of Western schools and therefore culturally biased (Kelly et al., 2007).

4.1.3 Haidt's social intuitionist model

In spite of this criticism, Nucci's and Turiel's work has been very influential and attracted many psychologists to the study of moral judgment. One the best known researchers in this field today is Jonathan Haidt. His view on human morality, however, is somewhat different from the earlier works in moral psychology. Consider the following scenario (Haidt, 2001, p. 814):

> Julie and Mark are brother and sister. They are traveling together in France on summer vacation from college. One night they are staying alone in a cabin near the beach. They decide that it would be interesting and fun if they tried making love. At the very least it would be a new experience for each of them. Julie was already taking birth control pills, but Mark uses a condom too, just to be safe. They both enjoy making love, but they decide not to do it again. They keep that night as a special secret, which makes them feel even closer to each other. What do you think about that? Was it OK for them to make love?

The vast majority of the people who read this scenario instantly state that it was wrong for the siblings to have sex. Then they begin searching for reasons. Some point out the danger of inbreeding, others argue that the siblings might become emotionally traumatized. However, they used birth control, and the story clarifies that no emotional worry befell them. Finally, people state that they cannot explain why they know that what Julie and Mark did was wrong. How can this phenomenon be integrated in the Kohlbergian tradition of moral judgment?

Haidt is convinced that moral intuitions have primacy over conscious reasoning when we form our moral judgments. It is important to point out that Haidt does not simply equate intuitions with emotions, however. He understands moral judgment as 'fast, automatic, and (usually) affect-laden processes in which an evaluative feeling of good-bad or like-dislike [...] appears in consciousness without any awareness of having gone through steps of search, weighing evidence, or inferring a conclusion' (Haidt, 2007, p. 998). In contrast, moral reasoning 'is a controlled and "cooler" (less affective) process; it is conscious mental activity that consists of transforming information about people and their actions in order to reach a moral judgment or decision' (Haidt, 2007, p. 998). Note that Haidt understands both as cognitive processes in the human mind. However, in his account, moral intuitions are the driving force in moral judgment, whereas moral reasoning refers to a post-hoc process in which people engage when they try to support or verbalize their initial intuition in retrospect. Haidt supports his view by stressing that '(i) people have nearly instant implicit reactions to scenes or stories of moral violations; (ii) affective reactions are usually good predictors of moral judgments and behaviors; (iii) manipulating emotional reactions, such as through hypnosis, can alter moral judgments; and (iv) people can sometimes be "morally dumbfounded" – they can know intuitively that something is wrong, even when they cannot explain why' (Haidt, 2007, p. 998). Moreover, Haidt's social intuitionist model follows an evolutionary logic. Since language and the ability to engage in conscious moral reasoning were probably not developed earlier than 100,000 years ago, he argues, evolutionary logic suggests affect primacy.

With his experimental efforts Haidt thus entered the old ethical debate between emotivists such as David Hume or Adam Smith and rationalists like Kant or Leibniz and was able to present robust evidence that moral intuitions and emotions play an important role in human morality. In addition, Haidt found moral intuitions to be highly sensitive to the individual's cultural environment, constituting a valuable contribution to the study of cultural diversity in moral judgment.

Critics claim, however, that Haidt's social intuitionist model fails to explain the relationship between the triggering situation and the corresponding moral intuition (Gräfenhain and Wiegmann, 2013). Therefore, they argue, it cannot accurately predict the outcome of moral intuitions to a particular situation, as, instance, the trolley cases.

4.2   In transition to Experimental Ethics

Even though Haidt has gathered much evidence in favor of his theory, he provides little explanation for why humans are able to judge against their intuitions and often do so. All theories we touched upon so far acknowledge that both moral reasoning and moral intuitions play a role in moral judgment. They merely disagree which process is considered to have primacy.

4.2.1   Greene's dual process theory

The dual process theory by Joshua Greene and colleagues ties in with these previous views and tries to mediate between more rationalist and more intuitionist approaches. Greene conducted several fMRI and reaction time studies in which participants were confronted with moral dilemmas (e.g., trolley cases) and non-moral dilemmas (Greene et al., 2001). He designed different scenarios, some of which are thought to be perceived as rather personal (e.g., the footbridge scenario) and others which are likely perceived as rather impersonal (e.g., the bystander at the switch scenario). According to Greene et al., a moral violation is personal if it fulfills the following criteria: '(i) likely to cause serious bodily harm, (ii) regarding a particular person, (iii) of such nature that the harm does not result from the deflection of an existing threat onto a different party' (Greene et al., 2001, p. 2107). Greene et al. then claim that personal moral violations should trigger affective responses which relate to deontological moral judgments whereas impersonal moral violations should trigger rational responses which relate to consequentialist responses (Greene et al., 2001; Greene and Haidt, 2002; Greene, 2007). Furthermore, Greene suspects that different moral judgments should be processed in different brain regions. And indeed, Greene and colleagues were able to present evidence of two different neurobiological correlates showing up when people contemplate a personal versus an impersonal moral dilemma. For personal dilemmas they found higher activity in emotion processing areas (such as the posterior cingulate cortex, the medial prefrontal cortex, and the amygdala), whereas for impersonal dilemmas a relatively higher neural activity in two brain areas classically associated with 'cognition' and working memory could be observed (such as the dorsolateral prefrontal cortex and inferior parietal lobe; Greene, 2007; Greene and Haidt, 2002).

Greene therefore supposed that high-conflict dilemmas, that is, those cases in which consequentialist intuitions are in severe clash with deontological ones, cognitive load would selectively interfere with consequentialist responses. In a follow-up study, Greene and colleagues thus added cognitive load to the presentation of moral dilemmas. The participants had to push a button each time the number '5' popped up in a sequence of numbers scrolling through the screen. In accord with Greene's prediction, results showed that reaction time only increased for consequentialist but not for deontological responses in the cognitive load condition (Greene et al., 2008). In a similar experiment Suter and Hertwig (2011) were able to manipulate the frequency of deontological judgments by reducing the time frame participants were given to make their judgment. Within reduced time frames, subjects were more likely to give deontological responses.

Greene endorses Haidt's claim that moral intuitions follow an evolutionary logic and played an important role during human evolution, but he claims that they are likely to be adapted to late Pleistocene conditions and not to the modern globalized world. Therefore, he argues, we cannot expect moral intuitions to correspond to modern problems. For this reason, deliberate moral reasoning seems even more important today. In Greene's perspective, both cognitive processes – deontological and consequentialist moral judgments – are adaptive, and both are shaped culturally at the same time. They merely differ in the sets of context variables which trigger them. Moreover, Greene's dual process theory is one step ahead with regard to dissecting moral judgment processes into their functional components and attempting to reconcile rationalist and emotivist approaches. The dual process theory clarifies that whether emotional or cognitive processes determine moral judgments largely depends on the specific structure of the moral dilemma.

Nevertheless, taking into account the divergent interpretations of the neuroimaging data, Greene's dual process theory seems not to be elaborated enough, yet. Moll and Oliveira-Souza (2007), for example, claim that the different brain activations may add up to higher level prosocial emotions which reintegrate emotional and cognitive processes, rather than putting them in conflict.

4.2.2   Universal moral grammar theory

Another approach which focuses on the details of the computational mechanisms which transfer situational input into moral judgments has been elaborated. In analogy to Chomsky's syntax theory, Mikhail and Hauser interpret morality as an evolved adaptation composed of innate, unconscious, and modularized computational processes that contain moral rules and principles (Hauser et al., 2007; Mikhail, 2007). Their universal moral grammar theory states that 'ordinary people are intuitive lawyers, who possess tacit or unconscious knowledge of a rich variety of legal rules, concepts, and principles, along with a natural readiness to compute mental representations of human acts and omissions in legally cognizable terms' (Mikhail, 2009, p. 29).

Mikhail and Hauser conducted a body of combined cross-species and cross-cultural research using neuroscientific methods as well as classical tools from moral psychology. For example, they conducted a study which presented 12 different trolley cases to more than 200,000 subjects from 120 different countries. They found that some moral judgments are widely shared across different cultures (for instance, subjects are less willing to push a person from the bridge than to throw the switch in the trolley scenarios; Mikhail, 2007; Mikhail, 2009). Mikhail's and Hauser's theory refines Haidt's and Greene's approaches by dissecting responses to the trolley cases by mapping them onto the underlying causal structures within the dilemmas. They specify the computational steps that transfer the stimuli present in the scenarios into an internal moral representation. In the bystander scenario, for example, the chronology of the events 'throwing a switch', 'diverting the train', and 'killing one man' are integrated into a causal chain representation by the subjects (Mikhail, 2007). By modifying these specific characteristics of moral dilemmas it is thus possible to analyze their morally relevant features, such as whether the death of the man is a side-effect or rather the intended aim of the act (Waldmann, Nagel, and Wiegmann, 2012). In this respect, universal moral grammar theory is the only account, so far, that makes clear predictions on individuals' responses to a particular dilemma.

Mikhail lists four arguments in favor of his theory (Mikhail, 2007, p. 143): (i) findings from developmental psychology suggest complex and well-developed intuitive legal codes which children develop from early childhood on and advance during ontogeny (Piaget, 1952 and 1997; Kohlberg and Kramer, 1969; Kohlberg, Levine and Hewer, 1983; Warneken and Tomasello, 2009); (ii) every language makes use of deontic principles, as for instance 'obligatory', 'permissible', or 'forbidden' (Bybee and Fleischman, 1995); (iii) prohibition of strong violence, such as murder and rape, appear to be universal, just like legal terms that are based on causation, intention, and volition (Mikhail, 2002); and finally, (iv) neuroimaging studies have led researchers to conclude that a specific set of brain regions is involved in the formation of moral judgments and found that if one of these is impaired or lesioned, moral judgment can be dramatically altered (Anderson et al., 1999).

Although universal moral grammar theory is still in its infancy, the precision of its predictions with respect to the trolley cases by far surmounts what other theories can offer so far. Simultaneously, however, its restriction to trolley cases heavily limits its general validity. Moreover, Waldmann, Nagel, and Wiegmann (2012) present several reasons that a theory of moral and deontic rules can easily work without the innateness and universality claims made by Hauser and Mikhail.

4.3 Key studies in current Experimental Ethics

In our brief historical overview of work which classifies as seminal for Experimental Ethics so far, Greene's dual process theory probably is the best candidate if one wished to mark a specific point in time at which the first more traditional philosophers really became interested in the newly established empirical results. Since then, Experimental Ethics as a branch within Experimental Philosophy has been growing steadily (see Figure 4.1 above). As of March 2014 philpapers.org lists more than 180 studies in Experimental Ethics. Since it would be a hopeless endeavor to try to review all of these here, we picked out four topics which are currently investigated bustlingly in this field of research.

4.3.1 Moral objectivism and Moral relativism

Most theories within moral psychology have focused on identifying moral preferences as elicited by particular cases (e.g., moral dilemmas). One long-lasting controversy in moral philosophy, however, concerns the question of how universal moral values are in general. Adding to the academic controversy on whether moral values are relative or objective, recent research in Experimental Ethics suggests that lay people tend to be rather objectivistic (Goodwin and Darley, 2008 and 2010; Nichols, 2004). Goodwin and Darley (2008), for example, conducted a study in which they presented participants with different statements expressing tastes and aesthetic preferences, social conventions, scientific facts, and moral issues. Participants rated these statements with respect to their objectivity and the extent to which they agreed with them. The results suggest that individuals tend to regard moral statements as considerably more objective than social conventions and tastes. Some moral statements are even judged to be as objective as scientific facts (Goodwin and Darley, 2008).

However, concluding that lay people are moral objectivists is not warranted by the data. Rather, subjects reliably exhibit a pluralism of metaethical views (Goodwin and Darley, 2012). Moreover, Sarkissian et al. (2011) demonstrated that lay people do not seem to be consistent in their moral objectivism. Instead, their participants offered progressively more relativist intuitions when they were confronted with cultural scenarios or ways of life that differed from their own, for example, when they were asked to evaluate the same scenario from an extraterrestrial organism's or hunter-gatherer tribe's perspective. The authors conclude that earlier results were biased because subjects' perspectives were restricted by the presented scenario (Sarkissian et al., 2011). Their more elaborate experimental procedure thus offers a more nuanced picture of folk metaethics.

4.3.2 Individual differences in moral judgment

As the just cited research on moral objectivism shows, lay people reliably exhibit pluralistic moral evaluations – that is, a multitude of answers that not only differs between subjects but also even within single individuals. What sorts of factors, then, determine which moral preferences humans develop? Feltz and Cokely (2008) conducted a series of studies on individual differences in folk psychology and moral judgment, showing that both are related to stable individual factors, such as personality traits and cognitive styles. As a starting point they used the scenarios developed by Nichols (2004). In addition, they assessed personality traits by means of a brief 'big five' personality measure (Gosling, Rentfrow, and Swann, 2003). They found a significant positive correlation between openness scores and relativistic responses to moral issues (Feltz and Cokely, 2008). In another scenario they tested whether high extraversion and affection scores are correlated with relativistic evaluations of socially abnormal acts which do not harm others (e.g., having sex with a dead chicken and eating it afterwards). Feltz and Cokely found that participants with high scores in extraversion judge socially abnormal behavior as morally wrong and harmful even though the scenario does not involve harming another person. In contrast, the majority of participants give relativistic responses. Feltz and Cokely therefore claim that people's moral preferences relate to individual social sensitivities, predicted by extraversion scores.

In another study, Arvan (2013a) tested whether there is a correlation between moral and political intuitions and the dark triad, abbreviated 'D-3', personality traits: psychopathy, Machiavellianism, and narcissism (relating to anti-social and destructive behavior). Arvan used a

17-item moral intuition survey in which every item either relates to liberal or conservative statements (e.g., statements about gay marriage, gun control, distribution of wealth, free markets, etc., as well as trolley dilemmas). Personality traits were assessed by the short D-3 personality inventory (Jones and Paulhus, 2010). The results show several significant positive correlations of high scores in the dark triad traits with conservative moral intuitions but not with liberal moral intuitions (Arvan, 2013a). Moreover, Arvan found that high scores in all D-3 categories are positively correlated with consequentialist responses in the footbridge scenario. In a methodologically advanced follow-up study with an expanded moral intuition survey and double the sample size, Arvan replicated his earlier findings (Arvan, 2013b).

However, not only personal traits can bias moral judgments. Nadelhoffer and Feltz (2008), for example, found an actor-observer bias in responses to the switch scenario. Participants tend to claim that it is more permissible for an observer to throw the switch than it would be for themselves. Feltz and Cokely (2008) took a closer look at this aspect and hypothesized that cognitively highly reflective individuals would be more sensitive to different perspectives on moral dilemmas compared to lowly or averagely reflective individuals. Participants with high scores on cognitive reflectivity are said to search problem space more widely and consider alternatives and options in problem-solving situations more thoroughly before making their decision. To initiate a change in perspectives, Feltz and Cokely therefore presented a moral dilemma either described from a second person/actor perspective ('you') or from a third/observer person perspective ('Jim/he'). Highly cognitive reflective participants now showed a reversed effect: they felt a stronger moral obligation to kill one person in order to save the group in the actor context than in the observer context. Thus, they felt they were more morally obligated to kill a person in order to save the group than an observer of the scene. The low and average scorers, however, showed the expected opposite actor-observer bias. They felt less morally obligated to kill one person in order to save the group as compared to an uninvolved observer.

4.3.3   Cross-cultural differences in moral judgment

Although the literature on contextual and personal factors influencing individual moral judgment is rapidly expanding, the majority of studies are restricted to convenience samples of Westerners from Educated, Industrialized, Rich and Democratic (WEIRD) societies. Recent cross-cultural research, however, has established that the cultural background also affects nearly all aspects of the human psyche (for a comprehensive review see Henrich, Heine, and Norenzayan, 2010). In Kohlberg's moral stage theory, for instance, the most advanced stage is the post-conventional level on which the individual no longer relies on external conventional standards but evaluates right and wrong by ethical principles of justice and individual rights. While this has been confirmed for most adults in WEIRD populations, cross-cultural researchers found little evidence of a post-conventional stage in non-Western societies (Al-Shehab, 2002; Snarey, 1985).

Culturally biased moral judgments were also found by Haidt in his research on moral principles. In WEIRD societies, subjects usually rely on justice/fairness- and harm/care-based principles when judging the moral status of an action. However, Western religious conservatives and more collectivistic non-Westerners rely on a far wider range of morally relevant principles (Haidt, 2007; Haidt and Graham, 2007). For instance, in collectivistic cultures moral evaluations are tightly linked to the individual's obligations toward its community. Hence, in-group/out-group distinctions and obligations toward in-group authorities are deemed far more important in these cultures.

Moreover, findings from economic cross-cultural experiments challenged the idea that WEIRD fairness preferences are universal. Numerous studies in different countries from WEIRD societies, for example, have established that participants in an ultimatum game typically offer 40–50 percent of the money they receive to an anonymous responder. Offers below 30 percent are usually rejected by the responder (Camerer, 2003; Fehr and Gächter, 1998). These allegedly robust findings were interpreted as universal adaptations in human psychology and were thought to have evolved for stabilizing fair social exchange (see, e.g., Nowak, Page, and Sigmund, 2000).

In reaction to these findings, Henrich and colleagues conducted ultimatum game and related other economic experiments in 23 small-scale societies all over the world with more than one thousand subjects including foragers, horticulturalists, pastoralists, and subsistence farmers, from Africa, Amazonia, Oceania, Siberia, and New Guinea (Henrich et al., 2001; Henrich et al., 2006). Henrich's results drastically contradicted earlier findings. For instance, offers made by Hadza, foragers from Tanzania, and Tsimane, forager-horticulturalists from the Bolivian Amazon, were only half as high as those of US Americans. Moreover, the rejection rates, which are usually interpreted as a proxy for a population's willingness to punish unfair offers, were five times higher in US participants and the Sursurunga from Papua New Guinea, who have a reputation for being very prosocial, than in 70 percent of the other societies.

In summary, all experimental measures used by Henrich et al. showed that large-scale societies occupy the extreme ends of the respective distributions of behavior. Further data analysis identified populations' degrees of market integration and their participation in a world religion as robust predictors of higher offers in the ultimatum game. Both account independently for much of the variation between populations (Henrich, Heine, and Norenzayan, 2010). These studies indicate that members of small-scale societies have quite different concepts of what constitutes fair and unfair social exchanges compared to WEIRD populations. As an explanation for these results, Henrich, Heine, and Norenzayan (2010) suggest that institutions regulating social exchange might have culturally co-evolved with market integration in expanding large-scale sedentary populations.

4.3.4   Asymmetries in folk concepts: The side-effect effect

One of the groundbreaking studies in Experimental Ethics, finally, found an unexpected asymmetry in judgments of whether an agent intentionally performed an action or not. The vast majority of people are more likely to judge that P did x intentionally if P is perceived as causing a harm (e.g., harming the environment) than if x is perceived as causing a benefit (e.g., helping the environment) – although, in both cases, P explicitly states no intention to bring about x (Knobe, 2003). The moral status of an action's consequences thus seems to influence our judgment of non-moral aspects of the action in retrospect.

Why is this the case? The so called 'side-effect effect', also known as 'the Knobe effect', challenges the traditional perspective of a unidirectional relationship between intentionality and morality, stating that the agent's intention determines the moral outcome of an act. Rather, the moral outcome also seems to alter the attribution of intention, and the relationship thus seems to be bidirectional. Various studies have replicated the side-effect effect and shown that it can be found in different cultures (Knobe and Burra, 2006), using various scenarios (Mele and Cushman, 2007), as well as in children from age three on (Pellizzoni, Siegal, and Surian, 2009). Moreover, Ditto, Pizarro, and Tannenbaum (2009) showed that individual differences in moral judgment lead to corresponding evolutions of whether an action is performed intentionally or not.

However, the side-effect effect does not only pertain to intuitions about intentionality. Recent studies demonstrated that the moral outcome influences various other folk-psychological concepts, as for instance knowledge (Beebe and Buckwalter, 2010), valuing (Knobe and Roedder, 2009), desire (Pettit and Knobe, 2009), weakness of will (May and Holton, 2012), and happiness (Phillips, Nyholm, and Liao, 2011). Thus, Knobe's original findings concerning the relationship between moral judgments and intentionality apparently are a characteristic of a far more pervasive effect regarding the influence moral judgment has on how individuals understand each other's minds.

Although researchers agree on the robustness of the side-effect effect, they offer diverging explanatory theories. According to Knobe's conceptual competence model, for example, the asymmetry between subjects' attributions arises during the judgment stage. In this perspective, moral evaluation is an integrative part of people's conception of intentionality and other concepts. Thus, moral status considerations are thought to be relevant to the application of folk psychological concepts in general (Beebe and Buckwalter, 2010; Knobe et al., 2012).

Sripada's deep self concordance model agrees with Knobe's model that the asymmetry arises during the judgment stage. However, it doubts an influence of normative concepts (the blameworthiness of harming the environment) on descriptive concepts (attributing an intended act) in general (Sripada, 2012). Instead, the model states that when participants determine if an action was intentional, they do not focus on the 'surface' self, but rather on the 'deep' self (Sripada, 2012). When the CEO in Knobe's original vignettes tells the vice-president that he does not care about the environment at all, this information is attributed to a deeply anti-environmental stance. Thus, when the CEO harms the environment, this is concordant with his anti-environment deep self. In contrast, benefiting the environment, as he does in Knobe's second scenario, is discordant with his anti-environment deep self.

Other approaches, as for instance Nadelhoffer's motivational bias model (Nadelhoffer, 2004), agree that the effect occurs during the judgment stage but interpret it as an emotional reaction by means of which people blame the agent by stigmatizing the outcome as intentional.

In summary, current research indicates that intentions play a far more pervasive and complex role in folk psychology than previously thought. Intentions are unobservable and therefore need to be inferred. Consequently, this process of inferring intentionality is intrinsically error-prone. Moreover, a broad network of factors (moral outcome, moral norms, causal structure, semantic aspects of language, etc.) is involved when individuals infer intentions.

4.4 Conclusions

Experimental Ethics is rapidly growing. Hence, giving a detailed overview of all areas of inquiry would exceed this chapter by far. For instance, experimental findings about well-being, happiness, and virtue ethics, as well as moral motivation and the broad field of applied ethics, could not be outlined here (see for instance, Phillips, Misenheimer, and Knobe, 2011; Doris, 1998; Batson, 2008).

One key feature of Experimental Ethics is its interdisciplinarity. Still, most research in this field comes from philosophy and psychology departments. Yet, other disciplines, such as biology, anthropology, economics, and cognitive neurosciences, also substantially contribute to the field (e.g., de Waal, 2012; Henrich, Heine, and Norenzayan, 2010; Singer and Steinbeis, 2009).

Even though some philosophers doubt that the field of Experimental Ethics can contribute anything substantial to moral philosophy, the publication rate within the field indicates otherwise. Yet, the field is still in infancy. Recent studies on the side-effect effect, for example, suggest that much more is to be examined here. Further research, however, is needed in every area of Experimental Philosophy.

What can we learn from this brief historical sketch of moral psychology and Experimental Ethics? It is clear that moral psychologists are no longer restricted to developmental aspects of morality today. Philosophers, for their part, are no longer constrained to theorizing. Both use a broad repertoire of empirical methods and combine it with the traditional theoretical concepts from moral philosophy. The boundaries between Experimental Ethics and moral psychology, we think, are completely blurred. Would it yield any benefit if we tried to find characteristic differences of the two? According to Knobe and colleagues (2012) the project of Experimental Philosophy should reject this kind of questions, as they only impede progress (see also Nadelhoffer and Nahmias, 2007; for contrasting perspectives, see Horvath, 2010; Kauppinen, 2007). We agree.

Finally, the important question arises how Experimental Ethics and other areas of Experimental Philosophy are related. Research on the side-effect-effect, for example, demonstrates that this effect is relevant to both the formation of a moral judgment, which is part of Experimental Ethics, and the attribution of intentions, which is part of experimental philosophy of mind. Moreover, the side-effect effect is at work in various other folk-psychological concepts (knowledge, valuing, desiring, weakness of will, and happiness; see 4.3.4). Again, these results seem to inform not only Experimental Ethics but also experimental philosophy of mind and experimental epistemology. This underlines that different fields of philosophy are more closely related in experimental philosophy than they seem to be in traditional philosophy. We hold that this is due to the simple fact that philosophy is, and always has been, the study of tightly intertwined questions concerning human being and thinking. These interconnections, however, recently became apparent again when philosophical concepts were finally tackled with empirical instruments.

References

Al-Shehab, A. J. (2002), 'A Cross-sectional Examination of Levels of Moral Reasoning in a Sample of Kuwait University Faculty Members', *Social Behavior and Personality*, 30, pp. 813–820.

Anderson, S. W., A. Bechara, H. Damasio, D. Tranel, and A. R. Damasio (1999) 'Impairment of Social and Moral Behavior Related to Early Damage in Human Prefrontal Cortex', *Nature Neuroscience*, 2, 11, pp. 1032–1037.

Arvan, M. (2013a) 'Bad News for Conservatives? Moral Judgments and the Dark Triad Personality Traits: A Correlational Study', *Neuroethics*, 6, 2, pp. 307–318.

Arvan, M. (2013b) 'A Lot More Bad News for Conservatives, and a Little Bit of Bad News for Liberals? Moral Judgments and the Dark Triad Personality Traits: A Follow-up Study', *Neuroethics*, 6, 1, pp. 51–64.

Batson, C. D. (2008) 'Moral Masquerades: Experimental Exploration of the Nature of Moral Motivation', *Phenomenology and the Cognitive Sciences*, 7, 1, pp. 51–66.

Beebe, J. R. and W. Buckwalter (2010) 'The Epistemic Side-effect Effect', *Mind and Language*, 25, pp. 474–98.

Bybee, J. L. and S. Fleischman (eds) (1995) *Modality in Grammar and Discourse* (Amsterdam and Philadelphia: John Benjamins Publishing).

Camerer, C. (2003) *Behavior Game Theory: Experiments in Strategic Interaction* (Princeton: Princeton University Press).

Cosmides, L. and J. Tooby (1994) 'Better Than Rational: Evolutionary Psychology and the Invisible Hand', *The American Economic Review*, 84, 2, pp. 327–332.

De Waal, F. B. (2012) 'The Antiquity of Empathy', *Nature*, 336, pp. 874–876.

Ditto, P. H., D. A. Pizarro, and D. Tannenbaum (2009) 'Motivated Moral Reasoning', *Psychology of Learning and Motivation*, 50, pp. 307–338.

Doris, J. (1998) 'Persons, Situations, and Virtue Ethics', *Nous*, 32, 4, pp. 504–540.

Fehr, E. and S. Gächter (1998) 'Reciprocity and Economics: The Economic Implications of Homo Reciprocans', *European Economic Review*, 42, 3–5, pp. 845–859.

Feltz, A. and E. T. Cokely (2008) 'The Fragmented Folk: More Evidence of Stable Individual Differences in Moral Judgments and Folk Intuitions', in *Proceedings of the 30th Annual Conference of the Cognitive Science Society*, pp. 1771–1776.

Goodwin, G. P. and J. M. Darley (2008) 'The Psychology of Meta-ethics: Exploring Objectivism', *Cognition*, 106, 3, pp. 1339–1366.

Goodwin, G. P. and J. M. Darley (2010) 'The Perceived Objectivity of Ethical Beliefs: Psychological Findings and Implications for Public Policy', *Review of Philosophy and Psychology*, 1, pp. 161–188.

Goodwin, G. P. and J. M. Darley (2012) 'Why Are Some Moral Beliefs Perceived to be More Objective Than Others?', *Journal of Experimental Social Psychology*, 48, pp. 250–256.

Gosling, S. D., P. J. Rentfrow, and W. B. Swann (2003) 'A Very Brief Measure of the Big-Five Personality Domains', *Journal of Research in Personality*, 37, pp. 504–528.

Gräfenhain, M. and A. Wiegmann (2013) 'Scientific Study of Morals', in C. Lutege (ed.) *Handbook of the Philosophical Foundations of Business Ethics* (Netherlands: Springer), pp. 1477–1501.

Greene, J. D. (2007) 'The Secret Joke of Kant's Soul', in W. Sinnott-Armstrong (ed.) *Moral Psychology, Vol. 3, The Neuroscience of Morality: Emotion, Brain Disorders, and Development* (Cambridge: MIT Press), pp. 35–79.

Greene, J. D., R. B. Sommerville, L. E. Nystrom, J. M. Darley, and J. D. Cohen (2001) 'An fMRI Investigation of Emotional Engagement in Moral Judgment', *Science*, 293, pp. 2105–2108.

Greene, J. D. and J. Haidt (2002) 'How (and Where) Does Moral Judgment Work?', *Trends in Cognitive Sciences*, 6, 12, pp. 517–523.

Greene, J. D., S. A. Morelli, K. Lowenberg, L. E. Nystrom, and J. D. Cohen (2008) 'Cognitive Load Selectively Interferes with Utilitarian Moral Judgment', *Cognition*, 107, pp. 1144–1154.

Haidt, J. (2001) 'The Emotional Dog and Its Rational Tail: A Social Intuitionist Approach to Moral Judgment', *Psychological Review*, 108, 4, pp. 814–834.

Haidt, J. (2007). 'The New Synthesis in Moral Psychology', *Science*, 316, pp. 998–1002.

Haidt, J. and J. Graham (2007) 'When Morality Opposes Justice: Conservatives Have Moral Intuitions That Liberals May Not Recognize', *Social Justice Research*, 20, pp. 98–116.

Hauser, M., F. Cushman, L. Young, R. Kang-Xing Jin, and J. Mikhail (2007) 'A Dissociation Between Moral Judgments and Justifications', *Mind & Language*, 22, 1, pp. 1–21.

Henrich, J., J. S. Heine, and A. Norenzayan (2010) 'The Weirdest People in the World?', *Behavioral and Brain Sciences*, 33, 2–3, pp. 61–83.

Henrich, J., R. Boyd, S. Bowles, H. Gintis, C. Camerer, E. Fehr, and R. McElreath (2001) 'In Search of Homo Economicus: Experiments in 15 Small-scale Societies', *American Economic Review*, 91, pp. 73–78.

Henrich, J., R. McElreath, J. Ensminger, A. Barr, C. Barrett, A. Bolyanatz, J. C. Cardenas, M. Gurven, E. Gwako, N. Henrich, C. Lesorogol, F. Marlowe, D. Tracer, and J. Ziker (2006) 'Costly Punishment Across Human Societies', *Science*, 312, 5868, pp. 1767–1770.

Horvath, J. (2010) 'How (Not) to React to Experimental Philosophy', *Philosophical Psychology*, 23, 4, pp. 447–480.

Jones, D. N. and D. L. Paulhus (2010) 'Differentiating the Dark Triad Within the Interpersonal Circumplex', in L. M. Horowitz and S. N. Strack (eds), *Handbook of Interpersonal Theory and Research* (New York: Guilford), pp. 249–267.

Kauppinen, A. (2007) 'The Rise and Fall of Experimental Philosophy', *Philosophical Explorations*, 10, 2, pp. 95–118.

Kelly, D., S. Stich, K. J. Haley, S. J. Eng, and D. M. T. Fessler (2007) 'Harm, Affect, and the Moral/Conventional Distinction', *Mind & Language*, 22, pp. 117–131.

Knobe, J. (2003) 'Intentional Action and Side Effects in Ordinary Language', *Analysis*, 63, 279, pp. 190–194.

Knobe, J. and A. Burra (2006) 'The Folk Concepts of Intention and Intentional Action: A Cross-cultural Study', *Journal of Cognition and Culture*, 6, 1–2, pp. 113–132.

Knobe, J. and S. Nichols (2008) 'An Experimental Philosophy Manifesto', in J. Knobe and S. Nichols (eds) *Experimental Philosophy* (Oxford: Oxford University Press), pp. 3–14.

Knobe, J. and E. Roedder (2009) 'The Ordinary Concept of Valuing', *Philosophical Issues*, 19, pp. 131–147.

Knobe, J., W. Buckwalter, S. Nichols, P. Robbins, H. Sarkissian, and T. Sommers (2012) 'Experimental Philosophy', *Annual Review of Psychology*, 63, pp. 81–99.

Kohlberg, L. and R. Kramer (1969) 'Continuities and Discontinuities in Childhood and Adult Moral Development', *Human Development*, 12, pp. 93–120.

Kohlberg, L., C. Levine, and A. Hewer (1983) *Moral Stages: A Current Formulation and a Response to Critics* (Basel, New York: Karger).

Libet, B., C. A. Gleason, E. W. Wright, and D. K. Pearl (1983) 'Time of Conscious Intention to Act in Relation to Onset of Cerebral Activity (Readiness-potential): The Unconscious Initiation of a Freely Voluntary Act', *Brain*, 106, 3, pp. 623–642.

May, J. and R. Holton (2012) 'What in the World Is Weakness of Will?', *Philosophical Studies*, 157, 3, pp. 341–360.

Mele, A. R. and F. Cushman (2007) 'Intentional Action, Folk Judgments, and Stories: Sorting Things Out', *Midwest Studies in Philosophy*, 31, 1, pp. 184–201.

Mikhail, J. (2002) 'Law, Science, and Morality: A Review of Richard Posner's "The Problematics of Moral and Legal Theory"', *Stanford Law Review*, 54, pp. 1057–1127.

Mikhail, J. (2007) 'Universal Moral Grammar: Theory, Evidence and the Future', *Trends in Cognitive Sciences*, 11, 4, pp. 143–152.

Mikhail, J. (2009) 'Moral Grammar and Intuitive Jurisprudence: A Formal Model of Unconscious Moral and Legal Knowledge', *Psychology of Learning and Motivation*, 50, pp. 27–100.

Moll, J. and R. de Oliveira-Souza (2007) 'Moral Judgments, Emotions, and the Utilitarian Brain', *Trends in Cognitive Sciences*, 11, pp. 319–321.

Nadelhoffer, T. (2004) 'On Praise, Side Effects, and Folk Ascriptions of Intentionality', *Journal of Theoretical and Philosophical Psychology*, 24, 2, p. 196.

Nadelhoffer, T. and E. Nahmias (2007) 'The Past and Future of Experimental Philosophy', *Philosophical Explorations*, 10, 2, pp. 123–149.

Nadelhoffer, T. and A. Feltz (2008) 'The Actor-Observer Bias and Moral Intuitions: Adding Fuel to Sinnott-Armstrong's Fire', *Neuroethics*, 1, 2, pp. 133–144.

Nichols, S. (2004) 'After Objectivity: An Empirical Study of Moral Judgment', *Philosophical Psychology*, 17, 1, pp. 3–26.

Nowak, M. A., K. M. Page, and K. Sigmund (2000) 'Fairness versus Reason in the Ultimatum Game', *Science*, 289, 5485, pp. 1773–1775.

Nucci, L. P. and M. S. Nucci (1982) 'Children's Responses to Moral and Social Conventional Transgressions in Free-play Settings', *Child Development*, 53, 5, pp. 1337–1342.

Nucci, L. P. and E. Turiel (1978) 'Social Interactions and the Development of Social Concepts in Preschool Children', *Child Development*, 49, 2, pp. 400–407.

Pellizzoni, S., M. Siegal, and L. Surian (2009) 'Foreknowledge, Caring, and the Side-effect Effect in Young Children', *Developmental Psychology*, 45, 1, pp. 289–295.

Pettit D. and J. Knobe (2009) 'The Pervasive Impact of Moral Judgment', *Mind and Language*, 24, 5, pp. 586–604.

Phillips, J., L. Misenheimer, and J. Knobe (2011) 'The Ordinary Concept of Happiness (and Others Like It)', *Emotion Review*, 71, pp. 929–937.

Phillips, J., S. Nyholm, and S. Liao (2011) 'The Ordinary Concept of Happiness' (New Haven, CT: Yale University), Unpublished manuscript.

Piaget, J. (1952) *The Origins of Intelligence in Children* (Madison: International University Press), Original work published 1936.

Piaget, J. (1997) *The Moral Judgment of the Child* (New York: Free Press), Original work published 1932.

Sarkissian, H., J. Park, D. Tien, J. C. Wright, and J. Knobe (2011) 'Folk Moral Relativism', *Mind & Language*, 26, 4, pp. 482–505.

Singer, T. and N. Steinbeis (2009) 'Differential Roles of Fairness- and Compassion-based Motivations for Cooperation, Defection, and Punishment', *Annals of the New York Academy of Sciences*, 1167, pp. 41–50.

Snarey, J. R. (1985) 'The Cross-cultural Universality of Social-moral Development: A Critical Review of Kohlbergian Research', *Psychological Bulletin*, 97, 2, pp. 202–232.

Sripada, C. (2012) 'Mental State Attributions and the Side-effect Effect', *Journal of Experimental Psychology*, 48, 1, pp. 232–238.

Suter, R. S. and R. Hertwig (2011) 'Time and Moral Judgment', *Cognition*, 119, 3, pp. 454–458.

Waldmann, M. R., J. Nagel, and A. Wiegmann (2012) 'Moral Judgment', in K. J. Holyoak and R. G. Morrison (eds) *The Oxford Handbook of Thinking and Reasoning* (New York: Oxford University Press), pp. 364–389.

Warneken, F. and M. Tomasello (2009) 'Varieties of Altruism in Children and Chimpanzees', *Trends in Cognitive Sciences*, 13, 9, pp. 397–402.

Part II

Applied Experimental Ethics: Case Studies

Introduction to Part II

Part I has set the stage for Experimental Ethics. The following part is supposed to provide the reader with a more concrete idea of what Experimental Ethicists do. It therefore presents five exemplary case studies that address concrete ethical questions with the experimental method.

In the first chapter, Eric Schwitzgebel investigates the question of whether professional ethicists behave differently than do non-ethicists of similar social background. The evidence he presents suggests that ethicists are no likelier to donate money, organs, or blood; choose a vegetarian diet; or return their library books. On some issues, however, such as charitable donation and vegetarianism, ethicists tend to endorse more stringent ethical norms than do non-ethicists. This pattern might fit with a view on which the role of the philosopher is only to espouse and defend ethical norms, not to live according to those norms.

Verena Wagner rejects the view that the famous 'Knobe effect' reveals an asymmetry within people's judgments concerning actions with good or bad side effects. She agrees with interpretations that see the ascriptions made by survey subjects as moral judgments rather than ascriptions of intentionality. On this basis, she provides an explanation as to why people are right in blaming and 'expraising' agents that acted on unacceptable motives, but praise and excuse agents who meet intersubjective expectations by acting on acceptable motives. The asymmetry only arises when blameworthiness and praiseworthiness are seen as instances of one and the same concept: moral responsibility.

Ezio Di Nucci analyzes the relationship between the *Doctrine of Double Effect* and the *Trolley Problem*. The former offers a solution for the latter only on the premise that killing the one in *Bystander at the Switch* is permissible. He offers both empirical and theoretical arguments against the permissibility of killing the one: firstly, by presenting data from empirical studies according to which the intuition that killing the one is permissible is neither widespread nor stable; secondly, by defending a normative principle according to which killing the one in Bystander at the Switch is not permissible. In conclusion, there just is no trolley *problem*.

Stephan Wolf and Alexander Lenger begin their chapter with a review of the debate between Rawls and Harsanyi over the 'right' distributive principle – maximin or utilitarianism – shows that different positive assumptions about the empirical world can have substantial effects on normative conclusions. They then refer to an experiment by Frohlich and Oppenheimer to study the validity of Rawls's and Harsanyi's competing normative claims by empirically challenging their underlying positive assumptions on human decision making. Consecutively, the authors present an original experiment where people chose distributional schemes in a production economy with social immobility. Behind a veil, subjects strongly tended toward income equalization, in line with Rawls's theory.

In the final chapter, Ulrich Frey addresses the ethical problem of environmental protection. He argues that while people are willing to protect natural resources, comparably little effort on an individual, national, and global level is observed. Frey discusses possible reasons for this discrepancy by discussing value assignments and presents experimental results on environmental values.

5
The Moral Behavior of Ethicists and the Role of the Philosopher

Eric Schwitzgebel

Professional ethicists appear to behave no differently than do non-ethicists of similar social background. However, ethicists also appear to embrace more stringent moral norms than do non-ethicists, at least on some issues. Part 1 will summarize the empirical evidence. Part 2 will discuss one possibly attractive response: that an ethicist's role is to espouse and defend moral norms, with no special obligation to live according to the norms she espouses and defends.

5.1 The moral behavior of ethicists

So far, all of the systematic empirical studies of the moral behavior of professional ethicists have been done by a single research group – the research group led by Joshua Rust and Eric Schwitzgebel, the author of this chapter. This will, then, be an embarrassingly self-centered review.

Our first study (Schwitzgebel and Rust, 2009) examined professional philosophers' opinions about the moral behavior of ethicists. We offered gourmet chocolate to passersby at a meeting of the Pacific Division of the American Philosophical Association in exchange for completing, on the spot, a '5 minute philosophical-scientific questionnaire'. There were two versions of the survey. One version asked respondents whether 'professors specializing in ethics tend, on average, to behave morally better, worse, or about the same as philosophers not specializing in ethics', with a seven-point response scale from 'substantially morally better' (marked 1) through 'about the same' (marked 4) to 'substantially morally worse' (marked 7). Opinion was divided: 35 percent of respondents circled a number on the 'better' side of the scale (1–3); 46 percent circled 4 'about the same', and 19 percent circled a number on the 'worse' side. The second version asked respondents to rate the overall moral behavior of an arbitrarily (alphabetically) selected ethicist from their own department and also to rate the overall moral behavior of a similarly selected specialist in metaphysics and epistemology: 44 percent rated the selected ethicist morally better behaved than the other selected philosopher, 26 percent rated them the same, and 30 percent rated the ethicist worse – a trend toward 'better' over 'worse', but not statistically significant in our sample.

We have directly examined moral behavior – or behavior that is arguably moral – using a wide variety of measures. Schwitzgebel (2009) examined the rates at which relatively obscure philosophy books – the kinds of books likely to be borrowed mostly by professors and advanced graduate students in the field – were missing from leading academic libraries in the US and Britain. Ethics books were substantially more likely to be missing than other types of philosophy books, even though the two groups of books were similar in overall age, check-out rate, and holdings per library. Schwitzgebel and Rust (2010) found that ethicists and political philosophers were no more likely to vote in public elections, as measured by state records of voter participation, than were non-ethicist philosophers or professors in fields other than philosophy or political science. (Political scientists, in contrast, did vote more often than other professors.) Schwitzgebel et al. (2012) found that ethicists were no more likely to behave courteously at professional meetings than were other philosophers, as measured by rates of talking audibly during the formal presentation, allowing doors to slam when entering or exiting mid-session, and leaving behind cups and trash at one's seat. Audiences in environmental ethics sessions did, however, leave behind less trash. Rust and Schwitzgebel (2013) found that ethicists were no more likely than other professors to respond to email messages designed to look like queries from students. Schwitzgebel and Rust (2014) found that non-ethicist philosophers were more likely to respond to a request to complete a survey when they were offered a charity incentive to do so ($10 to the respondent's choice of six major, well-regarded charities) than when they were not offered a charity incentive, but ethicists appeared to be unmoved by the charity incentive. Schwitzgebel (2013) found that ethicists were no more likely than other philosophers to pay their registration fees at meetings of the American Philosophical Association in the mid-2000s, when the APA relied upon an honor system for registration payment.

Schwitzgebel and Rust (2014) examined self-reports of moral attitudes and moral behavior, across several issues, in three groups of professors in five US states: philosophers specializing in ethics, philosophers not specializing in ethics, and a comparison group of other professors from the same universities. Some of the self-reports could be directly checked against objectively measured behavior, thus enabling a three-way comparison of self-reported attitude, self-reported behavior, and directly measured behavior for these three groups of professors. Schwitzgebel and Rust solicited self-reported attitudes and behavior on nine different issues: membership in one's main disciplinary academic society (such as the American Philosophical Association), voting in public elections, staying in touch with one's mother, regularly eating the meat of mammals, blood donation, organ donation, answering student emails, charitable giving, and honesty in responding to survey questions. The groups did not detectably differ in their self-reported rates of membership in disciplinary societies, in their self-reported voting rates, in their self-reported rates of blood or organ donation, in their self-reported responsiveness to student emails, or in their self-reported honesty in answering survey questionnaires. Non-philosophers reported more regular contact with their mothers than did the two groups of philosophers. Non-ethicist philosophers reported giving a lower percentage of their income to charity than did either ethicists or non-philosophers. And although ethicists reported eating the meat of mammals at fewer meals per week than did the other two groups, the three groups did not detectably differ in the rates at which they reported having eaten the meat of a mammal at their previous evening meal. Checking response accuracy in various ways (e.g., comparing self-reported vote rate with state recorded voting rates for the same respondents), the three groups did not appear to differ overall in the accuracy of their self-reports. Impressionistically, the aggregate result is approximately a tie. Schwitzgebel and Rust also mathematically aggregated the behavioral data in three different ways, finding no difference overall between ethicists and the other groups by any of the aggregate measures. Schwitzgebel and Rust (forthcoming) present a meta-analysis of all the studies described in this section and again find no tendency for ethicists to behave morally better or morally worse overall than other philosophers.

Schwitzgebel and Rust also examined correlations between self-reported normative attitude and both self-reported and directly measured behavior. Although ethicists showed a detectably higher correlation between attitude and behavior than did the other groups with respect to voting in public elections ($r = 0.36$, vs. 0.14 for non-ethicist philosophers and 0.01 for non-philosophers), they showed a detectably lower correlation between attitude and self-reported charitable giving ($r = 0.33$, vs. 0.46 for non-ethicist philosophers and 0.62 for non-philosophers). The aggregate attitude-behavior correlation did not detectably differ among the groups (r = 0.20 for ethicists, vs. 0.24 for non-ethicist philosophers and 0.16 for non-philosophers; all comparisons in this paragraph use Fisher's r-to-z conversion and a pairwise alpha level of 0.05).

The most notable group difference Schwitzgebel and Rust found was this: On several issues, ethicists appeared to endorse more stringent moral standards. Ethicists were more likely than other groups to rate blood donation and charitable donation as morally good, and they were more likely to rate meat-eating and failing to be an organ donor as morally bad. The results are especially striking for vegetarianism: 60 percent of ethicists rated 'regularly eating the meat of mammals, such as beef or pork' somewhere on the 'bad' side of a 1–9 scale from 'very morally bad' to 'very morally good', compared to 45 percent of non-ethicist philosophers and only 19 percent of professors from departments other than philosophy (χ^2 = 64.2, p < 0.001). When asked 'About what percentage of income should the typical professor donate to charity? (Enter "0" if you think it's not the case that the typical professor should donate to charity.)', only 9 percent of ethicists entered '0', compared to 24 percent of non-ethicist philosophers and 25 percent of other professors (χ^2 = 18.2, p < 0.001); and among those not entering '0', the geometric mean was 5.9 percent for ethicists vs. 4.8 percent for both of the two other groups (ANOVA, F = 3.6, p = 0.03). However, as mentioned above, these differences in normative attitude did not detectably manifest in behavior.

5.2   The role of the philosopher

If the role of the philosophical ethicist were to present her- or himself as a living model of wise conduct, these results might be alarming. However, most philosophers seem to be unalarmed and unsurprised by the results described in Part 1. Most philosophers' general idea of the role of the philosopher does not appear to be threatened by the possibility that ethicists behave overall no differently than do non-ethicists, or by the possibility that ethicists behave overall no more consistently with their espoused opinions, or by the possibility that ethicists espouse stringent moral views without tending to shift their behavior accordingly.

I think of Randy Cohen's farewell column as ethics columnist for the *New York Times Magazine*. Cohen writes:

> Writing the column has not made me even slightly more virtuous. And I didn't have to be.... I wasn't hired to personify virtue, to be a role model for kids, but to write about virtue in a way readers might

find engaging. Consider sports writers: not 2 in 20 can hit the curve-ball, and why should they? They're meant to report on athletes, not be athletes. And that's the self-serving rationalization I'd have clung to had the cops hauled me off in handcuffs.

What spending my workday thinking about ethics did do was make me acutely aware of my own transgressions, of the times I fell short. It is deeply demoralizing. (Cohen, 2011)

In light of the vegetarianism results described in Part 1, we might consider the following scenario: An ethicist philosopher considers the question of whether it's morally permissible to eat the meat of factory-farmed mammals. She reads Peter Singer. She reads objections and replies to Singer. In light of the considerations, she concludes – as the majority of U.S. ethicists seem to – that in fact it is morally bad to eat meat. She presents the material in her applied ethics class. Maybe she even writes on the issue. However, instead of changing her behavior to match her new moral opinions, she retains her old behavior. She teaches Singer's defense of vegetarianism, both inwardly and outwardly endorsing it, and then proceeds to the university cafeteria for a cheeseburger, perhaps feeling somewhat bad about it.

To the student who sees her in the cafeteria, our philosopher says: Singer's arguments are sound. It is morally wrong of me to eat this delicious cheeseburger. But my role as a philosopher is only to discuss philosophical issues, to present and evaluate philosophical views and arguments, not to live accordingly. Indeed, it would not be fair to expect me to live to higher moral standards just because I am an ethicist. I am paid to teach and write, like my colleagues in other fields; it would be an additional burden on me, not placed upon them, to demand that I also live my life as a model. Before accepting such an additional demand, I would require additional compensation.

Furthermore, our ethicist continues, the demand that ethicists live as moral models would create distortive pressures on the field that might tend to lead us away from the moral truth. If I feel no inward or outward pressure to live according to my publicly espoused doctrines, then I am free to explore doctrines that demand high levels of self-sacrifice on an equal footing with more permissive doctrines. If instead I felt an obligation to live as I teach, I would feel considerable pressure to avoid highly self-sacrificial doctrines. I would be highly motivated to avoid concluding that the wealthy should give most of their wealth to charity or that people should never lie out of self-interest. The world is better served if the intellectual discourse of moral philosophy is undistorted by such pressures, that is, if ethicists are not expected to live out their moral opinions.

Such a view of the role of the philosopher is very different from the view of most ancient ethicists. Socrates, Confucius, and the Stoics sought to live according to the norms they espoused and invited others to judge their lives as an expression of their doctrines.

It is an open and little discussed question which is the better vision of the role of the philosopher.

References

Cohen, R. (2011) 'Goodbye', *New York Times Magazine,* Feb. 27 issue, http://www.nytimes.com/2011/02/27/magazine/27FOB-Ethicist-t.html.

Rust, J. and E. Schwitzgebel (2013) 'Ethicists' and Nonethicists' Responsiveness to Student Emails: Relationships among Expressed Normative Attitude, Self-Described Behavior, and Empirically Observed Behavior', *Metaphilosophy*, 44, pp. 350–371.

Schwitzgebel, E. (2009) 'Do Ethicists Steal More Books?', *Philosophical Psychology*, 22, pp. 711–725.

Schwitzgebel, E. (2013) 'Are Ethicists Any More Likely to Pay Their Registration Fees at Professional Meetings?', *Economics & Philosophy*, 29, pp. 371–380.

Schwitzgebel, E. and J. Rust (2009) 'The Moral Behaviour of Ethicists: Peer Opinion', *Mind,* 118, pp. 1043–1059.

Schwitzgebel, E. and J. Rust (2010) 'Do Ethicists and Political Philosophers Vote More Often Than Other Professors?', *Review of Philosophy and Psychology*, 1, pp. 189–199.

Schwitzgebel, E. and J. Rust (2014) 'The Moral Behavior of Ethics Professors: Relationships among Self-Reported Behavior, Expressed Normative Attitude, and Directly Observed Behavior', *Philosophical Psychology*.

Schwitzgebel, E. and J. Rust (forthcoming) 'The Behavior of Ethicists', in W. Buckwalter and J. Sytsma (eds), *Blackwell Companion to Experimental Philosophy*.

Schwitzgebel, E., J. Rust, L. T.-L. Huang, A. T. Moore, and J. Coates (2012) 'Ethicists' Courtesy at Philosophy Conferences', *Philosophical Psychology*, 25, pp. 331–340.

6
Explaining the Knobe Effect

Verena Wagner

6.1 Introduction

Joshua Knobe famously conducted several case studies in which he confronted survey subjects with a chairman who decides to start a new program in order to increase profits and by doing so brings about certain foreseen side effects. Depending on what the side effect is in the respective case, either harming or helping the environment, people gave asymmetric answers to the question as to whether or not the chairman brought about the side effect *intentionally*. Eighty-two percent of those subjects confronted with the harm scenario judged the chairman to have *harmed* the environment intentionally, but only 23 percent of the subjects confronted with the help scenario judged the chairman to have *helped* the environment intentionally (Knobe, 2003). This at first sight surprising asymmetry is called the 'Knobe effect', and together with the explanation Knobe provided for his findings it gave rise to a great amount of responses in the literature. Many follow-up studies were conducted that were meant either to confirm or to reject the Knobe effect, and many comments were written on how to interpret the data correctly. Most of these very different responses share the view that the asymmetry is surprising and has to be explained: the chairman went through the same reasoning and decision process, both side effects are equally foreseen by the chairman, his motivation (which is making profit) is both times the very same, and there is no external influence that could explain why people judge his *harming* the environment to be brought about intentionally, but *helping* the environment not to be. The only difference seems to be that harming the environment is considered to be *bad* and helping the environment is considered to be *good*. Indeed, this asymmetry is in need of explanation.

In this paper I aim at providing an explanation of the Knobe effect that is based on the claim that people are in fact judging an agent morally when they ascribe intentionality to an agent's behavior. This kind of interpretation involves no new insight, and variations of it are given in several responses to the Knobe effect, for example in Adams and Steadman (2004a; 2004b). But unlike many other defenders of this claim, I do not think that this is sufficient for an explanation. Such an approach can be a first step, but it provides no explanation of the asymmetry itself because the same asymmetry arises when the chairman is judged to be *responsible* for harming, but *not* responsible for helping the environment. A sufficient explanation additionally requires either an explanation of why the *concept* of moral responsibility, in contrast to the concept of intentional action, contains an asymmetry that justifies people's diverging judgments; or it has to explain why people wrongly apply the concept of moral responsibility in an asymmetric way. There is no explanation given by merely stating that people judge the chairman to be responsible for the bad side effect but not to be responsible for the good one under the same circumstances. I defend the view that people – though being mistaken in their asymmetric ascription of *intentionality* – are doing the right thing in judging the harming chairman to be blameworthy, but the helping chairman to be not praiseworthy. However, I aim at showing that the ascriptions interpreted in this way do not involve an asymmetry after all. The asymmetry only arises when praise and blame are subsumed under one and the same concept: the concept of *moral responsibility*.

Among all the follow-up studies that were made after Knobe's original findings, there is one study I will refer to in detail. Joshua Shepherd conducted a series of surveys in 2012 that are based on Knobe's chairman cases and an example of Phelan and Sarkissian (2008) of a city planner who produces good or bad side effects in the course of cleaning an area from toxic waste. Shepherd's study is more conclusive than Knobe's because Shepherd varies the valence of the main goal (making profit, creating jobs, cleaning toxic area, etc.); the valence of the side effect (poisoning the groundwater, in-/decreasing joblessness, in-/decreasing cancer levels etc.); and the agent's verbally expressed attitude ('I don't care about', 'I feel terrible about', 'That's great news about', etc.).

6.2   Interpreting the data

Knobe's original study contains two case descriptions of a chairman who decides to start a new program in order to make profit. The only difference between the two descriptions concerned the respective side effect that resulted from starting this program: either the environment was helped or it was harmed.

> The vice-president of a company went to the chairman of the board and said, 'We are thinking of starting a new program. It will help us increase profits, but [and] it will also harm [help] the environment.' The chairman of the board answered, 'I don't care at all about harming [helping] the environment. I just want to make as much profit as I can. Let's start the new program.' They started the new program. Sure enough, the environment was harmed [helped]. (Knobe, 2003)

Knobe presented the following results after questioning survey subjects as to whether the chairman brought about the respective side effect intentionally: 82 percent of the subjects confronted with the harm scenario judged the chairman to have *harmed* the environment intentionally, but only 23 percent of the subjects confronted with the help scenario judged the chairman to have *helped* the environment intentionally. Knobe himself interprets his findings by stating that 'people's intuitions as to whether or not a behavior was performed intentionally can sometimes be influenced by moral considerations' and that 'when people are wondering whether or not a given behavior was performed intentionally, they are sometimes influenced by their beliefs about whether the behavior itself was good or bad' (Knobe, 2006, p. 205). In a later article, Knobe claims 'there is a psychological process that makes people more willing to apply the concept [e.g., of intentional action] in cases of morally bad side-effects and less willing to apply the concept in cases of morally good side-effects' (Pettit and Knobe, 2009, p. 590). For sure, moral considerations *do* play a role here, but it is doubtful whether Knobe is right that the application of concepts is generally *affected* by moral considerations about the goodness or badness of the side effect such that people are influenced in a way they should not be.

Adams and Steadman (2004a; 2004b) interpret the data by reference to a pragmatic usage of intentional language: while 'the folk do not normally possess a clearly articulated theory of the mental mechanisms of intentional action[, they] do possess a very clear notion of the pragmatic features of intentional action and talk of intentional action due to the role of talk of intention in social praise and blame' (2004a, p. 177). Further, Adams and Steadman contend:

> We suspect that what is going on in the minds of the folk is that they disapprove of the chairman's indifference to the harm of the

environment. They want to blame that indifference and they know that their blame is stronger and more effective at discouraging such acts, if the chairman is said to have done the action *intentionally*. (Adams and Steadman, 2004a, p. 178)

I agree with views like the one of Adams and Steadman that survey subjects actually ascribe blameworthiness to the harming chairman but withhold praiseworthiness from the helping chairman, and for this purpose they use the vocabulary of *intentionally* harming but *not* intentionally helping the environment. But subjects are mistaken here. It may be useful within a *pragmatic* context to ascribe intentionality toward an agent that is regarded as a proper target of blame ('It's your fault, you did it on purpose!') and to withhold the ascription of intentionality toward an agent who is seen as no proper target of praise ('It's not your credit, you didn't do it intentionally!') in order to emphasize the underlying moral judgment; nevertheless, this is no good reason to conclude that the concept of intentional behavior inherits a real asymmetry people refer to. Indeed, in both scenarios the chairman brought about the side effect intentionally: he intentionally harmed the environment and he intentionally helped the environment though he intended neither result. Albeit both chairmen brought about their respective side effect intentionally, the one is blameworthy for the produced harm, but the other is not praiseworthy for the produced help. The asymmetry within the ascription of intentionality leads back to this asymmetry between praise and blame. However, this explanation provides no answer to the question concerning the *source* of the asymmetry and merely locates the asymmetry somewhere else: in the concept of moral responsibility. In the following, I will refer to this asymmetry between the ascription of blame and praise rather than the asymmetry within subjects' ascription of intentional action. Further, I will argue that there is no such asymmetry when praise and blame are not subsumed under one concept.

6.3   Some Shepherd effects

In this section I will point out briefly in what way Shepherd extended Knobe's original setting and what effects resulted from these changes. Further, I will aim at explaining the Knobe effect and the additional effects found by Shepherd. In the surveys, Shepherd sticks to Knobe's original example of a chairman who starts a new program and produces environmental side effects. Additionally, he uses an example of Phelan and Sarkissian (2008, p. 296) in which a city planner starts a program in order to clean up toxic waste, which also produces certain side effects. Shepherd compares the original not caring but profit driven chairman with a chairman who is still profit driven but has another *attitude* toward the side effect: he either feels terrible about harming the environment or he is happy about helping the environment. Additionally, Shepherd compares all these cases with a chairman who has a nobler *main goal*: creating jobs for the homeless and disadvantaged. Correspondingly, Shepherd makes certain variations in the city planner's example: he manipulates the valence of the main goal (making profit vs. cleaning up toxic waste), the badness of the side effects (poisoning the groundwater vs. raising joblessness), and the goodness of the side effects (decreasing joblessness vs. decreasing cancer levels). Shepherd predicts that his results will show effects on the agent's *attitude*, on the valence of the *main goal* and on the valence of the respective *side effects*. Surprisingly, only an insignificant effect for the agent's attitude emerged when the side effect was bad, but there was a significant effect for the agent's attitude when the side effect was good. Changes of the respective valence of the main goal and the side effect did produce an effect when the side effect was bad, but none when the side effect was good. Shepherd interprets these findings as follows:

> While the valence of an agent's main goal or side effect significantly impacts folk ascriptions in harming cases, the agent's attitude does so in helping cases. [...] the asymmetry might result from the spontaneous triggering of a schema linking norm violations with intentionality – a schema not triggering by instances of helping. (Shepherd, 2012, p. 181)

In the following I will comment on Shepherd's assumptions and findings. I will start with my own explanation of the Knobe effect based on Shepherd's results. Then, I will discuss Shepherd's result that the agent's attitude seems to have an effect in helping cases though no significant effect in harming cases. I will not give further arguments for treating ascriptions and non-ascriptions of intentionality as moral judgments in the way Adams and Steadman propose. My central aim is to show that there is no asymmetry in blaming the harming chairman though not praising the helping chairman.

6.3.1 Subjective and intersubjective valence

Shepherd describes the valence of creating jobs for the homeless and disadvantaged as 'better' than the chairman's original main goal of making profit. In the same sense the side effect of poisoned ground-water is set as 'worse' than raising joblessness, and decreasing cancer levels is set to be 'better' than decreasing joblessness. Shepherd seems to assume that people commonly share this structure of valence in general; and he seems to assume an intersubjective agreement among people's judgments according to which a main goal or a side effect is judged to be good or bad, and according to which some are 'better' or 'worse' than others. This is a very important assumption because it shows on what basis survey subjects are invited to form their moral judgments. Further, it is this intersubjective agreement that underlies such valence talk that gives rise to certain moral expectations toward agents and their behavior in certain circumstances. If the valence of the side effect's occurrence is found to be worse than the non-achievement of an agent's main goal, it is expected from the agent that she refrains from performing the action in order to avoid the side effect. The profit-driven chairman is morally expected *not* to start the program in order to avoid environmental harm because the valence of harming the environment is seen as far worse than the valence of the chairman's not making profit. Correspondingly, avoidance of environmental harm is seen as far more important than the chairman's making profit. The chairman, of course, thinks other-wise. For him, not making profit is worse than harming the environment and, therefore, he starts the program disregarding the fact that by doing so the environment will be harmed. This does not necessarily mean that the chairman does not know about the intersubjective perspective and the corresponding expectations – as a matter of fact, the experimental setting makes sure that he is aware of this: the vice-president mentions the harming side effect as a potential problem, and the chairman affirms that he knows about the resulting harm. Nonetheless, the chairman rather acts on his main goal disregarding the intersubjective expecta-tion. That is why subjects judge him to be blameworthy for harming the environment. His *subjective* valence or preference structure 'making profit is more important than the environment' does not match the *intersubjective* expectation 'the environment is more important than making profit'. Because of this mismatch, the chairman is blamed for having started the program disregarding the resulting environmental harm. This mismatch does not only explain why the harming chairman is judged to be blameworthy (by means of ascribing intentionality), but also explains why the helping chairman is not found to be praiseworthy for the good side effect.

Blaming an agent is not the only negative reactive attitude: one can have a negative attitude toward a person who does bad *and* toward a person who does good. But of course, one cannot *blame* a person for producing good side effects even if she did not care about producing these. Yet, what one can do is to *withhold* moral praise. Withholding praise from a person is a negative attitude, too. This kind of resentment is what I call 'expraising' an agent; the practice of expraising an agent shall be understood in analogy to the practice of excusing an agent. An agent who is expraised is not judged as a proper target of praise as well as an agent who is excused is not a proper target of accusation or blame. The chairman who started the program in order to make profit and thereby, as a side effect, helped the environment has the very same *unacceptable* preference as the chairman who harmed the environment by starting the profitable program: neither of them cares about the environment, and both strongly prefer to make profit. The chairman's subjective preference 'making profit is more important than the environment' is not in accordance with intersubjective expectations. This is so independently of the respective goodness or badness of the outcome. The goodness or badness of the outcome does not change the *general negative reactive attitude*, but only determines whether an agent is to be blamed or expraised: since the action in the help scenario did not have a bad side effect, the chairman cannot be blamed for having done the action under his bad preference structure. However, he can be expraised from having performed the action that led to good side effects. Because both reactive attitudes – blaming and expraising an agent – are negative attitudes of resentment, there is no asymmetry in subjects' judgments concerning the chairman when they are read as moral judgments.

In the same way as we can have negative reactive attitudes toward agents who perform actions with bad side effects *and* toward agents who perform actions with good outcomes, it is possible to have positive reactive attitudes toward agents who perform actions with good outcomes *and* toward those who perform actions with bad outcomes. It is certainly debatable whether moral praise is reserved only for those who do better than what is morally expected or is also available for those who simply *meet* moral expectations in their actions. This is indeed an interesting and important question, but it shall not be a central question of this paper. What seems to be clear is that an agent is a proper target of moral praise only if she (at least) meets moral expectations. Knobe's original case descriptions do not provide for an agent who acts in accordance with intersubjective expectation. As I pointed out before, the chairman of the help scenario as well as the chairman of the harm scenario have unacceptable preferences: both do not care about the environment and strongly prefer making profit to caring about environmental issues. In both cases, survey subjects showed negative reactive attitudes of blame and expraise. Shepherd's extension makes us see positive attitudes toward an agent. In a variation of the help scenario, Shepherd makes the chairman say: 'That's great news about helping the environment! Ultimately, though, I want to make as much profit as I can' (Shepherd, 2012, p. 183). This caring chairman was judged by 62.5 percent of the subjects to have helped intentionally, while only 33.75 percent judged the not caring chairman to have helped the environment intentionally in a reproduction of Knobe's original study. Even if the results are not as high as in Knobe's own surveys, the difference between judgments about the caring and the not caring chairman is significant. Similarly but less significant, 54.67 percent judged the city planner to have brought about the good side effect intentionally when he expressed a positive attitude toward it, but only 26.67 percent agreed (and 60 percent disagreed) that the city planner brought about the good side effect intentionally when he explained his not caring about it. These results show that it is not only the *badness* of the side effect that triggers ascriptions of intentionality as Knobe claimed; when the agent shows sensibility to the goodness of the side effect, this agent is judged as having brought about the good side effect intentionally. When this ascription of intentionality is interpreted as an ascription of moral responsibility, the surveys' results indicate that the caring chairman is judged to be a proper target of praise and the caring city planner is at least considered as such. By stating that they consider it to be great news that their respective program will not only increase profit (or create jobs or clean an area from toxic waste) but additionally has good side effects, both agents at least meet the intersubjective expectation that the environment is something that has to be cared about.

After having discussed examples of positive reactions to good side effects, the question is whether there also is experimental support for my claim that people can have *positive* reactive attitudes toward an agent who performed an action that led to *bad* side effects. Again, Shepherd's study provides such a case: in the case description of the city planner who has as his main goal to clean an area from toxic waste, Shepherd changes the valence of the bad side effect from 'poisoning the groundwater' to the milder effect of 'increasing joblessness'. While 68.4 percent of the asked subjects agreed that the bad side effect of poisoned groundwater was brought about intentionally, only 47.5 percent agreed that increasing joblessness was brought about intentionally. Even if insignificant, there was also a difference between the city planner caring and the city planner not caring about increasing joblessness as a side effect of cleaning up toxic waste; nevertheless, Shepherd points out that this difference 'did approach significance' (Shepherd, 2012, p. 176). This may not be perfectly analogous to cases of positive reactive attitudes in the good side effects cases, but it seems to speak for the interpretation that survey subjects were inclined to accept the caring city planner's preference to clean an area from toxic waste over the comparatively mild side effect of raising joblessness. At least in parts, this city planner seems to be excused from having performed an action that led to bad side effects. It can be speculated that this effect would be more significant if the case description were modified in the following way: if the city planner decides against cleaning up the polluted area, many citizens would become ill due to the toxic waste in their neighborhood. Given this additional information, subjects would accept (if not expect from) any city planner to start the program even at the cost of increasing joblessness, because the consequences of not cleaning the area would be far worse. In this new scenario one can speculate that the city planner would be excused for having performed an action with bad side effects for a greater and intersubjectively accepted good. Survey subjects would refrain from ascribing intentionality to this city planner as a means to excuse him from having increased joblessness. Excusing an agent is, as is praising, a positive reactive attitude toward an agent's performing an action. Again, there is no asymmetry in help scenarios when we read subjects' ascription of intentionality as a moral judgment of an agent's praiseworthiness and the non-ascription of intentionality as a means to excuse an agent. In both scenarios, subjects express their *positive* attitude to the respective agent.

In summary, we have two pairs of reactive attitudes: the ascription of blame and expraise are negative reactive attitudes toward agents who act on unacceptable preferences that do not meet intersubjective expectations, and we have the ascription of praise and excuse as positive reactive attitudes toward agents who act on accepted or expected preferences. Maybe the ascription of moral praise has a special role here and requires from an agent not only to meet intersubjective expectations in her action but also to *exceed* these; yet, this is the topic of another article and cannot be discussed here.

Until now I based my explanation of the Knobe effect on Shepherd's results ignoring the fact that Shepherd explicitly separates effects that resulted from manipulating the agent's *attitude* and effects that resulted from manipulating the *valence* of the main goal and the side effect. One of his main results is that while there was a main effect on the verbally expressed attitude in help scenarios, there was none in harm scenarios;

and that there was an effect in harm scenarios when he manipulated the valence of the main goal or the side effect, but none in help scenarios. In short, the agent's attitude seems to make a difference when the side effect is good, while it is the valence of the main goal and the side effect that matter when the side effect is bad. How to explain that? Is that not undermining my explanation, which generally makes use of the subject's reference to the agent's attitude? In the next section I will discuss Shepherd's distinction of valence and attitude effects – a distinction I consider to be problematic.

6.3.2   Attitude as verbal expression

Shepherd separates the agent's attitude, on the one hand, and the valence of the main goal and the side effect on the other. In Shepherd's approach, the valence of the main goal and the valence of the side effect are treated like agent-external factors within the case description that are said to have an impact on survey subjects' judgments, but which are considered to be distinct from the agent's attitude concerning her own action and the resulting side effect. Note that the agent's attitude refers to her own action and the resulting side effect but must not be confused with 'reactive attitudes' survey subjects have when they morally judge the agent in a case description. Shepherd identifies the agent's attitude with the *verbal expression* that the agent gives in the case description: 'I don't care at all about [the side effect], I just want to [achieve the main goal]', 'I feel terrible about [the side effect] but priority one is [to achieve the main goal]' or 'That's great news about [the side effect], still priority one is [to achieve the main goal]'. As I pointed out before, it is an interesting result of Shepherd's study that 'the valence of an agent's main goal or side effect significantly impacts folk ascriptions in harming cases, [while] the agent's attitude does so in helping cases' (Shepherd, 2012, p. 181).

As I will point out in the following, it is problematic to treat the change of the agent's attitude and changes of the valence of the main goal and the side effect as if they had completely independent influences on what subjects conclude about the respective agent's motivation; the two must not be seen as distinct in the experimental setting. By changing the valence of the main goal or the side effect, the agent's preference structure is affected, too, when the agent acts on the motive to achieve the main goal. An agent who performs an action disregarding known bad side effects expresses by doing so her attitude that the achievement of the main goal is more important for her than the avoidance of the bad side effect. Merely adding a verbal expression of regret cannot overwrite the attitude that is expressed by performing the action, though a verbal expression may sometimes provide some missing details about the agent's attitude. Therefore, it is not surprising that in cases of bad side effects, in which the agent decides *for* the main goal and – in a way – *against* the avoidance of the side effect, there is no significant effect visible in the results when the agent verbally expresses regret about producing the bad side effect. The reason for this is simple: had the regret been serious or strong enough, the agent would have refrained from performing the action in the first place. But since she did not, subjects are not convinced that a merely *verbal* expression truly mirrors the agent's attitude – and rightly so. Though having expressed regret about the side effect, the chairman is still judged to be blameworthy for having harmed the environment. The reluctance to excuse the caring but still profit driven chairman explains the insignificance of an effect concerning the agent's verbally expressed attitude; this is simply not what the agent's attitude can be reduced to when the agent's action provides further and, in this case, more reliable information about the agent's motive.

Shepherd admits that it 'seems likely that in certain harming cases, an agent's attitude will have a significant impact.' Further, he adds that '[i]t is worth noting, however, that it seems that the impact will be much less than that of the valence' (Shepherd, 2012, p. 176). Against this interpretation, I think it is a mistake to conclude from the given data that in harm cases the agent's attitude has no impact on subjects' judgments and that only the valence of the main goal or the side effect has. When the side effect of the city planner's program is worsened from 'increasing joblessness' to 'increasing cancer levels', and in both scenarios the city planner says that he does not care about the respective harm, this is highly relevant for what kind of attitude is ascribed to the agent! The agent may give the very same verbal expression in both cases, but any judgment concerning the attitude of not caring about *x* and not caring about *y* depends on what *x* and *y* stand for and what their intersubjective valence is. An agent whose attitude does not reflect caring about increasing joblessness is bad enough, but somebody who does not care about increasing cancer levels is even worse. Here, it is the verbally expressed not caring attitude that – though syntactically identical in both cases – leads to different moral judgments concerning the agent. For judging an agent's attitude it is important *what* the agent does not care about.

After having explained why a change in the *verbal* expression of an agent's attitude does not lead to significant results, another question remains: why does a change in the agent's verbal expression have an impact on survey subjects' ascriptions of intentionality when the side effect is good? There is a difference between harm and help scenarios that concerns the agent's attitude and motivation. The agent's knowledge that a bad side effect will result from an action together with the performance of that action disregarding the consequences gives enough information about the agent's attitude: the achievement of the main goal is more important for her than the avoidance of the bad side effect. This conclusion cannot be made in help scenarios because there is no conflict between the main goal and the side effect such that it is inter-subjectively agreed upon that the action should be omitted for the sake of the side effect not to occur. The occurrence of a good side effect is as such never morally problematic as a bad side effect normally is. It is permissible to produce good side effects. However, there are intersubjective expectations also in help scenarios that concern the agent's attitude and motivation. A proper target of praise is required to (at least) meet these expectations. For example, the chairman who prefers making profit over environmental issues does not act on expected preferences even if the side effect turns out to be a good one. But in contrast to harm scenarios, it is not the case in help scenarios that the motive can be deduced from the performance of the action together with the agent's knowledge about the side effect. In help scenarios further information is needed in order to judge whether the agent is a proper target of praise or should rather be expraised. The verbal expression of the agent's attitude provides this sort of missing information in the helping scenarios, while it is redundant or overwritten in harm scenarios. While the information that the agent knows about the bad side effect in harm scenarios is sufficient for judging her morally when she performs the action in question, the verbal expression of the agent's attitude is required in the help scenario for that judgment. In cases where more information is required, the verbal expression determines whether subjects form a *positive* reactive attitude (praise) or a *negative* reactive attitude (expraise). That explains why manipulation of the verbal attitude has an effect in help scenarios but not a significant one in harm scenarios.

6.4   Why there seems to be an asymmetry

In the previous sections I argued against the common view that the effect Knobe and following experimenters found represents an asymmetry in survey subjects' judgments. In this section I will explain why the results can only be interpreted as an asymmetry when we try to explain the results within *one* concept, for example the concept of moral responsibility or the concept of intentional action. I will focus on the concept of moral responsibility here because I think that the asymmetric ascriptions of intentionality is a pragmatic means by which subjects strengthen their moral judgments. There is no asymmetry when we refer to positive and negative reactive attitudes and distinguish between praise and excuse, on the one hand, and blame and expraise on the other. When the judgment 'A is blameworthy' is replaced by the allegedly synonymous judgment 'A is morally responsible', and 'A is not praiseworthy' is replaced by 'A is not morally responsible', then the asymmetry arises: though an agent who is blamed or expraised is judged negatively in both cases, she is seen as morally responsible in one case but *not* morally responsible in the other. The same is true for positive judgments: an agent who is praised is seen as morally responsible but not when she is excused for having done so. Further, an agent who is judged to be morally blameworthy is, according to that synonymous treatment, not distinguishable from an agent who is judged to be praiseworthy if we do not refer to the goodness or badness of the relevant side effect. In both cases, the agent is morally responsible for her action and the resulting side effects. Accordingly, an agent who is expraised is not distinguishable from an agent who is excused, because both are seen as not morally responsible. But praising and blaming are completely different reactive attitudes as well as excusing and expraising are: while blaming and expraising are negative (or at least non-positive) judgments about an agent, praising and excusing are positive (or at least non-negative) judgments. That means that the goodness or the badness of an action or side effect does not determine whether the judgment is positive or negative, but only which kind of a positive or negative judgment is to be made.

It is the translation of expraise and excuse into '*not* morally responsible' and blame and praise into 'morally responsible' that makes an asymmetry appear. Even if most interpreters do not explicitly use moral responsibility as a synonym for either praise or blame, they treat the notions 'blameworthy' and 'not praiseworthy' as if there is one and the same underlying concept – one time in the affirmative and one time in the negative. Implicitly it is referred to the concept of moral responsibility that is assumed to unite praise and blame. However, this is no reason to arrive at any conclusions about an asymmetry within the concept of moral responsibility; we rather should conclude that the concept of moral responsibility is not suitable for uniting judgments like praise and excuse on the positive side, and blame and expraise on the negative side. Indeed, we should stop looking for general conditions of moral responsibility as such, and rather provide separate accounts for positive and negative moral attitudes. With the replacement of '(not) blameworthy' by '(not) responsible' and the replacement of '(not) praiseworthy' by '(not) responsible' the respective judgment's context becomes lost.

6.5   Conclusion

Similar to other contributors of the debate, I have argued for interpreting ascriptions of intentionality as moral judgments about the agent and her action, but this was not my main point. Though people are misled by the experimental setting in what question to answer and wrongly try to emphasize their moral judgment by ascription or non-ascription of intentionality, they are doing the right thing when they judge the not caring harming chairman to be blameworthy (via an ascription of intentionality) and the not caring helping chairman to be not praiseworthy (via a false ascription of non-intentionality). Knobe claims that it is the badness of the side effect as such that makes subjects generally more inclined to ascribe intentionality, while the goodness of the side effect makes subjects refrain from doing so. This could be transferred to moral judgment: while the badness of the side effect makes subjects generally more inclined to blame an agent, the goodness of the side effect makes subjects refrain from doing so. But Knobe's interpretation is flawed. As it can be seen in Shepherd's extended study, there are also reversed ascriptions of intentionality toward agents who perform actions with *good* side effects and non-ascriptions of intentionality toward agents who perform actions with *bad* side effects. Knobe's original scenarios of a helping and a harming chairman are restricted to *negative* judgments only: the chairman of the harm and the one of the help scenario act on unacceptable preferences that do not match intersubjective expectations because both do not care about the environment and both prefer to make profit. Whether a moral judgment is negative or positive is not determined by the goodness or badness of the side effect; it is the agent's *preference structure* that is decisive for this. However, the goodness or badness of the side effect determines whether the judgment is, if negative, a judgment of blame or expraise and, correspondingly, whether the judgment is, if positive, a judgment of praise or excuse. That means that there is no asymmetry between the negative attitudes of blame and expraise, on the one hand, and none between the positive attitudes of praise and excuse on the other. A natural divergence only arises between negative and positive attitudes, for example between praise as a positive attitude and expraise as a negative, and the same between blame as a negative attitude and excuse as a positive. An asymmetry between ascriptions of blame and expraise only arises if the two are read as 'morally responsible' and '*not* morally responsible'. When blame and expraise are read in this way, it cannot be seen that both of them are negative judgments and perfectly symmetric.

In this paper, I did not analyze the concept of moral judgment sufficiently but only tried to make sense of the experimental data provided so far. I am convinced that the interpretation of such data can be useful for philosophical inquiry concerning the concepts of praise and excuse as well as blame and expraise if we are interested in what people are *doing* when forming moral judgments. Lastly, the data clearly supports my claim that moral responsibility is not a concept under which praise and blame can be equally subsumed.

References

Adams, F. and A. Steadman (2004a) 'Intentional Action in Ordinary Language: Core Concept or Pragmatic Understanding?', *Analysis*, 64, pp. 173–181.

Adams, F. and A. Steadman (2004b) 'Intentional Action and Moral Considerations: Still Pragmatic', *Analysis*, 64, pp. 268–276.

Knobe, J. (2003) 'Intentional Action and Side Effects in Ordinary Language', *Analysis*, 63, pp. 190–193.

Knobe, J. (2006) 'The Concept of Intentional Action: A Case Study in the Uses of Folk Psychology', *Philosophical Studies*, 130, pp. 203–231.

Pettit, D. and J. Knobe (2009) 'The Pervasive Impact of Moral Judgment', *Mind and Language*, 24, pp. 586–604.

Phelan, M. and H. Sarkissian (2008) 'The Folk Strike Back; or, Why You Didn't Do It Intentionally, Though It Was Bad and You Knew It', *Philosophical Studies*, 138, pp. 291–298.

Shepherd, J. (2012) 'Action, Attitude, and the Knobe Effect: Another Asymmetry', *Review of Philosophy and Psychology*, 3, pp. 171–185.

7
Trolleys and Double Effect in Experimental Ethics
Ezio Di Nucci

7.1 Trolleys and double effect

In one of analytic philosophy's infamous thought experiments, a runaway trolley is about to kill five workmen who cannot move off the tracks quickly enough; their only chance is for a bystander to flip a switch to divert the trolley onto a side-track, where one workman would be killed. In a parallel scenario, the bystander's only chance to save the five is to push a fat man off a bridge onto the tracks: that will stop the trolley, but the fat man will die. Why is it permissible for the bystander to divert the trolley onto the one workman by pressing the switch while it is not permissible for the bystander to stop the trolley by pushing the fat man off the bridge? This is the so-called *Trolley Problem*, resulting from Judith Jarvis Thomson's (1976; 1985) adaptation of an example from Philippa Foot (1967). If it is permissible to intervene in the so-called *Bystander at the Switch* scenario while it is not permissible to intervene in the so-called *Fat Man* scenario, then the Trolley Problem arises and we must explain the moral difference between these two cases. And if the results of Marc Hauser's *Moral Sense Test* are to be believed, then according to public opinion it is indeed permissible to intervene in the former case (around 90 percent of respondents to the Moral Sense Test thought as much – Hauser, 2006, p. 139) while it is not permissible to intervene in the latter case (only around 10 percent of respondents thought it permissible to intervene).

The Doctrine of Double Effect is a normative principle according to which in pursuing the good it is sometimes morally permissible to bring about some evil as a side-effect or merely foreseen consequence: the same evil would not be morally justified as an intended means or end.[1] The Doctrine of Double Effect, it could be argued, offers a possible answer to the Trolley Problem because it can be deployed to argue that the difference in moral permissibility results from the one being killed as a means to saving the five in Fat Man; while in Bystander at the Switch the killing of the one is a mere side-effect of saving the five. In this respect, as long as the Trolley Problem remains 'unsolved' it offers dialectical support to the Doctrine of Double Effect. So the connection between the Doctrine of Double Effect and the Trolley Problem is dialectically very simple: the Trolley Problem counts as an argument in favor of the Doctrine in so far as it remains an unresolved problem and in so far as the Doctrine offers a possible solution to this unresolved problem.

The relationship between the Doctrine of Double Effect and the Trolley Problem can be then summarized as follows:

1. The Doctrine of Double Effect offers a solution to the Trolley Problem;
2. The two scenarios which constitute the Trolley Problem illustrate the distinction between 'means' and 'side-effects' which, according to the Doctrine of Double Effect, is morally relevant;
3. Widespread moral intuitions about the Trolley Problem suggest that, just as the Doctrine of Double Effect says, the distinction between 'means' and 'side-effects' is indeed morally relevant.

The philosophical debate on the Doctrine of Double Effect faces a continuing stall: on the one hand, the Doctrine has – intuitively – much to be said in its favor, but on the other hand, it cannot be coherently formulated and applied (as I have argued at length in my book *Ethics Without Intention*). How are we then to overcome this philosophical stall, which often leads to endorsement of the Doctrine notwithstanding its 'problems of application' (as Thomas Nagel put it)?[2] I think that it isn't enough to criticize the Doctrine of Double Effect; we must, in the spirit of Philippa Foot, also offer an alternative explanation of the cases, such as the Trolley Problem, which motivate it.[3]

To this end, here I defend both empirically and theoretically a recent argument for the claim that there is no trolley *problem* because even in Bystander at the Switch it is not permissible to intervene: on the empirical side of things, I present data showing that the intuition that intervening in Bystander at the Switch is permissible is neither stable nor widespread and that it is subject to some classic order effects. And on the theoretical side I defend the normative claim that intervening is not permissible.

7.2   The empirical argument against the permissibility of killing the one

There are two obvious ways to go about the Trolley Problem: one can either explain the moral difference between the two scenarios, or one can deny that there is such a difference, by either denying that it is permissible to kill the one workman in Bystander at the Switch or by denying that it is not permissible to kill the fat man in the other scenario. Interestingly, Thomson (2008) herself has recently argued that there is no Trolley Problem by denying that it is permissible to intervene in Bystander at the Switch. Thomson's argument moves from a variant in which you also have the chance to divert the trolley onto yourself (you are on a third track and you can't move off it quickly enough). If you would not be willing to divert the trolley onto yourself – sacrificing your own life to save the five – then it would be preposterous to sacrifice someone else: it is just not fair.

Someone who would not sacrifice herself in this new scenario ought not to sacrifice someone else in the original Bystander at the Switch; or so Thomson argues: 'Since he wouldn't himself pay the cost of his good deed if he could pay it, there is no way in which he can decently regard himself as entitled to make someone else pay it' (2008, p. 366). Here folk intuitions aren't clear-cut: 43 percent would still kill the one; 38 percent would commit self-sacrifice; and 19 percent would not act, letting the trolley kill the five (Huebner and Hauser, 2011).

If these numbers are to be believed, they can be used against Thomson's argument, since more than 40 percent would still kill the one; but also in favor of it, since almost 40 percent would commit self-sacrifice; and, perhaps more importantly, the majority (almost 60 percent) would now not kill the one, while in the traditional Bystander at the Switch it was only around 10 percent.[4]

But there is another respect in which the numbers are not decisive: Thomson's argument is about the effect of this new three-way scenario on the traditional two-way Bystander at the Switch. And these numbers are silent on that – what should then be tested is how folk intuitions would respond to the traditional scenario after having been subjected to the new three-way scenario: if the 9 to 1 proportion would even out somewhat, that would speak in favor of Thomson's argument.

Experiments that I conducted suggested just that: participants who were not previously familiar with any of the trolley scenarios were presented first with Thomson's new three-way scenario and then with the traditional Bystander at the Switch. Answers to Bystander at the

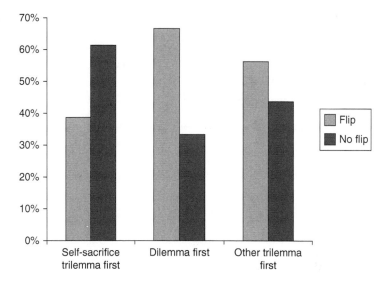

Figure 7.1   The Trolley Trilemma

Switch were radically different from the 9 to 1 proportion identified by Hauser, so much so that the majority (**61.34 percent**) opted to let the five workmen die.

For details on my studies please see Di Nucci (2013a): here I will just graphically sum up the results and then discuss them(see Figure 7.1).

So it seems that the apparently overwhelming intuition that intervening in Bystander is permissible disappears when subjects are presented with Bystander only after they have been asked about Thomson's new scenario. Indeed, after having considered a scenario in which they could also sacrifice themselves, a majority of subjects appear to think that intervening in Bystander is not permissible. As anticipated above, these results support Thomson's claim that her new scenario has a bearing on the permissibility of intervening in Bystander: we can suppose that subjects who have just been asked about the self-sacrifice scenario may overwhelmingly opt to let the five die in Bystander at the Switch because they now recognize that they may not do to the one what they would not do to themselves.

It may be objected that these results do not support Thomson's new argument; they rather just show that the relevant moral intuitions are very unstable. This is after all the conclusion Swain, Alexander, and Weinberg (2008) drew following their own experimental philosophy studies where the order in which the cases were presented affected results (see also, for other examples of this sort of effect, Petrinovich and O'Neill, 1996; Sinnott-Armstrong, 2008; Wiegmann, Okan, and Nagel, 2010). I think that the dialectic of Thomson's argument is such that our results do support it, because her argument is about the effect of the new case on the old one; but even if you disagree, then our results would show, in line with Swain, Alexander, and Weinberg (2008), that the Bystander intuition is unstable and that it depends on the order of presentation so heavily that it disappears (less than 40 percent have it) when Bystander is first introduced after Thomson's new self-sacrifice case.

Even if Hauser's data is reliable, then, the numbers are not decisive one way or another for Thomson's argument, because they can be interpreted both in favor of Thomson's argument and against it, and because the more relevant questions have not been asked – when the right questions are asked, then, as our numbers above show, intuitions seem to support Thomson's argument.[5]

7.3   The theoretical argument against the permissibility of killing the one

The empirical challenges against Thomson fail then, but there has also been a theoretical critique of Thomson's new argument. According to Thomson, her new case brings out the principle that 'A must not kill B to save five if he can instead kill himself to save the five' (2008, p. 365). William J. FitzPatrick has recently argued (2009) against this principle by suggesting that the values of equality and fairness that Thomson's argument appeals to can be captured by a weaker principle that does not support Thomson's conclusion. According to FitzPatrick, we need not accept, with Thomson, that 'A's respecting B as a moral equal requires that A not sacrifice B (without B's consent) for end E unless A would be willing to sacrifice himself for E if he could do so instead' (2009, p. 639). Moral equality may be satisfied by appeal to the weaker principle according to which 'A's respecting B as a moral equal requires that A not sacrifice B for end E unless A recognizes B's equal right to sacrifice A for E if their positions were reversed' (FitzPatrick, 2009, p. 639). On the former principle, I may not sacrifice the bystander if I would not be willing to sacrifice myself; but on the latter principle I may, as long as I recognize the bystander's right to sacrifice me if our positions were reversed. On this latter understanding, then, fairness would not support Thomson's argument that it is not permissible to intervene in Bystander at the Switch.

It may be argued that employing FitzPatrick's latter principle in the debate on the Trolley Problem is methodologically suspect because it introduces 'rights': what's at stake are exactly the sort of fundamental principles that may be deployed to justify rights, rather than the other way around. But there is a bigger worry with FitzPatrick's alternative principle: the problem is that this is no principle to capture fairness or, as FitzPatrick puts it, 'respecting others as moral equals' (FitzPatrick, 2009, p. 639). His principle amounts to the Law of the Jungle: it just says that whoever happens to find herself at the switch may take advantage of this (lucky or otherwise) circumstance and kill the other. It doesn't have anything to do with fairness or equality; it is sheer power and privilege. The point is not whether this perspective is defensible; it is just that, even if it is, this is not the point of view of fairness or 'respecting others as moral equals'. Here the dialectic of the argument is important: FitzPatrick doesn't argue for his alternative principle on the grounds that Thomson's own principle is flawed, but only on the grounds that his own less demanding principle also accounts for fairness and 'respecting others as moral equals'. That is why what is crucial is whether his principle does indeed account for fairness and 'respecting others as moral equals' rather than whether it is, in absolute terms, defensible.

This alternative principle does not support FitzPatrick's argument. What about the principle's intrinsic value, so to speak? In some particular set of circumstances, I may kill you only if I recognize your equal right to kill me if our positions were reversed. What may my recognition of your equal right to kill me amount to? Maybe if you were at the switch and diverted the trolley toward me, my recognition of your equal right to kill me means that I may not, as I die, swear at you; or that, as the trolley approaches, I should quickly try to write a note saying that I don't blame you. But wouldn't that problematically amount to consent? This would be problematic because the question is whether I may divert the trolley onto your track irrespective of your consent. But I think it is both complicated and uncharitable to test the principle's intrinsic value on the Trolley Problem. What about its more general application? The idea that I recognize your right to kill me if our positions were reversed must mean, for example, that if our positions were reversed, and you were threatening to kill me, I should not defend myself or try to stop you because I recognize your right to kill me, after all. And this isn't just weird, it is also against the spirit of the principle itself: if whoever gets to the switch first may kill the other, then you would expect that we are allowed to take advantage of our privileged positions, but then why should I let you kill me? In short, the principle bears contradicting responses: it asks us on the one hand to recognize the other's right to kill us, and on the other hand it justifies this right with the other's privileged position.

The principle is too Machiavellian to count as a principle of fairness or 'respecting others as moral equals', but it isn't Machiavellian enough to function as a workable and coherent moral or political principle. Therefore it works neither against Thomson's argument nor generally.[6] All in all, its absurdity as a principle of fairness explains why the principle yields the 'surprising' and 'paradoxical' (FitzPatrick's (2009, p. 640) own words) conclusion that it is permissible to divert the trolley onto another even if we are able but unwilling to divert it onto ourselves instead.

FitzPatrick's objection to Thomson does not work, then. But that, clearly, does not mean that Thomson's argument goes through. Specifically, FitzPatrick challenges also another aspect of Thomson's argument, where she argues that even those who would divert the trolley onto themselves in the three-way scenario, sacrificing their own lives, are not allowed to divert the trolley onto the one workman in the traditional Bystander at the Switch. Thomson claims that this sort of altruism is not 'morally attractive' (2008, p. 366), and that anyway the bystander may not suppose that the workman is similarly altruistic.

As we have seen, almost 40 percent of respondents to the Moral Sense Test declare that they would commit self-sacrifice in the three-way scenario; that's why this part of Thomson's argument is important. If Thomson's argument would apply only to those who would not be willing to commit self-sacrifice, and if the numbers are to be taken seriously, then that would be a problem for her general conclusion that intervening in Bystander at the Switch is not permissible: indeed, that conclusion could not be generalized to a large part of the population.[7] That is why this second part of Thomson's argument in which she argues that even those supposed altruists may not intervene in Bystander at the Switch also matters.

FitzPatrick challenges this part of Thomson's argument by arguing that her appeal to the notion of consent 'beg[s] the interesting questions ....Those who believe that it is generally permissible to turn the trolley obviously think that this is a special case where consent isn't necessary. So Thomson's quick appeal to consent won't gain any traction with those who don't already share her view' (2009, p. 642).

Thomson writes that 'the altruistic bystander is not entitled to assume that the one workman is equally altruistic, and would therefore consent to the bystander's choosing option (ii). Altruism is by hypothesis not morally required of us. Suppose, then, that the bystander knows that the one workman would not consent, and indeed is not morally required to consent, to his choosing option (ii)'[8] (2008, p. 367).

Here FitzPatrick is right to point out that appealing to consent is problematic – because the whole point of the Trolley Problem is the intuition that killing the one workman may be permissible even against his consent – but FitzPatrick is wrong to think that consent is what the argument actually relies on. In criticizing the sort of altruism that may motivate the bystander to turn the trolley toward herself in the three-way scenario, Thomson argues that dying for the sake of five strangers is not morally valuable. Thomson says that 'I would certainly not feel proud of my children if I learned that they value their own lives as little as that man values his' (2008, p. 367). It is this claim, which she cashes out in terms of altruism by devising her new three-way scenario, which is doing the philosophical work for Thomson: it is because dying for the sake of five strangers is not morally valuable that even the bystander that would sacrifice herself may not sacrifice someone else. Consent doesn't actually matter, as shown by the counterfactual that if dying for the sake of five strangers were morally valuable, then the bystander may turn the trolley against the one workman irrespective of the workman's consent.

In defusing FitzPatrick's challenge, then, we have uncovered the deep structure of Thomson's argument[9]: it is not about consent, but rather about the moral value of dying for strangers. Let me just say that here it will not do to object that in the traditional Bystander at the Switch both the one and the five are strangers for the bystander: that is addressed by Thomson's new scenario, which supposedly shows that the bystander may not sacrifice the one if she is not willing to sacrifice herself. This is just a point about fairness and treating others as moral equals, which we have here defended from FitzPatrick's weaker principle. But it is when Thomson addresses those who would be willing to sacrifice themselves that her stronger normative claim emerges: dying for the sake of strangers is not morally valuable. Since it is not morally valuable, those who wish to do it will have to appeal to individual liberty to justify it; but liberty will only justify self-sacrifice, and not sacrificing others. That is then why even those who would, in the three-way scenario, sacrifice themselves, may not sacrifice the one workman in the traditional Bystander at the Switch.

I have not only rebutted FitzPatrick's critique; I have also made explicit the crucial normative premise upon which Thomson's new argument is built: that it is not morally valuable to die for the sake of strangers. We see now that the real novelty in Thomson's new discussion of the Trolley Problem is not just the new three-way scenario involving self-sacrifice and its implications for the traditional scenario; Thomson has shown that we must defend the value of dying for the sake of strangers in order for the Trolley Problem to even arise. And because there is no moral value in dying for strangers, then there is no Trolley Problem. Here it is neither possible nor necessary to deal in depth with this sort of radical altruism: it is enough to have shown that the very existence of the Trolley Problem depends on taking a particular position on this radical altruism (and anyway, how many people do you know, for example, who have committed suicide so that their organs may be deployed to save the life of five strangers?[10]).

It may be objected that Thomson's dissolution of the Trolley Problem crucially depends on the characters involved being strangers. But, the objection goes, we can reformulate the Trolley Problem without this requirement, so that Thomson's argument would fail to dissolve this new version of the Trolley Problem because it could no longer rely on the point about dying for the sake of strangers. Let us then look at a variant on the Trolley Problem which includes the kind of features that, according to Thomson, may make self-sacrifice morally valuable: 'They're my children', 'They're my friends', 'They stand for things that matter to me', 'They're young, whereas I haven't much longer to live', 'I've committed myself to doing what I can for them': these and their ilk would make sacrificing one's life to save five morally intelligible.

> Consider, by contrast, the man who learns that five strangers will live if and only if they get the organs they need, and that his are the only ones that are available in time, and who therefore straightway volunteers. No reputable surgeon would perform the operation, and no hospital would allow it to be performed under its auspices. I would certainly not feel proud of my children if I learned that they value their own lives as little as that man values his. (Thompson, 2008, pp. 366–367)

Let us then take it that the five stuck on the main track are volunteers who have been trying to reach an isolated village in desperate need of water after an earthquake. And let us further suppose that the bystander knows the good work that the five have been doing through the years; the bystander thinks that the five are virtuous examples who must continue to provide an inspiration to society. The bystander concludes that, were she stuck on a third track toward which she could divert the runway trolley, she would sacrifice herself for the sake of the five. In order to maintain the symmetry of the original Trolley Problem, let us suppose that the one was also on her way to help the same isolated village, and that the bystander considers the one a virtuous example who must continue to provide an inspiration to society too. Is it now permissible for the bystander to sacrifice the one in order to save the five?

I see two problems here: firstly, once we have described the victims as exceptionally virtuous so as to provide an argument for self-sacrifice which the traditional Trolley Problem lacks, then the bystander may reasonably assume that the one would consent to being sacrificed; and on the other hand, if the bystander were to think that the one would not consent, then she may no longer regard it as exceptionally virtuous – so that the symmetry with the traditional Trolley Problem would be lost one way or the other. The second problem is with Fat Man: apart from the plausibility of a very fat man taking part to a rescue operation, in this version of the Trolley Problem it is no longer clear that it would be clearly impermissible to shove the fat man off the bridge – indeed, for the considerations above, it may have to be supposed that the fat man would himself jump and that if he didn't (jump or just give his consent to being pushed, as he might be too fat to climb the railing himself), the symmetry would no longer hold.

Here it may be objected that it is only by modeling the new variant on 'They stand for things that matter to me' (Thompson, 2008, p. 366) that we run into problems; other variants will work better. Let us try: 'They're my children' (2008, p. 366) will not do because, if all six have to be my children, then I can't compare myself to the one, which has a different relation to the five than I do. And in general we would be contaminating the Trolley Problem with parental and fraternal commitments and responsibility which would make the problem non-basic in a way so as to radically change its role in normative ethics. These two kinds of considerations also apply, respectively, to 'They're young, whereas I haven't much longer to live' (2008, p. 366) and 'I've committed myself to doing what I can for them' (2008, p. 366): the former because the symmetry between my relation to the five and the one's relation to the five would be altered; the latter because of the special responsibilities with which we would alter the Trolley Problem. Finally, 'They're my friends' (2008, p. 366) will also not do because of reasonable assumptions about consent in both Bystander and Fat Man. What this suggests is that it is constitutive of the Trolley Problem that it features strangers; but, as Thomson argues, since it features strangers, the Trolley Problem is not a problem because it is not permissible to kill the one in Bystander at the Switch.

Summing up, I have argued that criticizing the Doctrine of Double Effect will, alone, not do. We must also offer an alternative explanation for the cases, such as the Trolley Problem, that the Doctrine can deal with. On these grounds I have defended a proposed dissolution of the Trolley Problem. It may be objected that the Doctrine may still be preferred to Thomson's dissolution on the grounds that the former but not the latter explains the Trolley Problem by accounting for lay intuitions that Bystander is permissible but Fat Man is not permissible; the latter challenges lay intuitions by arguing that Bystander is not actually permissible. So only the Doctrine really does justice to lay intuitions; my proposed alternative does not. And on this ground one may still hang on to double effect.

It is true that the conclusion of Thomson's new argument, which I have here defended, is that Bystander is not permissible; while empirical evidence suggests that *the people* (as Steinbeck would have said) think that Bystander is permissible. But the relationship between Thomson's new argument and the intuitions which I have suggested here is different: my own experimental data suggest that the Bystander intuition is not basic in the way in which it has until now been suggested to be. When subjects answer the self-sacrifice scenario before they answer the Bystander scenario, then they no longer report the intuition that Bystander is permissible. So my proposal is not at a disadvantage against double effect on the grounds that the Doctrine does justice to wide-spread moral intuitions while my proposal does not: I have done justice to intuitions too by deploying Thomson's new argument to demonstrate that people don't really have the intuition that Bystander is permissible.[11]

Notes

1. Here are some representative definitions of the Doctrine of Double Effect (for more on the Doctrine please see Di Nucci, 2014):

   McIntyre in the *Stanford Encyclopedia of Philosophy*: 'sometimes it is permissible to bring about as a merely foreseen side effect a harmful event that it would be impermissible to bring about intentionally' (http://plato.stanford.edu/entries/double-effect/);

   Woodward in the Introduction to his standard anthology on double effect: 'intentional production of evil...and foreseen but unintentional production of evil' (2001, p. 2);

   Aquinas, which is often credited with the first explicit version of double effect: 'Nothing hinders one act from having two effects, only one of which is intended, while the other is beside the intention' (Summa II-II, 64, 7);

Gury: 'It is licit to posit a cause which is either good or indifferent from which there follows a twofold effect, one good, there other evil, if a proportionately grave reason is present, and if the end of the agent is honorable – that is, if he does not intend the evil effect' (Boyle's translation, 1980, p. 528);

Mangan: 'A person may licitly perform an action that he foresees will produce a good and a bad effect provided that four conditions are verified at one and the same time: 1) that the action in itself from its very object be good or at least indifferent; 2) that the good effect and not the evil effect be intended; 3) that the good effect be not produced by means of the evil effect; 4) that there be a proportionately grave reason for permitting the evil effect' (1949, p. 43).

2. 'I believe that the traditional principle of double effect, despite problems of application, provides a rough guide to the extension and character of deontological constraints, and that even after the volumes that have been written on the subject in recent years, this remains the right point of convergence for efforts to capture our intuitions' (Nagel, 1986, p. 179).

3. Foot originally suggested that we explain the trolley case in terms of the difference between positive and negative duties (1967); her proposal was refuted by Thomson (1976; 1985), which in doing so introduced the Trolley Problem as we know it today. Please see my book *Ethics Without Intention* for details on the history of this debate (Di Nucci, 2014).

4. Another consideration that is particularly relevant to this new case given that it involves self-sacrifice is the gap between the reports and what respondents would actually do were they really in such a situation.

5. My argument about the data has been admittedly quite quick here; please see Di Nucci (2013a; 2014) for more details.

6. I don't suppose that FitzPatrick ever meant it as a full-blown general principle because, understood as not only necessary but also sufficient, it justifies, amongst others, psychopaths, mass-murderers, and in general most if not all of the major wrong-doers of this world.

7. This should not be overstated as Thomson's general conclusion that intervening in Bystander at the Switch is not permissible clearly clashes with general intuition, as 90 percent of respondents disagree with Thomson. But fortunately we haven't yet reached a point where these kinds of surveys alone are sufficient to refute normative claims.

8. Option (ii) is diverting the trolley toward the one workman.

9. Here I leave unanswered the question of which interpretation is actually closer to Thomson's original: it may be that my interpretation is preferable, and then what I offer here is a defense of Thomson. Or it may be that FitzPatrick's interpretation is closer to the original, and then what I offer here is my own argument, based on one by Thomson (and there is certainly something to say in favor of FitzPatrick's interpretation, as Thomson, after having considered the value of dying for strangers, writes 'Perhaps you disagree. I therefore do not rely on that idea' (2008, p. 367), and goes on to talk about consent). I think this is just a question of copyright: nothing in the content of my argument hangs on whether it is more appropriately attributed to Thomson or myself.

10. No one else will save those on waiting lists: 'In the U.S. alone, 83,000 people wait on the official kidney-transplant list. But just 16,500 people received a kidney transplant in 2008, while almost 5,000 died waiting for one' (WSJ 8.1.10).
11. Here I could not get into much detail about the Doctrine of Double Effect. Those who are interested in what I have to say about the ethical and action-theoretical issues surrounding the Doctrine may look at: Di Nucci 2008; 2009; 2010; 2011; 2013a–d; 2014.

References

Aquinas. (1981) Summa Theologica. Christian Classics (translated by Fathers of the English Dominican Province).

Boyle, J. M. (1980) 'Toward Understanding the Principle of Double Effect', *Ethics*, 90, 4, pp. 527–538.

Di Nucci, E. (2008) *Mind Out of Action* (Saarbrücken: VDM Verlag).

Di Nucci, E. (2009) 'Simply, False', *Analysis*, 69, 1, pp. 69–78.

Di Nucci, E. (2010) 'Rational Constraints and the Simple View', *Analysis*, 70, 3, pp. 481–486.

Di Nucci, E. (2011) 'Automatic Actions: Challenging Causalism', *Rationality Markets and Morals*, 2, 1, pp. 179–200.

Di Nucci, E. (2013a) 'Self-Sacrifice and the Trolley Problem', *Philosophical Psychology*, 26, pp. 662–672.

Di Nucci, E. (2013b) *Mindlessness* (Newcastle upon Tyne: Cambridge Scholars Publishing).

Di Nucci, E. (2013c) 'Embryo Loss and Double Effect', *Journal of Medical Ethics*, 39, 8, pp. 537–540.

Di Nucci, E. (2013d) 'Double Effect and Terror Bombing', in M. Hoeltje, T. Spitzley, and W. Spohn (eds), *Was dürfen wir glauben? Was sollen wir tun?* Sektionsbeiträge des achten internationalen Kongresses der Gesellschaft für Analytische Philosophie e.V. DuEPublico.

Di Nucci, E. (2014) *Ethics Without Intention* (London: Bloomsbury).

FitzPatrick, W. J. (2009) 'Thomson's Turnabout on the Trolley', *Analysis*, 69, 4, pp. 636–643.

Foot, P. (1967) 'The Problem of Abortion and the Doctrine of the Double Effect', *Oxford Review*, 5, pp. 5–15.

Hauser, M. (2006) *Moral Minds* (New York: HarperCollins).

Huebner, B. and M. Hauser (2011) 'Moral Judgments About Altruistic Self-sacrifice: When Philosophical and Folk Intuitions Clash', *Philosophical Psychology*, 24, 1, pp. 73–94.

Mangan, J. T. (1949) 'An Historical Analysis of the Principle of Double Effect', *Theological Studies*, 10, pp. 41–61.

McIntyre, A. (2011) Doctrine of Double Effect. *Stanford Encyclopedia of Philosophy*.

Nagel, T. (1986) *The View from Nowhere* (Oxford University Press).

Petrinovich, L. and P. O'Neill (1996) 'Influence of Wording and Framing Effects on Moral Intuitions', *Ethology and Sociobiology*, 17, pp. 145–171.

Sinnott-Armstrong, W. (2008) 'Framing Moral Intuitions', in W. Sinnott-Armstrong (ed.) *Moral Psychology*, Volume 2, The Cognitive Science of Morality, pp. 47–76, Cambridge, MA: MIT Press.

Swain, S., J. Alexander, and J. Weinberg (2008) 'The Instability of Philosophical Intuitions: Running Hot and Cold on Truetemp', *Philosophy and Phenomenological Research*, 76, pp. 138–155.

Thomson, J. J. (1976) 'Killing, Letting Die, and the Trolley Problem', *The Monist*, 59, pp. 204–217.

Thomson, J. J. (1985) 'The Trolley Problem', *The Yale Law Journal*, 94, pp. 1395–1415.

Thomson, J. J. (2008) 'Turning the Trolley', *Philosophy and Public Affairs*, 36, pp. 359–374.

Tabarrok , A. (2010) The Meat Market. *The Wall Street Journal* (8th January).

Wiegmann, A., Y. Okan, and J. Nagel (2010) 'Order Effects in Moral Judgment', *Philosophical Psychology*, 25, pp. 813–836.

Woodward, P. A. (2001) (ed.) *The Doctrine of Double Effect* (Notre Dame: University of Notre Dame Press).

8
Utilitarianism, the Difference Principle, or Else? An Experimental Analysis of the Impact of Social Immobility on the Democratic Election of Distributive Rules

Stephan Wolf and Alexander Lenger

8.1 Introduction

Within ethics, distributive justice constitutes a central and controversial topic. Despite the rise of *positive approaches* to studying existing distributive preferences in society (see Konow, 2003), the question *how* different normative positions are justified is still fundamentally important for moral philosophers.[1] With John Rawls's *A Theory of Justice* (1971), a revival of normative theories of justice – including distributional aspects (see Nozick, 1974; Harsanyi, 1975) – has been observed. Even though much of the debate took place on an abstract-theoretical level, one must not overlook the crucial role of assumptions about the empirical world in this debate. At the end of the day, different normative conclusions are drawn partly because of the pre-election of different assumptions on an empirical level. An instructive example about the influence of positive assumption on normative theory is the debate between John Rawls (1971; 2001) and John Harsanyi (1953; 1955; 1975). Both used an *Original Position* to develop their normative conclusion, but due to different positive models of human decision making, the former derived his famous difference principle implying substantial redistribution, while the latter arrived at the utilitarian norm of maximizing average income. Given that both theories are mutually exclusive, Norman Frohlich and Joe A. Oppenheimer (1992; henceforth F/O) conducted an economics experiment to test which of the two distributive theories – together with two other principles discussed in Rawls (1971) – was able to explain collective decision making on how to share scarce resources, provided people chose behind an experimental *veil of ignorance*.

It is not the results alone which make this experiment so interesting for experimental ethics. In fact, it presents a general methodological framework which allows for constructing an indispensable bridge between normative theory and empirical input. Based on the initial F/O setup, a multitude of still highly controversial issues in normative justice theory can be investigated, creating necessary empirical input for philosophical reflection. For example, in a later design, F/O (1990) included productive effort into their distributional experiment since many considered potential merit considerations too important to be ignored. Even though this was an important step ahead, we argue that from both a theoretical and 'realism' perspective, certain additional factors need to be integrated. Rawls claims that the veil will make people want to neutralize differences, stemming from the 'lottery of life', no one is accountable for. Once society has installed institutions creating 'fair equality of opportunity' (Rawls, 1971), people shall be free to pursue their own interests. So the actual challenge for choosing a distributional principle behind the veil is that some factors influencing income are beyond individual control, and some within – just as in the empirical world for which principles are to be derived from an idealized viewpoint. To create an experimental setting in which such an interplay of factors is present, we designed a production economy in which social immobility diluted the influence of individual effort on income. People then had to vote on the degree of income inequality in two sequential rounds, between which the thickness of the veil naturally decreased.

Our experiment shows from a positive perspective that in such a decision making situation, people tend to equalize income as suggested by Rawls's difference principle. As soon as the veil is lifted, individuals egoistically choose in line with their post-veil interests: the unproductive individuals want to keep equality, while the productive ones on average shift toward merit-based rules. Nevertheless, since social immobility inflates income differences before the veil is lifted, the participants in our experiment equalize their income to quite a large extent. Generally, we think that such findings can enrich the theory development and even create policy implications, and hence be of genuine interest for (applied) moral and political philosophy.

The remainder of this paper is structured as follows: in Section 8.2, we present the debate between Rawls and Harsanyi on what distributive

principle rational people would agree behind a veil of ignorance. It illustrates how strongly normative theory and experimental empirical data
depend on each other and how economic experiments can be used as
a link. Section 8.3 presents the seminal 1992 experiment by F/O which
put the Rawls-Harsanyi dispute on empirical grounds. Based on this
study, a later F/O experiment, and one of our own experiments, we show
how this approach can be continued into a systematic research program:
under certain rather realistic circumstances, people tend toward Rawls's
difference principle to a substantial degree. Overall, we conclude in
Section 8.4 that experiments as such can create a useful, and even necessary, input for normative research, and that in the specific case of the
Rawlsian approach, such studies may help identify empirical conditions
under which Rawls's hypothetical construction seems to work.

8.2   Normative distributional theory and empirical evidence: difference principle, utilitarianism, and the Frohlich/Oppenheimer experiments

8.2.1   Rawls's justification of the difference principle and its critical perception

John Rawls's *A Theory of Justice* (1971) revitalized the philosophical
reflection on political issues which lay more or less dormant for about
one and a half centuries. Rawls resorted to an even older philosophical
paradigm: contractarianism. Despite the praise he received, Rawls has
been harshly criticized for many of his positions. Rawls' intention was
to provide a well-funded alternative to, and even solid rejection of,
utilitarianism. Especially following Kant, he argued that from a univer-
salized perspective, no rational individual would ever consent to utilitarianism as a social norm. Utilitarianism inherently puts at stake the
rights and well-being of any individual for the sake of some higher
goal, namely aggregate utility, respectively welfare. In the extreme case,
utilitarianism justifies misery for some as long as it is overcompensated
by enough pleasure for others, putting the well-being of individuals
permanently at risk. From an impartial perspective, no one could
rationally support this.

The most important tool in Rawls's argumentation is his 'veil of
ignorance' (1971). This veil, present in the *Original Position* (OP), is a
hypothetical construction behind which everyone is deprived of any
idiosyncratic information. Not knowing one's position in society,
people in the OP are forced to take into consideration any possible
social position. From this impartial viewpoint where any personal bias

is removed, the resulting principles can claim *general* validity, fulfilling the requirements of Kant's *Categorical Imperative* (Kant [1788/2005], as argued in Rawls (1971; see also Wolf and Lenger, 2013); similar arguments had been developed earlier by Adam Smith (1759/1976), referring to an 'impartial spectator's perspective', or with Rousseau's (1762/2010) *volonté générale*). Rawls concludes that in this case, the overriding of individual rights can never be rational for the respective decision maker, since he or she finally risks harming herself: if one cannot exclude being a slave in a slaveholder society, one cannot rationally agree to slavery behind the veil.

Rawls finally derives two principles of justice based on what a rational decision maker would choose behind the veil. The first one requires *maximum equal liberty* for everyone. The second one, being lexigraphically subordinate to the first, comprises two sub-principles, which are (i) 'fair equality of opportunity' concerning the access to public positions and offices, and his famous (ii) *Difference Principle* (DP). The DP means that all *primary goods* – all goods of which one wants more, not less – must be distributed to the advantage of the worst off individual, which in economics, other social sciences, but also in Rawls's (1971, p. 152) own work, is often formally represented as the decision-making rule called *maximin*.

For the remainder of the paper, we will concentrate on the interpretation of Rawls's theory, which narrows the discussion of the maximin rule, while being well aware of the stark under-complexity of this perception (even though Rawls himself [1971] suggested this heuristic in the context of social justice). In the narrow field of distributional justice, Rawls's program therefore shall be reduced to the following problem: given a certain set of alternative resource allocation schemes within a society, people should choose the one arrangement which maximizes the primary goods endowment of the worst-off individual. When discussing the F/O experiments, as well as our own one, we will even make one more simplifying assumption. In distributional contexts, we will only consider monetary income, standing as a – at least very important – proxy for material wealth in general. Before going into detail, the philosophical riposte on DP, an attempt to defend utilitarianism against Rawls's initial attack is presented (cf. Wolf and Lenger, 2013).

8.2.2 The utilitarian counterattack on Rawls

The rigorousness of the difference principle has attracted severe criticism (for a comprehensive summary, see Lamont and Favor, 2013). Especially John Harsanyi (1975) rejected the conclusion that individuals in an OP should resort to a maximin solution. Harsanyi was actually the first one to introduce the formalized perspective of veiled decision making in a hypothetical OP (Harsanyi, 1953; 1955). According to him, the factual maximin outcome, as suggested by Rawls's DP, is equivalent to veiled decision making by an infinitely *risk averse individual* (Harsanyi, 1975). Such behavior, he argues, can hardly be called 'rational' because maximin would imply the following: assume two options *A* and *B*. *A* stands for a nearly sure gain, but comes with a very small risk of losing a significant amount (or even one's life). *B* is a sure event realizing a very small gain, but hence not coming at the risk of any loss. According to Harsanyi, the Rawlsian maximin solution requires choosing *B*. Hence, one forgoes the nearly sure enormous gain (Harsanyi uses the example of an excellent paying job) because of *irrationally* fearing the smallest possible loss (in this case, the unlikely event of dying in a plane crash on the way to the new job). Following such a strategy, people would be doomed to never even cross a street (Harsanyi, 1975) – a kind of behavior which is neither observed in reality nor accepted as rational by anyone. A maximin-decider hence must occur to the reader as a neurotic fellow, but not rational in any sense. Even if, as Harsanyi continues, there are no clear probabilities given to the decider about how likely gains and – even existential – losses are, people would in any case estimate such probabilities, using their best (but of course limited) knowledge (which is perfectly in line with the findings of Kahneman and Tversky, 1979; and Kahneman, Slovic, and Tversky, 1982, stating that people most of the time rely on simplifying heuristics). Hence, the Rawlsian argument that a rational individual must always take only the worst case into consideration does not seem convincing, not even when basic matters of life are concerned. Harsanyi concludes that when facing several options with different outcomes, a first good guess is to assume equal probability for each event to occur. As long as there is no sufficient reason to argue otherwise, the rational decision maker behind the veil would act most rational by just assigning equal weight to each alternative. In mathematical terms, this amounts to drawing attention only to the *average* outcome (either in utility or monetary units). Since rational people want to maximize their outcomes, the rational decision rule behind the veil must therefore be *maximizing average utility* (or average income). This is equivalent to maximizing the sum as long as the population is static and, in this case, identical to maximizing aggregate welfare. Such behavior is, as Harsanyi (1955) highlights, perfectly in accordance with von Neumann's and Morgenstern's axioms of rational choice. Deviating from this rule may be explained by risk attitudes other than neutrality – being the rational default (Harsanyi, 1955) – which usually indicate some degree of *risk aversion*. As Roemer (1996) argued, the different results from veiled decisions concerning distributional rules – maximin versus maximizing the average – hence can be explained by different degrees of risk aversion (cf. Wolf, 2010). Consequently, rejecting infinite fear of risk implies rejecting the maximin rule as a rational option, and correspondingly Rawls's DP.

This interpretation even stands against Rawls's later defense of the DP. He argued that it is not risk aversion (Rawls, 2001), but the importance of the stakes involved, which lets people concentrate on the worst position. In decision theory terms, however, this is equivalent to (infinite) risk-aversion. It just concentrates on the special case of lotteries over differently sized stakes. Since the decision in the OP resembles a lottery – but without knowing the chances – risk-aversion or weighting stakes cannot be distinguished, neither in consequence nor in motivational terms.

8.2.3 From theory to empirics and back: Rawls vs. Harsanyi in the laboratory

The true problem in the above discussion is not if it is risk preferences or weighting stakes that drives people, but that both Rawls and Harsayni just *assume* certain individual tastes, respectively how people deal with uncertainty. In other words, their normative principles rely on some 'stylized facts' which are the basis for their respective philosophical anthropologies. Most central is their disagreement about how people deal with uncertainty, as summarized in Figure 8.1. But given the normative implications, it is highly relevant that the underlying assumptions are sufficiently realistic and robust. In the words of Buchanan and Mathieu (1986, pp. 43–44):

> [I]t would be a mistake to assume that progress toward a convergence of belief what is the most reasonable philosophical theory of justice can be achieved simply by refinements in philosophical thinking. On the contrary, it is becoming increasingly clear that philosophical disputes about justice cannot be resolved without significant contributions from the social sciences.

As we argue in this paper, such input from social sciences could be provided by empirical economic methods, above all economic experiments applied to moral questions. In experimental economics, hypotheses are systematically deduced from theory, which are then tested by

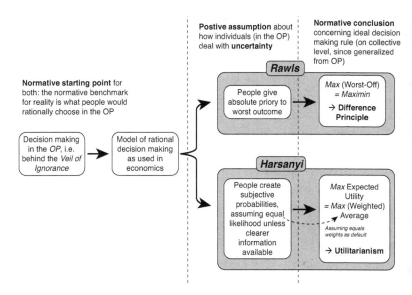

Figure 8.1 Different normative conclusions by Rawls and Harsanyi, derived from different positive models about human decision making (own compilation)

an adequately designed experiment (see Croson and Gächter [2010] for an introduction to experimental economics). The respective empirical results then allow for improving the theory, for example by increasing the validity of positive assumptions which affect, in our case, normative theory. Unlike other empirical methods like descriptive statistics, experiments enable the researcher to construct settings very close to the initial theoretical question, which seems especially interesting for philosophical work.

Norman Frohlich and Joe Oppenheimer argued that the *a priori* unresolved dispute between Rawls and Harsanyi could be partially clarified by letting real people, not idealized deciders in a hypothetical OP, decide on distributive principles behind a laboratory veil. In their 1992 book *Choosing Justice: An Experimental Approach to Ethical Theory*, they describe an experiment exactly addressing the question: if participating in a veil-approximating experiment, would individuals opt for the Rawlsian maximin solution or rather decide in accordance with Harsanyi's average maximization? Indeed, an experimental approach seems methodologically ideal: the necessary artificiality of the Rawls-Harsanyi veil forbids simply looking at some real life situation, where people are perfectly aware of their own position and situation. Hence, the best intermediary construction between empirical reality and the philosopher's mind can be a controlled laboratory setting, in which the OP is approximated as well as possible. The artificiality of an experimental environment – often considered problematic – turns out to be an enormous advantage, since it allows the construction of a counterfactual situation within the real world.

Nevertheless, such an empirical approach of course must raise criticism by philosophers. The idea of the OP and the veil, as the argument may go, is its non-empirical, hence transcendental nature. An empirical approach to the Rawlsian (and therefore also Harsanyian) construction hence necessarily must fail. With critical-rationalist counterarguments, one may point out that a theory, which tries to evade falsification and any contact with empirical content, is largely useless. Rawls (1971) himself does suggest that his theory must have relevance for 'reality', since it is supposed to affect the reflective equilibrium of individuals; and as argued above, Rawls's assumptions about human decision-making already do rely on assumptions about which empirical data can be – and should be – generated.

The design of the experiment was the following: F/O let groups of five persons unanimously decide on distributional principles. Unanimity is a necessity due to the contractarian core of the Rawlsian enterprise. In the ideal OP, the veil should actually make people identical. Stripped of all idiosyncratic information, including individual preferences, it does not matter who in the end makes the decision – everyone would argue and conclude the same. Equivalently, agreement by one individual then implies agreement by everyone (unanimity). In the realm of the laboratory this of course is not possible. As long as there is no consensus, the experimenters can be sure that there is no common, impartial perspective. Forced to deliberate before agreeing, the participants will exchange arguments and viewpoints, such that they will all come closer to a *generalizable* perspective. To some extent, this initial discussion comes close to a Habermasian *ethical discourse* (even though Rawls [1993] rejected the popular idea that *discourse ethics* could be a logical continuation of the OP). Apart from the inherent imperfection of this method, it seems to offer the best approximation of unbiased decision making in a laboratory setting so far.

In total, 85 student groups (five members per group) from the US and Poland participated in the experiment. The participants had to choose from four different income schemes, each containing five income classes

Table 8.1   Distributional schemes participants had to choose from, representing 'yearly dollar income for a household' (based on Frohlich and Oppenheimer, 1992, p. 38).

	Income Distribution			
Income Class	*1*	*2*	*3*	*4*
High	$32,000	$28,000	$31,000	$21,000
Medium High	27,000	22,000	24,000	20,000
Medium	24,000	20,000	21,000	19,000
Medium Low	13,000	17,000	16,000	16,000
Low	12,000	13,000	14,000	15,000
Average	*21,600*	*20,000*	*21,200*	*18,200*
Range	*20,000*	*15,000*	*17,000*	*6,000*

ranging from low to high. The hypothetical yearly income distributions the students were confronted with are presented in Table 8.1.

Before face-to-face discussion took place, students were introduced to the main distributional rules as discussed by Rawls (1971). Rawls had presented three alternatives to the DP, including utilitarianism, which he finally rejected in favor of the latter. F/O informed all participants about these four possibilities, but also allowed for the development of any other solution by the participants themselves. The four principles were

1. Maximizing average income.
2. Maximizing the average, subject to a minimum income (floor).
3. Maximizing the average, subject to a maximum distance between highest and lowest income (range).
4. The maximin-solution.

If group discussion and voting would not lead to consensus and people would declare unanimity impossible, a random selection of one principle would take place. If unanimity was found, each person would be allotted one of the above income groups by chance, and a fraction of the hypothetical yearly pay was received. The veil aspect of the experiment, as Frohlich and Oppenheimer argue, results from the *ex-ante* lack of knowledge in which position one later will end. Hence, individuals are forced to take *all* different positions into consideration when negotiating a solution, added by the discourse ethics elements described above.

How does Table 8.1 relate to the above principles? Assuming equal probability for ending up in any of the five income classes, the average income decreases from distribution 1 to 4, as well as the range between highest and lowest income. If a group unanimously favored the DP, the rational decision would be scheme 4. If the favorite principle were maximizing average income, then option 1 would be selected. If options 2 or 3 were preferred, a group had to specify a certain floor or range; otherwise, the decision would remain underdetermined. Additionally, individuals were asked privately for their own favorite scheme, again including a statement concerning floor or range if necessary.

The results from all 85 sessions were clear (Frohlich and Oppenheimer, 1992): both the maximin solution and the unconditional average maximization were rarely chosen. The overwhelming majority opted for a maximum average constrained by an income floor. This result was independent from cultural differences: the data was generated in the late 1980s, when Poland was under communist rule and the US represented the forefront of capitalist market economies. Figure 8.2 summarizes the outcomes.

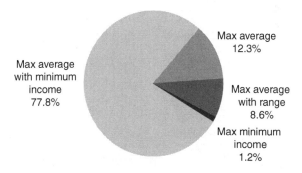

Figure 8.2 Choices for distributional schemes, percentages from all 85 groups (Frohlich and Oppenheimer, 1992, p. 60)

8.3 Extending the Frohlich/Oppenheimer approach: how social immobility affects distributional choices in the laboratory

8.3.1 Integration of production effort in the later Frohlich/Oppenheimer design

The first specification by F/O provoked substantial criticism. As long as participants receive income without any effort, apart from negotiating, the argument stands that the entire experiment is more a gamble than a decision on how to distribute income earned by labor. Therefore, F/O (1990) augmented the initial design and let students participate in a production game (counting spelling mistakes). The more points achieved in the production phase, the higher the final income. As in the initial setup, the group had to decide on potential redistribution of earned incomes after production via a tax and transfer system. Despite the fact that redistribution was no longer driven only by fortune, since money had to be earned, students still decided for distributional schemes that realized a minimum income, but with otherwise unconstrained income maximization (F/O, 1990; to avoid confusion, note that the book-length initial study was conducted earlier, but published only later in 1992).

8.3.2   Positive theory and normative conclusions beyond the veil: the effect of the 'economic model' on distributional decision making

Similar to the discussion in Section 8.2.3, one can argue that in the end it is again different *positive effects* which shape normative choices. In an experimental model society where income is not earned, but received without effort, people are likely to exhibit different distributional attitudes compared to a production setting. While, according to Rawls, people must not have any information about their own characteristics, they should be fully aware of the 'mechanics' of the society. When it comes to distributional choices, this especially holds for the economic system. So 'testing Rawls' (or Harsanyi) in the laboratory implies that the model economy simulated must include all features which may be important for decision making.

Therefore, augmenting the initial design by production effort indeed is a substantial improvement. In the initial design, no one could be blamed for receiving a low income, but in the second setting, individuals could *influence* their result by exerting more or less effort. This is a crucial point as we can conclude from Rawls's (1971) justification of the veil as such: an ideal society eliminates all effects a person is not responsible for because that is what people in the OP consider the only fair outcome. Consequently, 'responsibility sensitivity' (RS) (cf. Dworkin, 1981a; 1981b; Roemer, 1998; Lamont and Favor, 2013) is an integral part of Rawls's approach. In a fair society, 'brute luck' (Dworkin, 1981b) plays no systematic role anymore, but its effects are neutralized.

8.3.3   Effort vs. luck in the market: the case of social immobility

Actual market societies not only seem to fail reducing such inequalities. On the contrary, gaps are rather *reproduced* than leveled out, for example by education systems (Bourdieu and Passeron, 1964/1971;

Shavit, 2007) or welfare state measures (Marshall, 1949/1963; Johnson, 1996; Grusky and Kanbur, 2006). From a distributive justice and especially RS perspective, this seems problematic: if some people systematically receive low wages while others get high incomes, there seem to be forces working beyond individual control which need to be eliminated. Empirical data (Liebig, Lengfeld, and Mau, 2004; Kluegel, Mason and Wegener, 1995; Mason, Kluegel and Khakhulina, 2000) provide evidence that in many market societies with persistent social immobility, many are increasingly dissatisfied with the economic system. The example of the revolts in Greece and other Southern European countries show the increasing political importance of the problem. Therefore, we find it surprising how little attention is drawn to the interplay of normative theory and actual social immobility.

For us, the interesting question is: would people behind the veil want to accept a society in which income differences are reproduced over time? If the RS interpretation of veiled decision making is correct, then one should expect people to agree on institutional measures equalizing the brute luck of social immobility, since this is a force affecting people's income beyond individual control. Most straightforward, social immobility in a market society would – behind a veil – call for severe redistribution from rich to poor. In order to find out if this is the case, we ran an experiment based on the setup of F/O (1990).

8.3.4   An experimental approach to studying social immobility in market societies

In total, 105 students (11 groups, the initial group with 16, all others with nine members, and the data of one student had to be excluded since she had not understood the instructions) participated in our experiment, with a roughly even gender ratio amongst the group. Students were recruited on campus via flyers and announcements, and we ensured a mix from all disciplines (37 percent from natural sciences, mathematics, engineering, and medicine; 25 percent from economics and law, 34 percent from all other social sciences and humanities). Participants received a monetary compensation for participation, which amounted to 24 Euros for a 90 minute session.

The structure of the experiment was as follows: after explaining the design to the student participants, nine individuals (per group) had to collectively choose an income distribution scheme from the ones (A to D) presented in Table 8.2.

At the beginning of the experiment, people did not know about their later position, as they were only presented the different income schemes.

Table 8.2 Different income schemes the participants have to choose from (own compilation)

Position	Variant A	Variant B	Variant C	Variant D
1	300,000	240,000	250,000	120,000
2	240,000	230,000	190,000	120,000
3	190,000	140,000	130,000	120,000
4	140,000	130,000	120,000	120,000
5	120,000	120,000	100,000	120,000
6	60,000	110,000	90,000	120,000
7	50,000	50,000	90,000	120,000
8	30,000	40,000	70,000	120,000
9	10,000	30,000	50,000	120,000

After discussing the different schemes, participants had to choose one of the above presented by absolute majority. In the instance that none of the schemes received more than 50 percent, a run-off between the two most popular ones determined the choice.

After this, students had to participate in individual production games. They could choose between solving simple mathematical problems or a crossword puzzle. Each correct solution or word found yielded one point; the participants were then ranked according to the number of points they earned. The top rank then received income position one, the second highest position two, etc. Information about the individual result was then revealed to the participants privately: everyone knew his or her position, but not how exactly the others had performed.

Thereafter, the whole game was repeated: first the scheme for round two was chosen (the same as before or a different one), then people again participated in the production game (choosing the same occupation or switching); finally, their income was determined as in the previous round. To model social immobility in the experiment, however, the hypothetical income from this second round (Y_2) counted only 20 percent, while 80 percent of this round's payoff were 'inherited' from the first one (Y_1). Thus, the overall income of Y_{total} was:

$$Y_{total} = 1 \cdot Y_{Round1} + 0.8 \cdot Y_{Round1} + 0.2 \cdot Y_{Round2}$$

This amount was divided by 10,000 and, as usually done in economic experiments, paid to participants. Hence, individual income depended on the collective choice in which each person had a say as well as on individual work effort. A flowchart summary of the experiment can be found in appendix A (for the appendices, see Wolf and Lenger, 2014).

If compared to the F/O 1990 design, the readers will find that – apart from the indispensable inclusion of two rounds plus income transfer – we deviated from unanimity in addition to offering two possible production games. Both changes were motivated by an attempt to make the model more realistic, while nevertheless still relying on the veil construction as a crucial element. While the two production types seem unproblematic, majority instead of unanimity seems problematic from a theoretical perspective. The pro-side is that this way, we could detect far larger majorities in the first round (often unanimity) compared to the second, as the data in the appendix (Wolf and Lenger, 2014) shows. Generally, we could think of comparing the current design to an alternative specification with unanimity in groups of five. Nevertheless, the outcomes of the existing setup can still be interpreted well in line with our theoretical considerations. These results are the following:

1. Six out of eleven groups opted for complete equalization (D) in round 1 and then switched to the most unequal scheme (A). Also the remaining groups opted for only mildly inegalitarian options, as Figure 8.3 shows.
2. After the first round, those performing well tended toward less egalitarian schemes, while low-performers tended to income equalization.
3. Socioeconomic background factors had no significant effect on individual voting behavior.

The respective data and regression results are to be found in appendices B and C (Wolf and Lenger, 2014).

These findings suggest that the veil in the first round was rather thick. Behind this veil, people tended to choose egalitarianism. As soon as the veil was lifted, a separation occurred in line with people's self-interest. Hence, we conclude that it was not so much a concern for others (that is, social preferences) which drove people's initial choice of income equalization. The results can be interpreted perfectly in line with the risk aversion hypothesis suggested by Roemer (1996). In our case, people strongly tended toward equalization behind the veil, which is the rational strategy for risk-averse egoists. Nevertheless, not everyone opted for total income equalization behind the veil, which implies that the degree of risk-aversion was less than necessary to produce the Rawlsian maximin-solution, which in our design coincides with

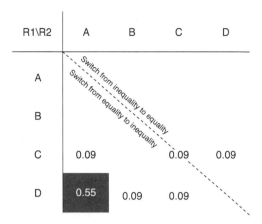

Figure 8.3   Combination of choices in round 1 and round 2. The vertical dimension shows the group decision in round 1 (only C and D chosen); horizontally, the group choice for round 2 is represented (all options from A to D realized). The numbers represent the frequency of a specific combination chosen, a darker grey background visualizing higher frequency. Outstanding is the combination 'D-A' with 6 out of 11 groups (about 55 percent of all) having chosen this particular sequence. Also most other combinations are found to the lower left of the dashed diagonal, showing a shift from more to less equality (own compilation)

choosing equality. Since in the second round, people knew far more about their relative talents, it was rational for above-average producers to vote for inequality, while below-average players tended toward equal incomes. The difference between veiled and unveiled decision making does not seem too surprising from a rational-choice viewpoint. As we argue in our conclusion, however, the stark orientation toward equality behind the veil is remarkable from a normative point of view.

8.4   Conclusion

Empirically, we found that the results of our experiment can to a large extent be explained by the working of the experimental veil approximating Rawls's veil of ignorance. Though the DP does not suggest complete income equalization, but leaves scope for inequality as long as it is in the interest of the worst off, the equalization tendency in our setting can be interpreted in a Rawlsian way: more equality improved the situation of the less productive participants on the expense of the more productive ones, just as the DP would imply. Of course, a more complex design might make clearer the distinction between equality and the DP. The fact that people separated into equality and inequality supporters after lifting the veil at least shows that the veil construction as such seems to work in the way that people are able to choose distributional rules in favor of the worse off, not because they are altruistic, but simply as 'mutually disinterested' (Rawls, 1971, p. 13) rational egoists behind a veil. In this case, individual fear of ending up in the lower end lets people opt for income equalization. However, people do not care about the worst outcome(s) only: in line with F/O, our results suggest that people are neither risk neutral nor infinitely risk-averse players. They chose a middle way between the possible extremes. Still, in our setting, the decisions were skewed toward equalization, a fact which can be explained by the working of social immobility, as RS theory suggests.

In general, we think that experiments like the ones presented can produce insightful results both for experimental ethics but also for more normatively oriented research. As the debate between Rawls and Harsanyi and the F/O studies show, there are situations in which empirical input is indispensable and where experiments can provide the necessary abstract and artificial environment needed, especially by a philosophical discipline such as ethics. The case of social immobility and our own experiment should have illustrated how the F/O approach can be meaningfully extended to dig deeper into the complex field between positive and normative justice research with empirical methods. In a nutshell, experimental approaches starting more closely from the status quo of the real world (democratic capitalistic systems with inequality, production games, and democratic decision making) seem to provide empirical evidence that when put behind an experimental veil, people begin to care for low-income positions for egoistic reasons, as suggested by Rawls. The above empirical results suggest that the degree to which people are concerned about the worst-off may be a function of individual responsibility, as well as the amount of information available behind the veil. In order to investigate the effect of the Rawls-Harsanyi veil in more depth, additional experiments could be conducted in which the degree of idiosyncratic information is varied respective to the importance of individual responsibility.

Note

1. Earlier versions of the paper were presented at a workshop on 'Experimental Ethics', organized by the German Association of Analytical Philosophy, September 2012, and a workshop on ethics and economics by Görres-Gesellschaft, held in

November 2013. We would like to thank the respective discussants for constructive criticism, as well as an anonymous referee's comments on an earlier extended abstract. Bernhard Neumärker and *Wissenschaftliche Gesellschaft der Albert-Ludwigs-Universität Freiburg* as well as the faculty of economics and business administration of the Goethe-University Frankfurt deserve special credits for providing financial support for our empirical research. Bernhard Neumärker and Robert Kappius provided helpful comments on earlier drafts of this final paper.

References

Bourdieu, P. and J.-C. Passeron (1964/1971) 'Die Illusion der Chancengleichheit. Untersuchungen zur Soziologie des Bildungswesens am Beispiel Frankreichs', (Stuttgart: Klett).

Buchanan, A. and D. Mathieu (1986) 'Chapter 2: Philosophy and Justice', in R. L. Cohan (ed.) *Justice: Views from the Social Sciences* (New York: Plenum Press).

Croson, R. and S. Gächter (2010) 'The Science of Experimental Economics', *Journal of Economic Behavior & Organization*, 73, pp. 122–131.

Dworkin, R. (1981a) 'Equality of Opportunity. Part 1: Equality of Welfare', *Philosophy and Public Affairs*, 10, 3, pp. 185–246.

Dworkin, R. (1981b) 'Equality of Opportunity. Part 2: Equality of Resources', *Philosophy and Public Affairs*, 10, 4, pp. 283–345.

Frohlich, N. and J. A. Oppenheimer (1990) 'Choosing Justice in Experimental Democracies with Production', *American Political Science Review*, 84, 2, pp. 461–477.

Frohlich, N. and J. A. Oppenheimer (1992) *Choosing Justice: An Experimental Approach to Ethical Theory* (Berkeley: University of California Press).

Grusky, D. B. and S. M. R. Kanbur (2006) *Poverty and Inequality* (Stanford: Stanford UP).

Harsanyi, J. (1953) 'Cardinal Utility in Welfare Economics and in the Theory of Risk-taking', *Journal of Political Economy*, 61, pp. 434–435.

Harsanyi, J. (1955) 'Cardinal Welfare, Individualistic Ethics, and Interpersonal Comparisons of Utility', *Journal of Political Economy*, 63, pp. 309–321.

Harsanyi, J. (1975) 'Can the Maximin Principle Serve as a Basis for Morality? A Critique of John Rawls's Theory', *American Political Science Review*, 69, pp. 594–606.

Johnson, D. T. (1996) *Poverty, Inequality and Social Welfare in Australia* (Heidelberg: Physica-Verlag).

Kahneman, D., P. Slovic, and A. Tversky (1982) *Judgment under Uncertainty: Heuristics and Biases* (Cambridge: Cambridge UP).

Kahneman, D. and A. Tversky (1979) 'Prospect Theory: An Analysis of Decisions under Risk', *Econometrica*, 47, 2, pp. 263–291.

Kant, I. (1788/2005) *Kritik der praktischen Vernunft* (Stuttgart: Reclam).

Kluegel, J. R., D. S. Mason, and B. Wegener (1995) *Social Justice and Political Change: Public Opinion in Capitalist and Post-Communist States* (Berlin: Walter de Gruyter).

Konow, J. (2003) 'Which Is the Fairest One of All? A Positive Analysis of Justice Theories', *Journal of Economic Literature*, 41, pp. 1188–1239.

Lamont, J. and C. Favor (2013) 'Distributive Justice', *Stanford Encyclopedia of Philosophy*, http://plato.stanford.edu/entries/justice-distributive/, date accessed January 13, 2014.

Liebig, S., H. Lengfeld, and S. Mau (2004) *Verteilungsprobleme und Gerechtigkeit in modernen Gesellschaften* (Frankfurt am Main: Campus Verlag).

Marshall, T. H. (1949/1963) 'Citizenship and Social Class', in T. H. Marshall (ed.) *Sociology at the Crossroads and Other Essays* (London: Heinmann).

Mason, D. S., J. R. Kluegel, and L. A. Khakhulina (2000) *Marketing Democracy. Changing Opinion About Inequality and Politics in East Central Europe* (Lanham: Rowman & Littlefield Publishers).

Nozick, R. (1974) *Anarchy, State, and Utopia* (Oxford: Basil Blackwell).

Rawls, J. (1971) *A Theory of Justice* (Cambridge, MA: Harvard UP).

Rawls, J. (1993) *Political Liberalism* (New York: Columbia UP).

Rawls, J. (2001) *Justice as Fairness. A Restatement* (Cambridge, MA: Harvard UP).

Roemer, J. (1996) *Theories of Distributive Justice* (Cambridge, MA: Harvard UP).

Roemer, J. (1998) *Equality of Opportunity* (Cambridge, MA: Harvard UP).

Rousseau, J.-J. (1762/2010) *Du Contract Social. Vom Gesellschaftsvertrag* (Stuttgart: Reclam).

Shavit, Y. (2007) *Stratification in Higher Education. A Comparative Study* (Stanford: Stanford UP).

Smith, A. (1759/1976) *The Theory of Moral Sentiments* (Empire Books).

Wolf, S. (2010) 'An Intergenerational Social Contract for Common Resource Usage: A Reality-Check for Harsanyi and Rawls', in *Constitutional Economics Network Papers*, 02–2010, pp. 1–8.

Wolf, S. and A. Lenger (2013) 'Choosing Inequality: An Experimental Analysis of the Impact of Social Immobility on the Democratic Election of Distribution Rules', in *Constitutional Economics Network Papers*, 03–2013. http://www.wipo.uni-freiburg.de/dateien/research/cen-papers/CENpaper2013_02

Wolf, S. and A. Lenger (2014) *Appendices A-C for 'Utilitarianism, the Difference Principle, or Else? An Experimental Analysis of the Impact of Social Immobility on the Democratic Election of Distributive Rules'* http://www.freidok.uni-freiburg.de/volltexte/9379/.

9
Value Assignments in Experimental Environmental Ethics

Ulrich Frey

9.1 The pressing cause of environmental protection

Among the most pressing problems of our time is environmental protection. Around the world natural resources are dwindling due to over-exploitation and degradation – and the loss of biodiversity caused by mankind is unprecedented. Pollution of the air, soil, and oceans has increased dramatically, and rising CO_2 emissions are at the top of the global agenda at climate conferences.

Important as these problems are, there is arguably too little effort in fighting them. On an individual level, examples of little effort include little or no change in life-styles; there is no change in the frequency of flying, in switching to less wasteful cars, etc. On a country level we witness the failure of countries like Brazil or Ecuador to protect their forests against economic interests. On a global level, the inability to come to an effective agreement to reduce emissions since 1992 with climate conferences is evident as well.

In fact, scientific assent is almost unanimous in stating that the environment should be protected more than it has been until now. While the importance of increased protective measures has undoubtedly been realized, appropriate actions lag far behind. Economic and technological concerns are often cited as reasons. However, these arguments seem to be flawed, since it has been convincingly demonstrated that with today's technical means it would be feasible to switch to 80–100 percent renewable energy by 2050, which might well mitigate global warming (Nitsch et al., 2012). It has also been demonstrated that economic concerns are misplaced. On the contrary, the later we will stop or slow climate change the more expensive it will become (Stern, 2009; Chum et al., 2011). One estimation assumes that about 2 percent of the global GDP (Gross

Domestic Product) is required for about fifty years to keep emissions under 500 ppm, compared to about 5–20 percent without action for every year to come (Stern, 2009).

Given these problematic economic arguments and the fact that the majority of individuals in many countries know and care about these problems (see Section 9.5), *environmental ethics* become particularly relevant. Environmental ethics is at its root concerned about questions of environmental values. However, as a branch of philosophy, namely applied ethics, philosophers in environmental ethics have traditionally been more concerned about whether and how non-human entities can be targets of moral considerations and how to justify that than about looking at actual value assignments.

This article tries to complement these efforts by stressing that knowing more about *actual* environmental values by laymen is important, too. It may not be too important for questions of justification, but it is central for almost all *actual* decisions on environmental questions – be they on an individual, country, or global level. In order to explore this topic, this contribution takes a philosophical perspective about *experimental methods and data* (e.g., from surveys) about environmental value assignments. By broadening the scope of environmental ethics to practical decisions, for example which values motivate people to act concerning environmental questions, this article hopes to gain more insight in which values people actually have and whether and how this may be measured. These results translate back to traditional philosophical problems like justification, for example, by shifting the burden of proof.

I will argue that given the many pressing environmental problems such an analysis is crucial for an adequate protection of the environment – apart from fundamental differences within the field of environmental ethics itself (see Section 9.2). We should know about actual values, and we should know which entities are valued and how that translates into action or inaction toward the environment. To answer these questions, an interdisciplinary approach is chosen, since methods how to measure such values are available in economics (see Section 9.3). It will also be shown that these methods – although ingenious in trying to 'measure the unmeasurable' – are afflicted with serious problems (see Section 9.4).

Thus, I hope to show that such experimental evidence is a valuable contribution to moral philosophy in general and environmental ethics in particular, since it complements existing research in environmental ethics and contributes to the literature of experimental philosophy by critically discussing experimental methods in philosophy.

9.2   Environmental protection is not a priority

In order to understand why humans care about the environment at all, we are immediately referred to the reasons behind them. What philosophical reasons are there to protect the environment? This leads to a central point of debate in environmental ethics, whether natural entities possess value by themselves (non-anthropocentric positions) or are only means to us humans (anthropocentric positions). This is quite a sharp divide. The first position – in fact it splits up in many different positions – maintains that natural entities do have an intrinsic value independent of their value for human needs. Therefore, to conserve, for example, a rare plant does not need any further appeal other than its rarity. However, there is considerable debate about the *scope* of such supposed intrinsic values – is it only animals, or plants as well? What about whole ecosystems?

A notable biocentric approach within non-anthropocentrism has been put forward by Paul Taylor (1986; 2003). He argues that humans are part of Earth's complex and interconnected community of life, while at the same time there is no sound biological argument for any kind of our superiority (Taylor, 2003). Thus, it follows for him that our interests have to be balanced against those of other organisms. Their intrinsic good in turn can be deduced from their evolutionary goals: to thrive and to reproduce:

> We can think of the good of an individual non-human organism as consisting in the full development of its biological powers. (Taylor, 2003, p. 75)

Differences within non-anthropocentrism are also about whether only those entities that possess the ability to feel should be assigned intrinsic value. Another large division is about holism and individualism:

> Holists argue in contrast that individualism or sentientism is inadequate for an environmental ethic because it fails to offer directly reasons for the moral consideration of ecosystems, wilderness, and endangered species – all top priorities for the environmental movement. (Light, 2002, p. 431)

In contrast, an anthropocentric position asserts that natural entities are only indirectly morally considerable – by their value for humans. Natural entities possess value only insofar as they are in some way useful to us. In short, they have *instrumental value* and can be used as resources (Desjardins, 2006). Taking the example above, whether we should conserve a rare plant is not about its rarity, but more about its potential to serve, for example, as a cancer cure. This has to remain a very rough sketch. (For a more comprehensive overview of these discussions within environmental ethics, see Light and Rolston, 2003; Light, 2002.)

The crucial point to make here is that *irrespective* of which line of approach is followed in environmental ethics, all argue *for* the protection of the environment, albeit for different reasons and with different arguments. Anthropocentric perspectives may in general be considered the least environmental conservation-friendly, because each protection effort has to be weighted against other, mostly economic interests. However, even here environmental protection is very important. Three anthropocentric arguments are shortly outlined to clarify this logic: first, it is in our own economic interests to harvest natural resources like fish or forests in a sustainable way (Krewitt and Schlomann, 2006) because the long-term benefits usually outweigh the short-term gains by far. Second, we should care about the loss of biodiversity because the cautionary principle applies: extinctions are irreversible, and with the present scientific knowledge we simply do not know the *potential* uses and benefits of the majority of organisms. Third, for reasons of intergenerational justice, it is not justifiable to use up resources like oil completely or to pollute the earth (Ott, 2010). (For more arguments, see Light and Rolston, 2003.)

However, as stated above (see Section 9.1), it seems that not enough efforts are put into environmental protection, neither on a global nor country nor individual level:

- failure of climate conferences lead to climate goals not being met around the globe (Edenhofer et al., 2011),
- forests are rapidly destroyed worldwide (Geist and Lambin, 2002),
- we face an extreme loss of biodiversity (Ehrlich and Wilson, 1991),
- many fish species are overexploited on a global scale (Gutiérrez, Hilborn and Defeo, 2011),
- there is a slow or no transition to renewable energies although they are competitive price-wise and technologically feasible (Krewitt and Schlomann, 2006), and
- we see little or no change toward a more sustainable lifestyle in post-industrialized countries (frequent flying, meat consumption, wasteful cars, etc.).

This list is by no means exhaustive. On the other hand, we do see conservation efforts:

- global agreements on environmental protection,
- emission trading,
- creation of nature reserves,
- implementation of recycling systems,
- successful introduction of renewable energies,
- stated-wide programs and individual efforts to waste less energy, and
- bans on many toxic substances.

Since both anthropocentric and non-anthropocentric approaches agree on the importance of environmental protection, if not on the way, there is no fundamental conflict and therefore no reason to suspect that it may be missing support for a particular philosophical approach that leads to little protection. Still, many other possibilities have been considered.

The first and most simple explanation is that *a majority of people do not know* about the urgent scientific pleas to establish greener measures on a global scale. This might be dismissed on the basis of survey data. For example, a representative survey of German people finds that 93 percent know about the 'Energiewende', which is a country-wide shift to renewable energies (Verbraucherzentrale Bundesverband, 2013).

A second explanation assumes this knowledge but asserts that *most people don't care* (for whatever reasons). Again, this can be dismissed on world-wide survey data. *Globally*, the vast majority supports

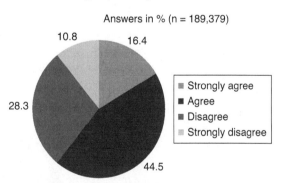

Figure 9.1 Answer distribution to question b001 in the World Values Survey 1981–2008 (5 waves)

environmental protection measures and would accept restrictions to have them instituted (Inglehart, 2009, own calculations).

A third contention sees mostly *pragmatic problems* as obstacles to more protection. It might be argued, for example, that climate conferences fail mainly due to the sheer complexity to get hundreds of countries to an agreement. Similarly, deforestation, overfishing, or land encroachment follow basic necessities – if there is barely enough to eat for the surrounding communities, which is the rule for many natural resources in developing countries, nature conservation has understandably no priority. While these are certainly valid points, there are examples of successful agreements on a global scale. One famous example is the Montreal protocol from 1987 to protect the ozone layer. There are also quite a few examples of communities engaging in successful long-term management (Ostrom, 1990).

Fourth, *ideological* reasons have been advanced, blaming the western life-style of post-industrialized countries with its positive emphasis on economic growth, scientific progress, and disproportionate consumption. It is argued that we lost the wisdom of indigenous people and should go 'back to nature', the noble-savage-hypothesis. While it is largely unclear how much our life-style is *cause* of the problem, it is undisputed that to revert to a more 'simple and natural' way of life is – from a purely practical point – unfeasible, and false from a historic/ evolutionary point. Modern anthropology dispenses with this myth quite thoroughly that indigenous people live in harmony with nature, harvest in a sustainable way, and protect the environment (Alvard, 2007; Penn and Mysterud, 2007).

Fifth, serious protection efforts are hindered by *discounting*. This means that short-term interests are weighted more heavily in comparison to future benefits. It is well known from evolutionary biology that humans do indeed discount steeply (Warner and Pleeter, 2001; Weitzman, 1994), so this is certainly one important aspect. In particular, if individuals fight for survival, protecting the environment understandably has no if any priority.

Sixth, *economic reasons* prevent more protection. Although short-sighted and not profitable in the long-term, because not sustainable, overharvesting resources like fish, trees, or soil can be very profitable in the short-term for the harvesting individuals, leading to the infamous *tragedy of the commons* (Ostrom, 1990). This may indeed be seen as one of the main reasons.

Seventh, the structural logic of this social dilemma prevents initiative – a single individual may hesitate to cooperate by *not* overharvesting because such efforts will only work if a majority follows his or her example. On a larger scale like a country, individual efforts look insignificant and for that very reason may not get started in the first place.

It can be concluded that – besides the other reasons discussed above – it seems of major importance to understand why positive attitudes toward the environment *do not translate* into environmental protection despite the obstacles. At the heart of the problem seems to be the fact that environmental protection *is not a priority*. Whenever interests clash between humans and nature, environmental protection does not take precedence in most cases.

One reason may be that environmental protection in its widest sense has a very low value compared to our other values. From a practical stand-point interested in a more adequate protection, it is therefore important to know why knowledge (about norms, about the prudence to protect, about technological means to do so) does not translate into practice. To understand this and to inform environmental political decisions, this article suggests looking more closely at laymen's decisions and intuitions about environmental values. The remaining article thus reviews value assignments both from an environmental ethics and an economic perspective. In particular, the methods of measurement and their associated problems will be analyzed. This analysis could thus serve as a bridge between experimental ethics, economics, and environmental ethics. In addition, it tries to amend the deplored insignificant role of environmental ethics in advancing environmental protection (e.g., Light, 2002).

9.3   Environmental value assignments

9.3.1   Value assignments in environmental ethics

According to an *anthropocentric* view, value is assigned exclusively in terms of conventional ethics (Ott, 2010), that is, according to its usefulness to humans. This creates numerous problems: *who* decides which values are assigned? If there are competing interests, and often there are, whose take precedence? Given the global nature of environmental conservation problems and the simultaneous diversity of interests, finding a solution seems virtually impossible.

A second problem is *which* value should be assigned to which organism? Since in most cases the potential uses are not known to us and *a fortiori* we do not know their values for future generations, this problem seems unsolvable, too. This is especially so, because we have to know the value of all organisms for a working ranking system (Ehrenfeld, 1997).

In a non-anthropocentric perspective, natural entities possess intrinsic value (Curry, 2011). However, the origin of such values remains deeply problematic. Where do they come from? How can they be justified? Should all organisms be included? Does inclusion depend on the ability to feel pain or some other trait? Do values only extend to individuals or also species or ecosystems? (See, e.g., Taylor, 1986.)

Due to these fundamental differences and unsolved questions, it may be profitable to look elsewhere to advance on these questions. For moral philosophers, actual decisions of individuals are of minor interest because not acting on a moral imperative could simply be attributed to some psychological failure in executing a moral decision. The moral justification for that action would remain untouched, and the problem would be in another realm (psychology).

However, since this article is interested in exploring environmental attitudes and moral intuitions and since we do assign values to natural entities all the time, it could be a step forward to include this data in the discussion. One strong argument in favor is the enormous impact of political environmental decisions. Examples are the planned wide-spread exploitation of tar sands in Canada with a disastrous environmental impact or the decision of Ecuador to abandon a historic plan to leave pristine forests untouched and not to exploit the oil reserves within.

Other arguments are familiar from the debate of experimental philosophy. Philosophers often rely on their commonsense intuitions to start a philosophical analysis, assuming that others share this intuition (Knobe, 2008). It is therefore good to know more about whether these intuitions are *in fact* shared by a majority. Not surprisingly, the field of experimental philosophy is full of examples where many familiar philosophical assumptions have been challenged because most people do not think this way. If a theory goes against commonsense intuitions, this usually counts as a counter-argument (e.g., free will); therefore if nothing else, the burden of proof shifts.

Additionally, experiments and surveys are appropriate tools to unlock the enormous diversity of beliefs concerning even basic concepts, depending on age, gender, culture, religion. This helps to overcome the WEIRD bias (western, educated, industrialized, rich, democratic) that we know is problematic in some scientific disciplines. Samples, but also the researchers themselves (adding another bias: predominantly male) are WEIRD, which biases results (for examples of even basic concepts, see

Henrich, Heine, and Norenzayan, 2010). This criticism can be applied to philosophy as well (Cf. Knobe, 2008).

Finally, experiments do not aim to replace traditional philosophical ways of analysis, but try to add another tool in order to arrive at a more pluralistic approach to a specific problem (Knobe, 2008). They could also help to bridge the gap between philosophy and natural sciences.

9.3.2   Value assignments in economics

In economics, the problem of assigning values to natural resources has received a lot of attention:

> The central problem in the application of standard economic tools to the provision of environmental goods, whether indirectly through regulation or directly through public provision, is placing a monetary value on them. Because these goods are not routinely bought and sold in the market, actual cost/sales information is seldom available. (Carson, 2000, p. 1413)

It is an important problem how to assign monetary values to non-market goods like natural reserves or the value of a forest relating to recreation, carbon sequestration, or preventing biodiversity loss (Elsasser, 2004). One prominent example is the evaluation of the damages to the environment of the Exxon Valdez oil spill (Carson et al., 1992). There are two prominent ways to estimate, for example, the values of environmental changes. One is to measure the actual behavior toward a marketed good that is connected to a non-market good (also called *revealed preferences*). The other way is to describe a hypothetical market in a survey or questionnaire and ask respondents about their *willingness to pay*, for example, for a change in status quo (Hanley, Mourato, and Wright, 2001), therefore asking about *stated preferences*. Two methods measuring stated preferences are worth mentioning. The first one is *contingent valuation* (CV) (Carson, 2000), where respondents typically rate alternatives or answer open-ended questions. Another method is called *choice experiments*. Here, two or more alternatives with different attributes including a status quo choice have to be ranked, scored or chosen in between (Hanley, Mourato, and Wright, 2001). The table below (Table 9.1) describes an example (adapted from Adamowicz et al., 1998) about a preserve describing four varying attributes in columns and four choices in rows, the second row being the status quo. Respondents are asked which choice they prefer.

(Another informative case study about choice experiments and ecotourism in Costa Rica can be found in Hearne and Salinas, 2002.)

Table 9.1 Alternatives with attributes in a choice experiment

Wilderness area	Forest industry employment	Recreation restrictions	Changes to provincial income tax
100,000	450	No restrictions	$50 decrease
150,000 (current level)	900 (current level)	Activities in designated areas (current level)	No change (current level)
220,000	1,200	No hunting, fishing	$50 increase
300,000	1,250	No hunting, fishing, camping, horses	$150 increase

While not without problems, contingent valuation methods have been in use for over 35 years, CV studies have taken place in over 50 countries, and descriptions of CV have been published in more than 2000 scientific articles. Many federal and state agencies routinely use CV methods. There are extensive databases listing more than 3000 records of actual CVs (https://www.evri.ca/Global/HomeAnonymous.aspx) (Carson, 2000). It can thus be concluded that stated preference methods are a successful and established way to get at environmental values – with certain important caveats (see Section 9.4).

9.4 Methodological problems in surveys and experiments

Results from surveys and experiments may be criticized for a number of reasons. I will confine this section to methodological problems. Such criticisms involve contesting the role of intuition, the exceptional position of a trained philosophy expert versus laymen, the weakness of a majority verdict, semantic confusion, and others. (For more general criticism and refutations of the experimental approach in philosophy, please see Kauppinen, 2007; Knobe, 2008; Sosa, 2007.)

In my opinion, one of the more apt criticisms about experimental philosophy is about technical concerns. There are indeed a lot of things that can go wrong in surveys, experiments, and questionnaires. The following section gives an overview of some problems and errors that may occur.

First, there are technical shortcomings. In what Cullen calls 'Survey-Driven Romanticism' he specifically addresses studies from experimental philosophy and their somewhat naive interpretation of results (Cullen, 2010). In general, this points to a neglect of typical survey-problems.

However, although grave errors, these could be overcome quite easily, since there is a long methodological tradition in Psychology about just those problems and good practices (see, e.g., Groves et al., 2009, for a comprehensive overview about survey techniques, etc.).

Second, answers in surveys and experiments are influenced by many factors that have nothing to do with the answer or decision, for example, the order in which the answers are presented. Additionally, humans use context-specific heuristics for many problems which may introduce a heavy bias. This has been pointed out since the 1970s. There is a huge literature just about heuristics and biases (e.g., Gigerenzer, Todd, and ABC Research Group, 1999; Tversky and Kahneman, 1981; Gilovich, Griffin, and Kahneman, 2002).

Third, these criticisms also apply to tested designs like contingent valuation and choice experiments (Hanley, Mourato, and Wright, 2001). Most designs are, for example, not robust against anchoring or framing effects (Chapman and Johnson, 2002; Kühberger, 1998) or a number of other biases (Frey, 2007). This can be confirmed by own experiments, where the designs of choice experiments and contingent valuation were compared. Depending on the frame, *the same attributes* were judged in a different way leading to contradictory declarations. For these and other reasons, some researchers even think they are not appropriate for what they intend to measure at all (Diamond and Hausman, 1994). However, there have been attempts to react to such criticism, most notably a panel of economists with two Nobel laureates, who recommended several improvements in the design of contingent valuation surveys (Arrow et al., 1993).

9.5   Experimental results on environmental values

The most comprehensive survey on attitudes is the World Values Survey, initiated in 1981 by Ronald Inglehart (http://www.worldvaluessurvey. org/) covering nearly 90 percent of the world's population in almost 100 countries. Its data is used here to demonstrate that environmental-friendly attitudes are globally known and wide-spread. As mentioned above, out of 189,379 respondents the great majority would give part of their income for the environment (see Figure 9.1). Similarly, almost 82 percent of 105,139 respondents answered that 'human beings should coexist with nature' whereas only 18 percent answered 'human beings should master nature'. Other results corroborate this evidence that people are motivated to protect the environment as well.

In addition, there are many other professional surveys with a host of information about environmental values and attitudes that could be used as useful starting points for experimental environmental ethics (e.g., for the United States the General Social Survey; for Germany the 'Repräsentativumfrage zu Umweltbewusstsein und Umweltverhalten im Jahr 2010').

Even more instructive than surveys are experiments because they can be tailored to specific philosophical problems. To demonstrate the use of experiments in environmental ethics, two experiments are introduced that were conducted in May 2012 in Germany. Both are relevant to central points of debate in environmental ethics and to value assignments in particular.

The first experiment puts the 'last people' thought experiment of Routley (Routley, 2003) into practice. The question asked was: 'Please imagine that humanity has lost its fertility once and for all (e.g., through an epidemic). Should the last generation, who does not have any responsibility toward future generations, still conserve the environment?' Possible answers were: Yes; More likely yes; Partly yes, partly no; More likely no; No; and No answer. Seventy persons (n = 70) of all ages (mean: 38.9 years) and education levels, with an equal gender distribution (55.4 percent female, 44.6 percent male) took part. The surprising result is depicted in Figure 9.2.

This result sheds some light on one central question in Experimental Ethics, since an overwhelming majority (92.8 percent) (of western people) thinks that even without obligations to future generations it is a moral duty to conserve the earth. The intuition of western people

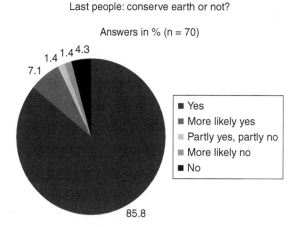

Last people: conserve earth or not?

Answers in % (n = 70)

- Yes
- More likely yes
- Partly yes, partly no
- More likely no
- No

1.4 1.4 4.3
7.1
85.8

Figure 9.2 Survey result for Routley's 'last people' thought experiment

seems to be along the lines of a non-anthropocentric view. This may lend credibility to the argument of Routley that a traditional anthropocentric approach to environmental values is not sufficient for an adequate protection. However, not too much weight should be put on this result, since two potential confounding effects could have influenced the result: the 'Yes'-answers could be due to a heuristic that cannot be switched off in a thought experiment, or they could be the result of expectancy effects.

The second experiment we conducted tries to shed some light at the different dimensions behind environmental value judgments, here in the context of species preservation (unpublished data). Why are some species considered to be more worthy of protection than others? We tested a number of possible candidates for preferences. These dimensions were: usefulness for humanity, resemblance to humans, rarity, attractiveness, and usefulness for the ecosystem.

For this, the same sample of participants as in the first experiment were asked to rank twelve animals (elephant, bonobo, dolphin, giraffe, common mouse, domestic cattle, grasshopper, honeybee, mandrill, proboscis monkey, ant, and earthworm) according to whether they deserve protection (from most to least deserving in comparison to the others, i.e., a forced ranking). The participants did so by sorting twelve pictures of the animals to make the task cognitively undemanding. It was made sure that the pictures and the animals were of the same size. Posture and facial expression were as neutral as possible. Only *after* participants finished sorting, they were asked to fill out a matrix of the above mentioned five dimensions for each animal (yes/no) whether the animal in question possesses this attribute or not (e.g., for a bonobo resemblance to humans would be yes, for a Grasshopper it would be no).

Some interesting results emerged. First of all, there were no significant correlations between demographic variables and ranking order. Second, the dimensions largely agreed with what would be expected; for example, 0.98, 0.91, and 0.86 percent of respondents agreed that the three apes resembled humans, whereas 0 percent said that for Grasshopper and Earthworm. Third, none of these dimensions is able to explain a significant portion of variance in regard to the actual ranking in terms of deserving protection. However, the sum of the mean of each of these five dimensions is a nearly perfect predictor for the actual ranking ($p = 0.000$; $r = 91.2$). This can be interpreted as evidence that these five dimensions or value assignments really do make up the decision which organism to protect and which not.

9.6   The value of experimental environmental ethics for moral philosophy

This article started out asking why on the one hand environmental degradation is perhaps the biggest challenge of our time and on the other hand comparably little efforts are put in to stop it. This problem refers us to our environmental *values* – morally justified values discussed in moral philosophy but also actual intuitions and values of laymen and politicians – that have to stand behind conservation efforts. While all major factions in environmental ethics agree on the importance and give different arguments *for* environmental protection, their impact has, unfortunately, been negligible (Light, 2002). In addition, there are a number of problems with the justification of values in traditional environmental ethics. It is suggested that this approach may be complemented by information from surveys and experiments.

Experiments and surveys allow to 'measure the unmeasurable'; people are asked about their attitudes or decisions to find out their environmental values. Particularly in economics, methods have been developed to put a monetary value on non-market goods, for example values like the recreation value of a forest. These methods have been outlined, but seem – despite their long time in use – to be somewhat unreliable as discussed above. In general, experiments with monetary incentives seem to be more precise than studies without. In addressing the methodological problems with surveys and experiments this article hopes to improve reliability. This clearly shows that they are not a cure-all, but another tool that has to be used with care and diligence. However, they are one of the few tools able to get at the phenomena in question at all.

Two experiments about environmental value assignments have been discussed to demonstrate the usefulness of experiments in moral philosophy in general and environmental ethics in particular. The results show that a majority of German people seem to believe in intrinsic values and that it is possible to get at the values behind environmental moral decisions.

As a conclusion, I would like to discuss in what ways environmental ethics and experimental philosophy can profit from such an approach described above. The first point I want to make is about interdisciplinarity. Interdisciplinarity or even transdisciplinarity is very often emphasized in abstract terms, but markedly less often actually implemented in scientific projects (Frey, 2010). It has been demonstrated that methods from economics and methodological knowledge from psychology may be of considerable use in experimental philosophy. However, interdisciplinarity is not restricted to methods, but it pays to look for data in other disciplines that may be of relevance in the field of philosophy. This has also been demonstrated by using the World Values Survey. This survey contains data – for example, religion, ethics, and environmental attitudes – relevant for various philosophical disciplines.

So, both methods and data are available that can be used for philosophical questions. In this article, the various results shed light on the question why comparably little effort goes into environmental protection. Various hypotheses could be eliminated by looking at various disciplines: it is neither a lack of knowledge, nor lack of motivation or willingness to do something about it, nor ideological reasons. Further steps need to explore how the disposition of individuals to belief in intrinsic values can be used to further the motivation to engage in conservation efforts. Another step toward that goal could be further decomposing the values behind such efforts (as in experiment 2).

Based on the arguments above, I suggest that philosophy could profit from an experimental approach because the latter complements traditional ways well (Cf. Knobe and Nichols, 2008). If nothing else, traditional philosophy could benefit in learning more about intuitions and why they might differ between philosophers and laymen, take some surprising results as new starting points for further reflection (e.g., Knobe, 2003), and advance metaphilosophy on the divergences between those standpoints (Sosa, 2007). On a more optimistic note, to which I want to ascribe, the combination of these two perspectives on the same problems has great potential that has yet to be exploited.

References

Adamowicz, W. P., P. Boxall, M. Williams, and J. Louviere (1998) 'Stated Preference Approaches for Measuring Passive Use Values: Choice Experiments and Contingent Valuation', *American Journal of Agricultural Economics*, 80, 1, pp. 64–75.

Alvard, M. S. (2007) 'Evolutionary Ecology and Resource Conservation', in D. J. Penn and I. Mysterud (eds) *Evolutionary Perspectives on Environmental Problems* (New Jersey: Transaction Publishers).

Arrow, K., R. Solow, P. R. Portney, E. E. Leamer, R. Radner, and H. Schuman (1993) *Report of the NOAA Panel on Contingent Valuation*, http://www.cbe.csueastbay.edu/~alima/courses/4306/articles/NOAA%20on%20contingent%20valuation%201993.pdf, date accessed November 7, 2013.

Carson, R. T. (2000) 'Contingent Valuation: A User's Guide', *Environmental Science & Technology*, 34, 8, pp. 1413–1418.

Carson, R. T., R. C. Mitchell, W. M. Hanemann, R. J. Kopp, S. Presser, and P. A. Ruud (1992) *A Contingent Valuation Study of Lost Passive Use Values Resulting From the Exxon Valdez Oil Spill*, http://are.berkeley.edu/~gh082644/Exxon%20Valdez%20Oil%20Spill.pdf, date accessed November 7, 2013.

Chapman, G. B. and E. J. Johnson (2002) 'Incorporating the Irrelevant: Anchors in Judgments of Belief and Value', in T. Gilovich, D. Griffin, and D. Kahneman (eds) *Heuristics and Biases: The Psychology of Intuitive Judgment* (Cambridge: Cambridge University Press).

Chum, H., A. Faaij, J. Moreira, G. Berndes, P. Dhamija, H. Dong, B. Gabrielle, A. G. Eng, W. Lucht, M. Mapako, O. M. Cerutti, T. McIntyre, T. Minowa, and K. Pingoud (2011) 'Bioenergy', in O. Edenhofer, R. Pichs-Madruga, Y. Sokona, K. Seyboth, P. Matschoss, S. Kadner, T. Zwickel, P. Eickemeier, G. Hansen, S. Schlömer, and C. von Stechow (eds) *IPCC Special Report on Renewable Energy Sources and Climate Change Mitigation* (Cambridge: Cambridge University Press).

Cullen, S. (2010) 'Survey-Driven Romanticism', *Review of Philosophy and Psychology*, 1, 2, pp. 275–296.

Curry, P. (2011) *Ecological Ethics: An Introduction*, 2nd edn (Cambridge: Polity Press).

Desjardins, J. R. (2006) *Environmental Ethics: An Introduction to Environmental Philosophy*, 4th edn (Belmont, CA: Thomson Wadsworth).

Diamond, P. A. and J. A. Hausman (1994) 'Contingent Valuation: Is Some Number Better Than No Number?', *Journal of Economic Perspectives*, 8, 4, pp. 45–64.

Edenhofer, O., R. Pichs-Madruga, Y. Sokona, K. Seyboth, P. Matschoss, S. Kadner, T. Zwickel, P. Eickemeier, G. Hansen, S. Schlömer, and C. von Stechow (eds) (2011) *IPCC Special Report on Renewable Energy Sources and Climate Change Mitigation* (Cambridge: Cambridge University Press).

Ehrenfeld, D. (1997) 'Das Naturschutzdilemma', in D. Birnbacher (ed.) *Ökophilosophie* (Stuttgart: Reclam).

Ehrlich, P. R. and E. O. Wilson (1991) 'Biodiversity Studies: Science and Policy', 253, 5021, pp. 758–762.

Elsasser, P. (2004) 'Economic Valuation of Non-Market Forest Benefits in Germany', in F. Andersson, Y. Birot, and R. Päivinen (eds) *Towards the Sustainable Use of Europe's Forests – Forest Ecosystem and Landscape Research: Scientific Challenges and Opportunities* (Joensuu: European Forest Institute).

Frey, U. J. (2007) *Der blinde Fleck – Kognitive Fehler in der Wissenschaft und ihre evolutionsbiologischen Grundlagen* (Heusenstamm: Ontos).

Frey, U. J. (2010) 'Im Prinzip geht alles, ohne Empirie geht nichts-Interdisziplinarität in der Wissenschaftstheorie', in M. Jungert, E. Romfeld, T. Sukopp, and U. Voigt (eds) *Interdisziplinarität: Theorie, Praxis, Probleme* (Darmstadt: Wissenschaftliche Buchgesellschaft).

Geist, J.-C. and E. F. Lambin (2002) 'Proximate Causes and Underlying Driving Forces of Tropical Deforestation', *Bioscience*, 52, 2, pp. 143–150.

Gigerenzer, G., P. M. Todd, and ABC Research Group (eds) (1999) *Simple Heuristics That Make Us Smart* (Oxford: Oxford University Press).

Gilovich, T., D. Griffin, and D. Kahneman (eds) (2002) *Heuristics and Biases: The Psychology of Intuitive Judgment* (Cambridge: Cambridge University Press).

Groves, R. M., F. J. Fowler, M. Couper, J. M. Lepkowski, E. Singer, and R. Tourangeau (2009) *Survey Methodology*, 2nd edn (Hoboken, NJ: Wiley).

Gutiérrez, N. L., R. Hilborn, and O. Defeo (2011) 'Leadership, Social Capital and Incentives Promote Successful Fisheries', *Nature*, 470, 7334, pp. 386–389.

Hanley, N., S. Mourato, and R. E. Wright (2001) 'Choice Modelling Approaches: A Superior Alternative for Environmental Valuation?', *Journal of Economic Surveys*, 15, 3, pp. 435–462.

Hearne, R. R. and Z. M. Salinas (2002) 'The Use of Choice Experiments in the Analysis of Tourist Preferences for Ecotourism Development in Costa Rica', *Journal of Environmental Management*, 65, 2, pp. 153–163.

Henrich, J., S. J. Heine, and A. Norenzayan (2010) 'The Weirdest People in the World?', *Behavioral and Brain Sciences*, 33, pp. 61–135.

Inglehart, R. (2009) *World Values Survey 1981–2008, official aggregate v.20090901*, www.worldvaluessurvey.org, date accessed July 3, 2012.

Kauppinen, A. (2007) 'The Rise and Fall of Experimental Philosophy', *Philosophical Explorations*, 10, 2, pp. 95–118.

Knobe, J. (2003) 'Intentional Action and Side Effects in Ordinary Language', *Analysis*, 63, 279, pp. 190–194.

Knobe, J. (2008) 'An Experimental Philosophy Manifesto', in J. Knobe and S. Nichols (eds) *Experimental Philosophy* (Oxford: Oxford University Press).

Knobe, J. and S. Nichols (eds) (2008) *Experimental Philosophy* (Oxford: Oxford University Press).

Krewitt, W. and B. Schlomann (2006) *Externe Kosten der Stromerzeugung aus erneuerbaren Energien im Vergleich zur Stromerzeugung aus fossilen Energieträgern. Gutachten im Rahmen von Beratungsleistungen für das Bundesministerium für Umwelt, Naturschutz und Reaktorsicherheit*, http://www.dlr.de/Portaldata/41/Resources/dokumente/institut/system/publications/ee_kosten_stromerzeugung.pdf, date accessed November 20, 2013.

Kühberger, A. (1998) 'The Influence of Framing on Risky Decisions: A Meta-analysis', *Organizational Behaviour and Human Decision Processes*, 75, pp. 23–55.

Light, A. (2002) 'Contemporary Environmental Ethics From Metaethics to Public Philosophy', *Metaphilosophy*, 33, 4, pp. 426–449.

Light, A. and H. I. Rolston (eds) (2003) *Environmental Ethics* (Malden, MA: Blackwell).

Nitsch, J., T. Pregger, T. Naegler, D. Heide, D. Luca de Tena, F. Trieb, Y. Scholz, and K. Nienhaus (2012) *Langfristszenarien und Strategien für den Ausbau der erneuerbaren Energien in Deutschland bei Berücksichtigung der Entwicklung in Europa und global*, http://erneuerbare-energien.de/files/pdfs/allgemein/application/pdf/leitstudie2011_bf.pdf, date accessed November 7, 2013.

Ostrom, E. (1990) *Governing the Commons: The Evolution of Institutions for Collective Action* (Cambridge: Cambridge University Press).

Ott, K. (2010) *Umweltethik zur Einführung* (Hamburg: Junius).

Penn, D. J. and I. Mysterud (eds) (2007) *Evolutionary Perspectives on Environmental Problems* (New Jersey: Transaction Publishers).

Routley, R. (2003) 'Is There a Need for a New, an Environmental, Ethic?', in A. Light and H. I. Rolston (eds) *Environmental Ethics* (Malden, MA: Blackwell).

Sosa, E. (2007) 'Experimental Philosophy and Philosophical Intuition', *Philosophical Studies*, 132, 1, p. 99–107.

Stern, N. H. (2009) *Der Global Deal: Wie wir dem Klimawandel begegnen und ein neues Zeitalter von Wachstum und Wohlstand schaffen* (München: Beck).

Taylor, P. W. (1986) *Respect for Nature: A Theory of Environmental Ethics* (Princeton: Princeton University Press).

Taylor, P. W. (2003) 'The Ethics of Respect for Nature', in A. Light and H. I. Rolston (eds) *Environmental Ethics* (Malden, MA: Blackwell).

Tversky, A. and D. Kahneman (1981) 'The Framing of Decisions and the Psychology of Choice', *Science*, 211, 4481, p. 453–458.

Verbraucherzentrale Bundesverband (2013) *Verbraucherinteressen in der Energiewende: Ergebnisse einer repräsentativen Befragung*, http://www.vzbv.de/ cps/rde/xbcr/vzbv/Energiewende_Studie_lang_vzbv_2013.pdf, date accessed November 14, 2013.

Warner, J. T. and S. Pleeter (2001) 'The Personal Discount Rate: Evidence from Military Downsizing Programs', *American Economic Review*, 91, 1, p. 33–53.

Weitzman, M. L. (1994) 'On the "Environmental" Discount Rate', *Journal of Environmental Economics and Management*, 26, 2, p. 200–209.

Part III
On Methodology

Introduction to Part III

This part reflects on the new methodology of Experimental Ethics. In this vein, it addresses the problem of how to gauge moral intuitions, characterizes methodological approaches used in Experimental Ethics, and raises the question of how to bring reflective equilibrium to the lab.

Almost all work in recent moral psychology studies explicit answers to moral questions, although moral judgments and actions also depend on moral attitudes that can be hidden either by motivated reasoning or as unconscious processes. Strohminger et al. survey methods of studying implicit moral attitudes, including an implicit association test (IAT), an affect misattribution procedure (AMP), a process dissociation procedure (PDP), eye-tracking, and brain scanning with functional magnetic resonance imaging (fMRI). If developed successfully, they argue, these methods can be used for testing theories that refer to implicit moral attitudes and may also help for understanding, treating, and predicting crimes by psychopaths and others who hide what they really think about morality.

Bruder and Tanyi argue that examining folk intuitions about philosophical questions lies at the core of experimental philosophy. They emphasize the requirement of both a good account of what intuitions are and methods allowing assess to them. The authors propose to combine philosophical and psychological conceptualizations of intuitions by focusing on three of their features: immediacy, lack of inferential relations, and stability. Once this account is at hand, they move on to propose a methodology that can test all three characteristics without eliminating any of them. Finally, Bruder and Tanyi propose implementations of the new methodology as applied to the experimental investigation of the so-called overdemandingness objection to consequentialism.

Bunge and Skulmowski distinguish between pragmatic and descriptive levels of empirical ethics and provide a characterization of the main methodological approaches used in this field. While research into the pragmatic dimension involves the investigation of strategies to promote moral conduct and design humane institutions, research at the descriptive level makes use of methods required to appropriately measure and analyze moral behavior. The authors highlight the cognitive prerequisites of moral behavior, including concepts, judgment, and decision-making, and discuss how their situated nature can be fully appreciated in holistic research paradigms. Shortfalls of current research are presented and some alternatives are proposed, such as dialogical surveys and virtual reality experiments.

The aim of Aguiar, Gaitán, and Rodríguez Lopez is to explore a way of bringing reflective equilibrium into the lab. They argue that any experimental approach that purports to use Rawls's model of theoretical justification with the aim of getting subjects' considered judgments has to be enriched with the methods of experimental economics. The authors proceed by introducing the different currents of the so-called 'experimental philosophy project', attending to an influential criticism by Kauppinen. According to Kauppinen, experimental philosophy would not be able to identify the robust conceptual intuitions of speakers. Although partially endorsing Kauppinen's concern, they argue that what he takes to be an insurmountable obstacle for the prospects of experimental philosophy (and ethics) assumes in fact a narrow methodological focus.

10
Implicit Morality: A Methodological Survey

*Nina Strohminger, Brendan Caldwell, Daryl Cameron,
Jana Schaich Borg and Walter Sinnott-Armstrong*

A large hunk of research in moral psychology is devoted to self-reports, which represent the end product of a complex and diverse bundle of underlying cognitive processes.[1] There is more to the moral processing, however, than what can be discerned from introspection or straightforward paper-and-pencil methodologies. A complete account must include all of the processes – explicit or implicit, articulated or unspoken – that go into everyday moral responses.

Those parts of moral judgment that are more obscured from view provide special challenges for the researcher, as their scientific discovery requires more finesse than standard surveys. There are two major ways that moral competence might be hidden from direct observation: *motivated moral reasoning* and *unconscious processes*.

The social unacceptability of lying, cheating, sexual promiscuity, racial prejudice, homophobia, and any of a variety of other crimes of thought or deed impacts the candor with which individuals may disclose their true beliefs and desires. This results in a barrier between the researcher and the full story of a subject's moral attitudes. The desire to conform to social norms can vary in its level of deliberate calculation from outright lying to subtler forms of self-deception, but collectively these sorts of behaviors are known as motivated moral reasoning (Ditto, Pizarro, and Tannenbaum, 2009). Since by their very nature moral beliefs and actions have a socially desirable response, the issue of candor is especially pressing in the study of morality.

One powerful example of this problem occurs when studying clinical populations such as psychopaths. Studies show that psychopaths typically perform normally on self-report tests of morality (Cima, Tonnaer, and Hauser, 2010; Schaich Borg and Sinnott-Armstrong, 2013), perhaps because psychopaths know what others take to be the 'correct' answer so they deliver accordingly. However, the psychopath's abstract knowledge of the rules of human morality may not be a critical dimension of their moral competence. Implicit tests may therefore be particularly useful to assessing these sorts of moral deficits (Snowden et al., 2004; Cima, Tonnaer, and Lobbestael, 2007; Meier, Sellborn, and Wygant, 2007; Polaschek et al., 2010), and perhaps even for predicting and treating psychopaths' misbehavior.

While dissimulation takes place above the threshold of conscious awareness, many processes underlying moral judgment are not accessible through introspection (Nisbett and Wilson, 1977; Cushman, Young, and Hauser, 2006; Schaich Borg et al., 2006). Moral intuitions and other 'gut feelings' represent an output whose underpinnings are introspectively inaccessible; the reasons that a person gives for them are often little more than a post hoc confabulation (Haidt, 2001). Moral judgment is at least partly a product of these fast, automatic, affective, and often unconscious cognitive processes – though deliberative, slow, flexible, controlled processing also plays a role. Dual process theories, which hold that judgments draw upon both kinds of processes, form the basis of many recent theoretical accounts of moral judgment (Gawronski and Bodenhausen, 2006; Strack and Deutsch, 2004; Cushman, Young and Greene, 2010). The extent to which each contributes is a matter of some debate, ranging from theories that self-reported judgments reflect only a fraction of moral beliefs (Haidt, 2001) to those where they have a more critical influence on moral judgments (Paxton and Greene, 2010). Although the degree to which automatic processes motivate moral judgment is still hotly debated, most theories are in agreement that implicit processes play at least some sort of role in these proceedings. This suggests a pressing need for research programs that disentangle the role of automatic and controlled processes in moral judgment.

Thus, implicit moral processes include phenomena that are introspectively inaccessible to the individual and those that go unreported because the individual is unwilling to admit they are present. It may not always be possible to distinguish between these two types of implicit morality (Fazio and Olson, 2003), but some methods are moving in this direction, for example fMRI (discussed later in this chapter).

This chapter focuses on some of the more promising tools researchers have at their disposal to investigate and uncover implicit morality. The scope is not intended to be exhaustive, but rather we focus on noteworthy and useful examples. Understanding the role implicit phenomena have in moral judgment and behavior will have significant benefits for the study of morality. Not only will it allow more complete theoretical models of moral judgment, it will also allow us a better understanding of the neural mechanisms at play and facilitate more effective interventions for those with compromised moral abilities. But how can we verify the presence or absence of implicit moral attitudes? We will discuss three classes of techniques that have been used to assess implicit moral attitudes: implicit judgment tasks, eye-tracking, and functional magnetic resonance imaging.

10.1 Implicit judgment tasks

In the 1990s, a new wave of psychological tasks were devised to capture automatic processes. A common feature of these tasks is that they examine how the judgment of a target stimulus is impacted by the unintended influence of a prime stimulus (Degner and Wentura, 2009). Among the most popular of these tasks are the implicit association test (Greenwald, McGhee, and Schwartz, 1998), the affect misattribution procedure (Payne et al., 2005), and evaluative priming (Fazio and Williams, 1986; Bargh, 1994; Higgins, 1996). They can capture individual differences in automatic attitudes toward different social objects (e.g., racial prejudice), converge with explicit attitudes (Hofmann et al., 2005), and predict behaviors above and beyond self-reported attitudes (Greenwald et al., 2009; Cameron, Brown-Iannuzzi, and Payne, 2012).

10.1.1 The IAT

The Implicit Association Test (IAT) is designed to identify the degree to which there is a mental association between two target concepts (e.g., 'flower' and 'insect') and two attributes (e.g., 'pleasant' and 'unpleasant'). During the IAT, a participant is presented with a succession of words or images and asked to sort them into their appropriate category using a keystroke. When two highly associated categories (e.g., 'flower' and 'pleasant') share a response key, participants can quickly and accurately sort the stimuli. When two negatively associated categories share a response key, participants sort more slowly and less accurately. The IAT has been used extensively in social psychology to measure implicit attitudes (Greenwald et al., 2009), and an increasing number of studies have used the IAT to probe implicit moral attitudes.

Implicit bias against homosexuality, as measured by a standard Sexuality IAT (Nosek et al., 2007), has been shown to correlate with general disgust sensitivity (Inbar et al., 2009). The previously established link between disgust and moral judgment suggests that this IAT may be tapping into implicit moral evaluations of homosexuality, even without employing moral concepts explicitly. Even moral decisions that are cooler and more deliberative – such as choosing whether a hypothetical company should sacrifice a modest profit in order to preserve corporate charitable donations – can be predicted by the implicit association test (Marquardt and Hoeger, 2009).

The IAT has been used to study psychopaths, whose moral competence is especially difficult to assess with explicit measures (Cima et al., 2003; Cima, Tonnaer, and Hauser, 2010). Using an IAT designed to measure the degree to which an individual implicitly associated 'moral' with 'good' and 'immoral' with 'bad', it was found that a weaker relationship between these concepts predicted a higher psychopathy score (Cima, Tonnaer, and Lobbestael, 2007). fMRI research supports the idea that these implicit moral attitudes are associated with emotional processing and impulse inhibition (Luo et al., 2006).

The IAT has also been used to test the constituent parts of morality. While some researchers have claimed that morality is divisible into five distinct domains (harm, fairness, loyalty, authority, purity), the evidence for this conclusion has mostly been provided on the basis of self-reports (Graham, Haidt, and Nosek, 2009). There is preliminary evidence, at least, that these divisions hold at an implicit level, since the association with wrongness of these foundations correlates with explicit self-reports of wrongness across individuals (Graham, 2010). A competing hypothesis holds that all morality ultimately stems from a concern with harm and that even when no harm is observed, people implicitly impute it to the situation or actor (Gray, Schein, and Ward, in press). Correspondingly, it has been shown that moral violations in the purity domain nonetheless are implicitly associated more with harm than failure (a non-moral negative concept). The IAT is particularly well suited to resolving this debate, since it measures the relative strength of implicit associations, thus allowing us to compare the strength of one's implicit associations of wrongness with one foundation compared to the other foundations. One could even construct an IAT that compares each individual foundation to the others by assigning each of them to separate target categories; an IAT of this sort has already been used in other contexts (Greenwald, 2005; Sriram and Greenwald, 2009). An adaptation of this type of IAT could provide us with a more detailed picture of a person's implicit attitudes with regards to the moral foundations.

10.1.2   The AMP

Another popular implicit measure is the affect misattribution procedure (AMP), which is a more reliable measure of implicit processes than the IAT (Payne et al., 2005). In this task, people are briefly shown a prime image, followed by an ambiguous Chinese symbol. Subjects are asked to ignore the prime image, and instead judge whether the symbol is pleasant or unpleasant. People tend to misattribute feelings they have about the prime images to the target symbols; if they feel positive about the prime image, they tend to rate a subsequent Chinese symbol as pleasant. The AMP has been used to measure racial bias (Payne et al., 2005), responses to smoking cues (Payne, McClernon, and Dobbins, 2007) and drinking cues (Payne, Govorun, and Arbuckle, 2008), and to predict voting in the 2008 US Presidential election (Payne et al., 2010). The AMP has also been used to measure automatic affective responses to morally salient primes, which in turn predicts anticipated guilt in a moral dilemma (Hofmann and Baumert, 2010).

While the foregoing evidence is suggestive, none of these measures were adapted to directly assess moral judgment. Rather, they assessed automatic associations between morality and concepts, or morality and valence, which may not be equivalent to moral judgment. Consider the case where a person shows negative associations (as measured by the IAT or AMP) between homosexuality and negative valence. This could be due to an implicit belief that homosexuality is wrong, but it could just as well signal that the person thinks that homosexuality is unpleasant or that others view it as wrong. While an inference from the association to either a judgment or behavior is possible, neither necessarily follow. Convergent evidence is required to disentangle these possibilities, for example by showing that a person with negative implicit attitudes about homosexuals is also more likely to explicitly judge homosexuality to be morally wrong or to discriminate against them in the real world.

10.1.3 The PDP

Typically, researchers use separate tasks to study explicit and implicit processes. Verbal report might be used to study explicit processes, and the IAT or AMP might be used to study implicit processes. One assumption inherent to this approach is that implicit judgment tasks only capture automatic (but not controlled) processes, whereas self-report measures only capture controlled (but not automatic) processes. Yet it is likely that both kinds of process contribute to performance on any kind of task. Thus, it is desirable to design measurement techniques that allow for a comparison of the relative contributions of automatic and controlled processes within a single task.

The process dissociation procedure (PDP) allows for the measurement of the independent contribution of automatic and controlled processes within a single task. Process dissociation is an analytic technique originally pioneered to study implicit and explicit memory (Jacoby, 1991; for applications in social psychology, see reviews in Payne, 2008; Payne and Cameron, 2014). This analysis technique requires using a task that has some conditions in which automatic and controlled processes suggest the same response (congruent), and some conditions in which they suggest different responses (incongruent).

For instance, in a racial bias task, people might see prime images of Black or White faces, before having to identify whether a subsequently presented object is a gun or a tool (Payne, 2001). On trials in which a Black face precedes a gun, both the automatic stereotype response to the Black face and controlled identification of the target object point to saying 'gun' as the response. On trials in which a Black face precedes a tool, then only the automatic stereotype response suggests saying 'gun', whereas the controlled response suggests saying 'tool'. Performance on congruent and incongruent trials allows for the independent contribution of controlled and automatic processes to be calculated.

The PDP uses error rates (or ratings) to algebraically solve for numerical estimates of the probability of intentional control (C) and the probability of an automatic bias (A) (for a detailed review, see Payne, 2008). The control estimate is the probability that a person exerts intentional control, and the automatic estimate reflects the conditional probability that a person shows a systematic, unintended bias when control falters.

An important step in using PDP is validating that the estimates of automaticity and control are sensitive to theoretically predicted manipulations and measures of related cognitive processes. Controlled processes are usually resource-heavy and slow, whereas automatic processes are resource-efficient and fast (Bargh, 1994). Thus, imposing time pressure, cognitive load, or ego depletion should decrease the C estimate but not the A estimate, which is what the research finds (Cameron et al., 2014; Conway and Gawronski, 2013; Govorun and Payne, 2006; Payne, 2001). The control estimate correlates with voluntary attention (Payne, 2005) and neurophysiological signals of control (Amodio et al., 2004; Cameron et al., 2014).

Although originally developed for the study of memory, process dissociation has been used to study racial bias (Payne, 2001; 2005), heuristics in decision-making (Ferreira et al., 2006), and moral judgments (Cameron et al., 2014; Conway and Gawronski, 2013). A sequential priming task has been used to assess automatic and controlled moral judgments using process dissociation. In this task, subjects are asked to complete a series of trials in which they see two words in rapid succession. The first, prime word either represents a non-controversially morally wrong action (e.g., murder) or neutral action (e.g., baking), as does the second, target word (Cameron et al., 2014). Participants are instructed to judge the target word as morally wrong without being influenced by the prime word. Although subjects intend to make accurate judgments about the target words, they show a biased response: when a morally wrong prime precedes a neutral target (e.g., 'murder' precedes 'baking'), accuracy in judging target words drops to nearly chance levels. Process dissociation analyses revealed that imposing fast response deadlines reduced controlled but not automatic moral judgment, consistent with dual-process theories, and automatic moral judgment was stronger on trials with morally wrong prime words than on trials with morally neutral prime words, suggesting the role of emotion and intuitions in the identification of moral items.

These metrics can be connected with morally salient personality traits and behaviors. For instance, sub-clinical psychopathy predicts deficits in automatic, but not controlled, moral judgments, consistent with the idea that psychopaths lack the affective spark toward moral violations that would motivate moral behavior (Cameron et al., 2014). Current work in our lab is focused on applying this method to clinical samples, such as incarcerated psychopaths (Kiehl, 2007) and patients with damage to brain regions typically associated with emotional processing (such as the ventromedial prefrontal cortex; Koenigs et al., 2007) in order to investigate potential deficits in automatic and controlled moral judgment in these populations.

This work can also be extended to actions whose moral status is more controversial. One such hotly contested issue is the legalization of gay marriage. In an exit poll field study, we found that automatic wrongness judgments about gay marriage predicted voting in favor of a North Carolina state amendment to define marriage as between one man and one woman (Cameron, Payne, and Sinnott-Armstrong, 2013). Undoubtedly, there will be a great deal of future work using these techniques to explore implicit moral attitudes about complex moral questions.

10.2   Eye-tracking

In the previous section, we discussed one technique, the IAT, that uses reaction times to draw inferences about implicit processes. Eye-tracking also makes use of reaction times, but with two dimensions added: an X and a Y coordinate. This added dimensionality makes eye-tracking a powerful, but also complex, tool for studying implicit moral processes.

Since most visual information must be acquired serially and at the center of the visual field, eye gaze is a fairly direct measure of overt visual attention (Holmqvist et al., 2011). While the phenomenal experience of visual scanning is that of fluid motion, eye gaze behavior is actually a series of swift motor movements (saccades) punctuated by static focus on a single area of interest (fixations) typically lasting a few hundred milliseconds (Rayner, 1998; Henderson and Hollingworth, 1998). Though eye movements can be voluntary, they are more often not consciously controlled. Although scanpaths reflect a combination of bottom-up, stimulus driven mechanisms and top-down processes that collect and track goal-relevant information, even the top-down processes tend to be subconscious (Weierich, Treat, and Hollingworth, 2008). Eye movements thus reflect the unstated knowledge, intentions, and desires of the observer.

Modern eye-tracking systems use cameras with rapid sampling rates (60Hz or more) to collect two types of data: gaze location and pupil size. Gaze location can be used in several ways, depending upon the design and aims of the experiment. Gaze parameters shown to be related to implicit cognitive processes include the location of first fixation, location of last fixation, number of fixations, length of fixations, distance between saccades, and dynamic temporal patterns (Holmqvist et al., 2011; Hayes, Petrov, and Sederberg, 2011). Most eye-tracking systems also measure pupil dilation. Pupil diameter can reflect cognitive effort (including cognitive load), emotional intensity, psychophysiological arousal, stress, and pain (Wang, 2011). Thus, pupillometry is best suited to study designs that can reasonably rule out alternative explanations, or where one is modeling behavior without needing to know what the pupil response signifies (see, e.g., Wang, Spezio, and Camerer, 2010).

Eye gaze can be guided by evaluative judgments. People preferentially look at beautiful paintings and attractive faces, an effect that corresponds to self-reported enjoyment (Maner et al., 2003; Plumhoff and Schirillo, 2009; Leder et al., 2010). Gaze reflects preferences of which people might not be aware: adults who have been exposed to high testosterone levels in the womb (as measured by digit ratio) spend more time viewing stereotypically male toys (Alexander, 2006).

Eye gaze can also influence evaluative judgment. For example, having someone look toward neutral or positive targets increases preference for them (Shimojo et al., 2003; Krajbich, Armel, and Rangel, 2010; Bird, Lauwereyns and Crawford, 2012; though see Nittono and Wada, 2009; Isham and Geng, 2013), and placing objects in a visual field where subjects are more likely to look at them increases preference for those objects (Reutskaja et al., 2011; Atalay, Bodur, and Rasolofoarison, 2012; Ashby, Dickert, and Glöckner, 2012). In the other direction, forcing gaze toward strongly negative information biases judgment against it even further (Armel, Beaumel, and Rangel, 2008).

However, eye gaze may not reflect preference so much as emotional salience. People orient more quickly toward, and spend more time viewing, positive and negative imagery compared with neutral images (Nummenmaa, Hyönä, and Calvo, 2006), a pattern that is especially strong in anxious individuals (Calvo and Avero, 2005). Similarly, people spend the most time looking at the worst outcome of a losing gamble, suggesting that this information might contribute to decisions about losses (Venkatraman, Payne, and Huettel, 2012).

Eye gaze does not reflect preference so much as emotional salience. People orient more quickly toward, and spend more time viewing, positive and negative imagery compared with neutral images (Nummenmaa, Hyönä, and Calvo, 2006), a pattern that is especially strong in anxious individuals (Calvo and Avero, 2005). Similarly, people spend the most time looking at the worst outcome of a losing gamble, suggesting that this information is the driving factor in decisions about losses (Venkatraman, Payne, and Huettel, 2012).

The information-gathering function of visual attention means that eye gaze does not just reflect emotional salience, but also the goals of the viewer. When free-viewing faces, people fixate on core features such as the eyes and lips (Walker-Smith, Gale, and Findlay, 1977; Luria and Strauss, 1978), a behavior that is missing in people with social impairments such as autism (Pelphrey et al., 2002; Boraston and Blakemore, 2007). Likewise, people look more at dominant faces, especially when dominance is linked with mating goals (Maner, DeWall, and Gailliot, 2008). Whether people look more at old photographs or new photographs depends on whether they are judging the photos for their newness or their oldness (Schotter et al., 2010).

Eye-tracking can function in an atheoretical mode; that is, simply as an instrument for making behavioral predictions. Previous work indicates that eye-tracking could be used to build models predicting implicit racial prejudice (Mele and Federici, 2013), sexual orientation (Hall, Hogue, and Guo, 2011), aesthetic taste (Glaholt, Reingold, and Wu, 2009), and deception (Wang, Spezio, and Camerer, 2010). Thus, it is not difficult to imagine this technology being applied to moral contexts, to make predictions about lie detection, motivated moral reasoning, and the moral competence or behavior of psychopaths.

More often, though, eye-tracking is used to identify and explore cognitive mechanisms. For instance, a well-known finding in cultural psychology is that East Asians are more likely to describe and remember holistic, interconnected aspects of scenes (Masuda and Nisbett, 2001); this effect is mediated by increased visual fixations toward global features of the environment (Chua, Boland, and Nisbett, 2005; Masuda et al., 2008). Patients with amygdala damage lose the ability to judge fear in others, an effect that can be explained by the fact that these patients no longer focus on the eyes when viewing faces (Adolphs et al., 2005; Spezio et al., 2007). The mechanism of the own-race memory bias appears to occur at encoding, when people expend more cognitive effort (as measured by pupil dilation) on faces in a different racial category than their own, while also spending less time viewing these faces (Wu, Laeng, and Magnussen, 2012).

Eye-tracking can be used to test competing hypotheses about underlying psychological processes. In decisions involving uncertainty, people are more likely to choose the option looked at first, which has been used to argue for the role of automatic processing in these intuitions (Innocenti, Rufa, and Semmoloni, 2010). Similarly, fear of seeming racist, but not racism itself, predicts initial saccades toward African-American faces (Bean et al., 2012), suggesting that motivation to appear non-prejudiced takes place at an early stage of processing. Generally speaking, eye-tracking can be used to choose between competing theories whenever those theories make contrasting predictions about patterns of attention, effort, or information-seeking (see for instance Pochon et al., 2008; Reutskaja et al., 2011; Ellis, Glaholt, and Reingold, 2011; Chua, Hannula, and Ranganath, 2012; Quaschning, Pandelaere, and Vermeir, 2013).

Some of these principles are starting to be applied to the study of moral cognition. For example, people spend more time viewing the target of harm rather the agent, and pupils dilate more to intentional (as opposed to accidental) harm, and more when the victim is a person (Decety, Michalska, and Kinzler, 2012). These pupillometry results may indicate higher affective arousal for intentional, pain-inducing harm – though they may also indicate higher cognitive effort. The increased attention toward the victim suggests that people place a greater importance on inspecting the target of damage rather than the actor, though this could also reflect preference differences (such as if the victim is more sympathetic). The tendency to look more at positive (because pleasant) and negative (because important or emotionally salient) information means that fully crossed designs are required to distinguish between these two possibilities.

Following a moral decision-making task, Kastner (2010) found that people look away from those they have decided to kill or let die, and toward those they have decided to save or let live. One explanation for this finding is that it reflects preference: people look toward objects they like, and away from those they do not like. However, these recordings were taken after the moral decision was made, so this may represent a confirmation bias rather than the values leading up to the decision. Settling this question will require studies that measure eye gaze while the moral judgment is being made.

Eye-tracking can also be used to test different models of morality. Prominent theories of morality hold that emotional, intuition-based moral judgments are fairly insensitive to rational, utilitarian information (Greene et al., 2001; Haidt, 2001). However, a recent study has found that people who choose the deontological (intuition-based) option in a moral dilemma spend an increased amount of time inspecting utilitarian information, suggesting that this information is not discounted but rather weighed and considered throughout the decision process (Strohminger, de Brigard, and Sinnott-Armstrong, 2014). This is consistent with models of moral cognition that argue for hidden cost-benefit analyses in highly emotionally charged judgments, even when people self-report these factors not to be under consideration (Bartels, 2008).

Initial forays into the application of eye-tracking to moral psychology offer intriguing hints at what this technology can bring to the field. In addition to theory-testing between different models of moral judgment, eye-tracking has the potential to illuminate (and distinguish between) the early stages of moral processing, give shape to the role visual attention plays in various aspects of moral cognition, and act as an instrument for prediction of implicit moral processes.

10.3   Functional magnetic resonance imaging

Functional magnetic resonance imaging (fMRI) has several possible applications to the study of implicit morality. It is particularly useful for identifying instances when people's implicit moral attitudes or feelings are inconsistent with their explicit self-reports. fMRI can indicate when participants are likely to be exerting cognitive control, detecting conflict, or experiencing reflexive brain responses, which can provide converging evidence that people are lying, experiencing unreported internal conflict, or having automatic intuitions during moral processing, respectively. By providing information about what the brain is doing while engaged in such tasks, fMRI may also help us identify the dynamic mechanisms that permit conscious and unconscious influences to independently contribute to moral performance.

fMRI is already being used, albeit controversially, to detect when people are telling lies. Most work implicates the prefrontal cortex in lying (other brain regions have been implicated in lying as well, but with less consistency and accuracy; Abe, 2011). Prefrontal cortex activity is evoked by intentional deception, both when participants are instructed to lie (Bhatt et al., 2009; Lee, Raine, and Chan, 2010; Monteleone et al., 2009) and when participants lie by their own volition (Greene and Paxton, 2009). Further, pathological liars have increased prefrontal cortex white matter volume compared to control populations (Yang et al., 2005; 2007). Such correlational studies raise the possibility that the prefrontal cortex could play a causal role in deception. Consistent with this hypothesis, manipulating prefrontal cortex activity with transcranial magnetic stimulation affects how efficient (as measured by reaction time) participants are at deception (Mameli et al., 2010; Karim et al., 2010; Priori et al., 2008). These studies clearly indicate the prefrontal cortex plays an important role in deception.

Although it is not yet known how and why the prefrontal cortex influences lying (Christ et al., 2009), its function might be related to the fact that the prefrontal cortex is also active when giving explicit, but not implicit, evaluations (Falk and Lieberman, 2013). Importantly, this pattern holds for moral stimuli. When people are asked to judge socially relevant concepts as good or bad (e.g., 'murder', 'happiness', 'abortion', 'welfare'; Cunningham, Nezlek, and Banaji, 2004), or judge pictures of moral violations according to severity (Harenski et al., 2010), the prefrontal cortex is more active when judging socio-moral items than when judging control items. However, this disparity in prefrontal cortex activity disappears when subjects are asked to judge the same stimuli according to non-moral criteria.[2] On the other hand, other brain regions – including the insula, amygdala, and temporo-parietal junction – are involved with both explicit and implicit moral evaluation and judgments (Cunningham, Nezlek, and Banaji, 2004; Harenski et al., 2010). These same regions are active during the observation of morally trustworthy people, even when participants aren't explicitly asked to judge their trustworthiness (Singer et al., 2004). These results suggest that the insula, amygdala, and temporo-parietal junction, but likely not the prefrontal cortex, could be useful targets for detecting implicit moral processing.

The model that lying or explicitly assessing the moral nature of stimuli is associated with increased prefrontal cortex activation is useful for designing and refining new research directions, but should be pursued with appropriate recognition of its caveats. Although the term 'prefrontal cortex' was used in the paragraphs above for simplicity, the prefrontal cortex is comprised of many different subsidiary regions with distinct functions (the dorsolateral prefrontal cortex, the dorsomedial prefrontal cortex, the frontal poles, and so forth). Although *some* region of the prefrontal cortex has been implicated in most studies of lying and explicit versus implicit processing, the precise regions vary widely from study to study and differ depending on the type of task (Falk and Lieberman, 2013), type of question asked (Priori et al., 2008), or stimuli used (Rameson, Satpute, and Lieberman, 2010; Mameli et al., 2010). Task-relevant prefrontal cortex activity also varies across individuals based on their specific anatomy, subjective experiences, or cognitive strategies, perhaps explaining why no one brain region has been shown to accurately predict lying across all subjects (Monteleone et al., 2009). Further, even if we could pinpoint which prefrontal brain region was most consistently involved in lying or explicit processing, that region's involvement could be due to functions as diverse as working memory, arousal, self-monitoring, or conflict detection, making it difficult to determine how to interpret activity in that region across multiple tasks. Therefore, prefrontal activity does not necessarily indicate conscious or explicit moral knowledge.

Another caveat is that brain activity detected by fMRI can be consciously manipulated. fMRI is most useful for assessing implicit moral sentiments when it can provide an objective (if indirect) measurement of brain function that is resilient against impression management. However, we do not yet know that fMRI is completely immune to such concerns. To the contrary, people might be able to learn how to manipulate their brain activity in the same way they learn to manipulate their behavioral responses (Ganis et al., 2011).

These considerations suggest that fMRI is best considered a powerful tool to be used in combination with other tools to assess the likelihood of moral thoughts or feelings that are inconsistent with self-reports. In addition, fMRI will be most useful for determining how groups of people (clinical populations or people with certain personality types) respond to moral stimuli rather than how an individual person responds to a single stimulus. For example, although fMRI cannot likely provide convincing evidence that an individual psychopath is purposely lying about a specific moral sentiment, learning that groups of psychopaths use their prefrontal cortex more than non-psychopaths when explicitly responding to moral stimuli provides unique and informative evidence supporting clinical observations that psychopaths intentionally manipulate their moral judgments to impress experimenters. We will discuss some of the other ways fMRI can be used in combination with other methods to measure implicit moral attitudes in the next and last section of this chapter.

10.4   Conclusion

The preceding sections detail a variety of methods that may be employed to measure implicit moral attitudes. While we have outlined the strengths of each approach, it is important to bear in mind that no single method is sufficient for measuring this construct. Rather, a multi-method, integrated approach is preferable. Combining the available methods allows for each to complement the relative strengths and weaknesses of the other, thus leading to more inferential power than any of these measures when considered in isolation. As such, the remainder of this chapter is devoted to how these various implicit measures might be combined to complement each other, thus providing a rough outline for future research on implicit moral attitudes.

At a basic level, these measures aim at implicit moral attitudes insofar as they assess aspects of moral cognition that subjects are either unwilling or unable to self-report. They are therefore theoretically unified by a shared assumption in the explicit/implicit processing distinction made by dual-processing models of social cognition, and the assumption that moral cognition can be categorized as a sub-type of social cognition.

However, these measurement techniques differ in the extent to which they evaluate the same construct. Because implicit attitudes cannot be observed directly, the only way to establish that a particular method is measuring those implicit attitudes is by comparing its results with the theoretically predicted results and the results of other, previously established, implicit measures. If two methods measure the same construct, we should see a convergence between them when they are used in the same experiment. Thus, a basic test of a measure's construct validity is whether it exhibits convergent validity – that is, it correlates with other implicit measures of the same construct (Greenwald and Nosek, 2001). Moreover, utilizing multiple measures of a single construct when analyzing a latent variable has been shown to provide more accurate estimates than can be provided by any of the individual measures (Little, Lindenberger, and Nesselroade, 1999).

This method has been successfully applied to implicit attitudes in the past. Cunningham, Preacher, and Banaji (2001) contrasted two implicit judgment tasks with the intention of examining their construct validity. By comparing conceptually similar IATs and evaluative priming tasks, they were able to establish that the implicit measures correlated with each other and more importantly, that they both were evaluating the same latent construct, verifying the construct validity of each.

Although it has yet to be directly examined, there is some evidence to suggest a similar convergence between implicit judgment tasks and brain scanning techniques. Consistent with the aforementioned fMRI research, several studies have shown the IAT to be correlated with activity in the amygdala (Phelps et al., 2000), cingulate cortex, and parts of the prefrontal cortex (Chee et al., 2000). Performance on a moral IAT corresponds to activation in both the amygdala and medial orbit-ofrontal cortex during the sorting of moral stimuli (Luo et al., 2006), suggesting that implicit judgment tasks like the IAT – and the concept it measures – have a distinct neural signature.

There is also support for a convergence between implicit judgment tasks and eye-tracking data. Individuals with different implicit associations should process the information in an implicit judgment task differently, which will be reflected in eye movements. As one would expect, eyetracking data can be used to predict IAT scores (Mele and Federici, 2013). This finding suggests that the processes measured in the IAT bleeds into the top-down, goal-directed processes involved with eye gaze.

Of course, the differences between these implicit measures can be just as critical. Different measures seem to focus on different aspects of moral intuitions. While implicit judgment tasks and eye-tracking both limit their analyses to the level of implicit cognition, fMRI focuses on neuronal activity. Successfully identifying the brain areas activated by these other implicit measures is therefore a promising way to fill out this part of the overall picture. Additionally, the extant fMRI research finds that dishonest moral assessment and unconscious evaluation of moral stimuli have different activation patterns. Data from fMRI studies therefore may allow us to distinguish whether a participant is unwilling or unable to report a moral attitude; something that cannot be done via implicit judgment tasks.

Eye-tracking has the unique benefit of providing us with more detailed picture of the information processing that goes into the formation of a moral intuition. By looking at eye-gaze and pupil dilation, we can identify what information about a moral scenario is being processed, and in what order.

There are even relevant differences between various implicit judgment tasks. The IAT provides us with a comparative assessment of implicit attitudes; that is, it measures how an individual implicitly evaluates one category compared to another category. In contrast, the AMP and evaluative priming task provide us with an absolute measure of implicit evaluation. Thus, the IAT is more effective when the implicit moral attitude we want to measure is comparative (e.g., an individual's implicit moral attitude toward gay marriage compared to straight marriage), while the AMP and evaluative priming task are more effective when we want to test whether an implicit moral attitude is present at all (e.g., do psychopaths have moral intuitions?).

Because the IAT focuses on implicit evaluations of categories, it may be more effective at predicting attitudes and behaviors at the category level, such as attitudes toward social policies targeted at specific groups (e.g., gay marriage). By contrast, priming methods such as AMP focus on implicit evaluations of individual items that are exemplars of a larger category. Such implicit measures may be more effective at predicting attitudes and behaviors toward exemplars of a social category (e.g., a homosexual person; Fazio and Olson, 2003).

Overall, these methods contribute collectively toward a complete picture of moral intuitions and moral beliefs. Incorporating implicit measures into moral psychology will be an important step forward in coming years.

Notes

1. N. Strohminger and B. Caldwell contributed equally to this chapter.
2. In Cunningham's study, participants were asked to judge whether or not socially relevant concepts were abstract or concrete. In Harenski's study, participants were asked whether the moral violations represented in the pictures were occurring indoors or outdoors.

References

Abe, N. (2011) 'How the Brain Shapes Deception: An Integrated Review of the Literature', *The Neuroscientist*, 17, 5, pp. 560–574.

Adolphs, R., F. Gosselin, T. W. Buchanan, D. Tranel, P. Schyns, and A. R. Damasio (2005) 'A Mechanism for Impaired Fear Recognition After Amygdala Damage', *Nature*, 433, 7021, pp. 68–72.

Alexander, G. M. (2006) 'Associations Among Gender-linked Toy Preferences, Spatial Ability, and Digit Ratio: Evidence From Eye-tracking Analysis', *Archives of Sexual Behavior*, 35, 6, pp. 699–709.

Amodio, D. M., E. Harmon-Jones, P. G. Devine, J. J. Curtin, S. L. Hartley, and A. E. Covert (2004) 'Neural Signals for the Detection of Unintentional Race Bias', *Psychological Science*, 15, pp. 88–93.

Armel, K. C., A. Beaumel, and A. Rangel (2008) 'Biasing Simple Choices by Manipulating Relative Visual Attention', *Judgment and Decision Making*, 3, 5, pp. 396–403.

Ashby, N. J., S. Dickert, and A. Glöckner (2012) 'Focusing on What You Own: Biased Information Uptake Due to Ownership', *Judgment and Decision Making*, 7, 3, p. 254.

Atalay, A. S., H. O. Bodur, and D. Rasolofoarison (2012) 'Shining in the Center: Central Gaze Cascade Effect on Product Choice', *Journal of Consumer Research*, 39, 4, p. 848.

Bargh, J. A. (1994) 'The Four Horsemen of Automaticity: Awareness, Efficiency, Intention, and Control in Social Cognition', in R. S. Wyer and T. K. Srull (eds.) *Handbook of Social Cognition*, 2nd ed., p. 1, Hillsdale, NJ: Erlbaum.

Bartels, D. (2008) 'Principled Moral Sentiment and the Flexibility of Moral Judgment and Decision Making', *Cognition*, 108, 2, p. 381.

Bean, M. G., D. G. Slaten, W. S. Horton, M. C. Murphy, A. R. Todd, and J. A. Richeson (2012) 'Prejudice Concerns and Race-based Attentional Bias New Evidence From Eyetracking', *Social Psychological and Personality Science*, 3, 6, p. 722.

Bhatt, S., J. Mbwana, A. Adeyemo, A. Sawyer, A. Hailu, and J. Vanmeter (2009) 'Lying About Facial Recognition: An fMRI Study', *Brain and Cognition*, 69, 2, p. 382.

Bird, G. D., J. Lauwereyns, and M. T. Crawford (2012) 'The Role of Eye Movements in Decision Making and the Prospect of Exposure Effects', *Vision Research*, 60, pp. 16–21.

Boraston, Z. and S.-J. Blakemore (2007) 'The Application of Eye-tracking Technology in the Study of Autism', *The Journal of Physiology*, 581, 3, pp. 893–898.

Calvo, M. G. and P. Avero (2005) 'Time Course of Attentional Bias to Emotional Scenes in Anxiety: Gaze Direction and Duration', *Cognition Emotion*, 19, 3, pp. 433–451.

Cameron, C. D., J. L. Brown-Iannuzzi, and B. K. Payne (2012) 'Sequential Priming Measures of Implicit Social Cognition: A Meta-analysis of Associations with Behavior and Explicit Attitudes', *Personality and Social Psychology Review*, 16, 4, pp. 330–350.

Cameron, C. D., B. K. Payne, and W. Sinnott-Armstrong (2013) *Modeling Moral Intuitions: Using Process Dissociation to Understand Automatic and Controlled Moral Judgment*, unpublished manuscript.

Cameron, C. D., B. K. Payne, W. Sinnott-Armstrong, J. Scheffer, and M. Inzlicht (2014) *A Study of Implicit Moral Attitudes*, unpublished manuscript.

Chee, M. W., N. Sriram, C. S. Soon, and K. M. Lee (2000) 'Dorsolateral Prefrontal Cortex and the Implicit Association of Concepts and Attributes', *Neuroreport*, 11, 1, pp. 135–140.

Christ, S. E., D. C. Van Essen, J. M. Watson, L. E. Brubaker, and K. B. McDermott (2009) 'The Contributions of Prefrontal Cortex and Executive Control to Deception: Evidence From Activation Likelihood Estimate Meta-analyses', *Cerebral Cortex*, 19, 7, pp. 1557–1566.

Chua, H. F., J. E. Boland, and R. E. Nisbett (2005) 'Cultural Variation in Eye Movements During Scene Perception', *Proceedings of the National Academy of Sciences of the United States of America*, 102, 35, pp. 12629–12633, doi: 10.1073/pnas.0506162102.

Chua, E. F., D. E. Hannula, and C. Ranganath (2012) 'Distinguishing Highly Confident Accurate and Inaccurate Memory: Insights About Relevant and Irrelevant Influences on Memory Confidence', *Memory*, 20, 1, pp. 48–62, doi: 10.1080/09658211.2011.633919.

Cima, M., H. Merckelbach, S. Hollnack, and E. Knauer (2003) 'Characteristics of Psychiatric Prison Inmates Who Claim Amnesia', *Personality and Individual Differences*, 35, 2, pp. 373–380.

Cima, M., F. Tonnaer, and J. Lobbestael (2007) 'Moral Emotions in Predatory and Impulsive Offenders Using Implicit Measures', *Netherlands Journal of Psychology*, 63, 4, pp. 133–142.

Cima, M., F. Tonnaer, and M. D. Hauser (2010) 'Psychopaths Know Right From Wrong but Don't Care', *Social Cognitive and Affective Neuroscience*, 5, 1, pp. 59–67.

Conway, P. and B. Gawronski (2013) 'Deontological and Utilitarian Inclinations in Moral Decision Making: A Process Dissociation Approach', *Journal of Personality & Social Psychology*, 104, 2, pp. 216–234, doi: 10.1037/a0031021.

Cunningham, W. A., K. J. Preacher, and M. R. Banaji (2001) 'Implicit Attitude Measures: Consistency, Stability, and Convergent Validity', *Psychological Science*, 12, 2, pp. 163–170.

Cunningham, W. A., J. Nezlek, and M. R. Banaji (2004) 'Implicit and Explicit Ethnocentrism: Revisiting the Ideologies of Prejudice', *Personality and Social Psychology Bulletin*, 30, pp. 1332–1346.

Cushman, F., L. Young, and M. Hauser (2006) 'The Role of Conscious Reasoning and Intuition in Moral Judgment Testing Three Principles of Harm', *Psychological Science*, 17, 12, pp. 1082–1089.

Cushman, F., L. Young, and J. Greene (2010) 'Multi-system Moral Psychology', in J. Doris and the Moral Psychology Research Group (eds.) *The Moral Psychology Handbook*, pp. 47–71, New York: Oxford University Press.

Decety, J., K. J. Michalska, and K. D. Kinzler (2012) 'The Contribution of Emotion and Cognition to Moral Sensitivity: A Neurodevelopmental Study', *Cerebral Cortex*, 22, 1, pp. 209–220.

Degner, J. and D. Wentura (2009) 'Not Everybody Likes the Thin and Despises the Fat: One's Weight Matters in the Automatic Activation of Weight-related Social Evaluations', *Social Cognition*, 27, 2, pp. 202–221.

Ditto, P., D. Pizarro, and D. Tannenbaum (2009) 'Motivated Moral Reasoning', in D. Bartels, C. Bauman, L. Skitka, and D. Medin (eds.), *Psychology of Learning and Motivation*, 50, pp. 307–338, Burlington, MA: Academic Press.

Ellis, J. J., M. G. Glaholt, and E. M. Reingold (2011) 'Eye Movements Reveal Solution Knowledge Prior to Insight', *Consciousness & Cognition*, 20, 3, pp. 768–776, doi: 10.1016/j.concog.2010.12.007.

Falk, E. B. and M. D. Lieberman (2013) 'The Neural Bases of Attitudes, Evaluations, and Behavior Change', in F. Krueger and J. Grafman (eds.) *The Neural Basis of Human Belief Systems*, pp. 71–94, New York: Psychology Press.

Fazio, R. H. and C. J. Williams (1986) 'Attitude Accessibility as a Moderator of the Attitude-perception and Attitude-behavior Relations: An Investigation of the

1984 Presidential Election', *Journal of Personality and Social Psychology*, 51, 3, pp. 505–514, doi: 10.1037/0022-3514.51.3.505.

Fazio, R. H. and M. A. Olson (2003) 'Implicit Measures in Social Cognition Research: Their Meaning and Use', *Annual Review of Psychology*, 54, 1, pp. 297–327.

Ferreira, M. B., L. Garcia-Marques, S. J. Sherman, and J. W. Sherman (2006) 'Automatic and Controlled Components of Judgment and Decision Making', *Journal of Personality & Social Psychology*, 91, 5, pp. 797–813.

Ganis, G., J. P. Rosenfeld, J. Meixner, R. A. Kievit, and H. E. Schendan (2011) 'Lying in the Scanner: Covert Countermeasures Disrupt Deception Detection by Functional Magnetic Resonance Imaging', *Neuroimage*, 55, 1, pp. 312–319, doi: 10.1016/j.neuroimage.2010.11.025.

Gawronski, B. and G. V. Bodenhausen (2006) 'Associative and Propositional Processes in Evaluation: An Integrative Review of Implicit and Explicit Attitude Change', *Psychological Bulletin*, 132, 5, p. 692.

Glaholt, M. G., E. M. Reingold, and M.-C. Wu (2009) 'Predicting Preference From Fixations', *Psychology Journal*, 7, 2, pp. 141–158.

Govorun, O. and B. K. Payne (2006) 'Ego-depletion and Prejudice: Separating Automatic and Controlled Components', *Social Cognition*, 24, 2, pp. 111–136.

Graham, J. (2010) *Left Gut, Right Gut: Ideology and Automatic Moral Reactions*, unpublished manuscript.

Graham, J., J. Haidt, and B. A. Nosek (2009) 'Liberals and Conservatives Rely on Different Sets of Moral Foundations', *Journal of Personality & Social Psychology*, 96, 5, pp. 1029–1046.

Gray, K., C. Schein, and A. F. Ward (in press) 'The Myth of Harmless Wrongs in Moral Cognition: Automatic Dyadic Completion From Sin to Suffering', *Journal of Experimental Psychology: General*. Advance online publication. http://dx.doi.org/10.1037/a0036149

Greene, J. D. and J. M. Paxton (2009) 'Patterns of Neural Activity Associated With Honest and Dishonest Moral Decisions', *Proceedings of the National Academy of Sciences of the United States of America*, 106, 30, pp. 12506–12511, doi: 10.1073/pnas.0900152106.

Greene, J. D., R. B. Sommerville, L. E. Nystrom, J. M. Darley, and J. D. Cohen (2001) 'An fMRI Investigation of Emotional Engagement in Moral Judgment', *Science*, 293, 5537, pp. 2105–2108.

Greenwald, A. G. (2005) *Implicit Assessment of Multifactor Traits*, unpublished manuscript.

Greenwald, A. G. and B. A. Nosek (2001) 'Health of the Implicit Association Test at Age 3', *Zeitschrift Für Experimentelle Psychologie*, 48, 2, pp. 85–93.

Greenwald, A. G., D. E. McGhee, and J. L. K. Schwartz (1998) 'Measuring Individual Differences in Implicit Cognition: The Implicit Association Test', *Journal of Personality & Social Psychology*, 74, 6, pp. 1464–1480.

Greenwald, A. G., T. A. Poehlman, E. L. Uhlmann, and M. R. Banaji (2009) 'Understanding and Using the Implicit Association Test: III: Meta-analysis of Predictive Validity', *Journal of Personality & Social Psychology*, 97, 1, pp. 17–41.

Haidt, J. (2001) 'The Emotional Dog and Its Rational Tail: A Social Intuitionist Approach to Moral Judgment', *Psychological Review*, 108, 4, p. 814.

Hall, C., T. Hogue, and K. Guo (2011) 'Differential Gaze Behavior Towards Sexually Preferred and Non-preferred Human Figures', *Journal of Sex Research*, 48, 5, pp. 461–469, doi:10.1080/00224499.2010.521899.

Harenski, C. L., Antonenko, O., Shane, M. S., and Kiehl, K. A. (2010). A functional imaging investigation of moral deliberation and moral intuition. *Neuroimage*, 49, 3, pp. 2707–2716.

Hayes, T. R., A. A. Petrov, and P. B. Sederberg (2011) 'A Novel Method for Analyzing Sequential Eye Movements Reveals Strategic Influence on Raven's Advanced Progressive Matrices', *Journal of Vision*, 11, 10, pp. 1–11.

Henderson, J. M. and A. Hollingworth (1998) 'Eye Movements During Scene Viewing: An Overview', in G. Underwood (ed.) *Eye Guidance in Reading and Scene Perception*, 11th edn, pp. 269–293, Oxford, UK: Elsevier.

Higgins, E. T. (1996) 'Knowledge Activation: Accessibility, Applicability, and Salience', in E. T. Higgins and A. W. Kruglanski (eds.) *Social Psychology: Handbook of Basic Principles*, pp. 133–168, New York: Guilford Press.

Hofmann, W., B. Gawronski, T. Gschwendner, H. Le, and M. Schmitt (2005) 'A Meta-analysis on the Correlation Between the Implicit Association Test and Explicit Self-report Measures', *Personality and Social Psychology Bulletin*, 31, 10, pp. 1369–1385.

Hofmann, W. and A. Baumert (2010) 'Immediate Affect as a Basis for Intuitive Moral Judgement: An Adaptation of the Affect Misattribution Procedure', *Cognition and Emotion*, 24, 3, pp. 522–535.

Holmqvist, K., M. Nyström, R. Andersson, R. Dewhurst, H. Jarodzka, and J. Van de Weijer (2011) *Eye Tracking: A Comprehensive Guide to Methods and Measures* (Oxford, UK: Oxford University Press).

Inbar, Y., D. A. Pizarro, J. Knobe, and P. Bloom (2009) 'Disgust Sensitivity Predicts Intuitive Disapproval of Gays', *Emotion*, 9, 3, p. 435.

Innocenti, A., A. Rufa, and J. Semmoloni (2010) 'Overconfident Behavior in Informational Cascades: An Eye-tracking Study', *Journal of Neuroscience, Psychology, & Economics*, 3, 2, pp. 74–82, doi: 10.1037/a0018476.

Isham, E. A. and J. J. Geng (2013) 'Looking Time Predicts Choice but Not Aesthetic Value', *Plos One*, 8, 8, pp. 1–7, doi: 10.1371/journal.pone.0071698.

Jacoby, L. L. (1991). A process dissociation framework: Separating automatic from intentional uses of memory. *Journal of Memory and Language*, 30, 5, pp. 513–541.

Karim, A. A., M. Schneider, M. Lotze, R. Veit, P. Sauseng, C. Braun, and N. Birbaumer (2010) 'The Truth About Lying: Inhibition of the Anterior Prefrontal Cortex Improves Deceptive Behavior', *Cerebral Cortex*, 20, 1, pp. 205–213.

Kastner, R. M. (2010) 'Moral Judgments and Visual Attention: An Eye-tracking Investigation', Chrestomathy: Annual Review of Undergraduate Research, School of Humanities and Social Sciences, School of Languages, Cultures, and World Affairs, College of Charleston, 9(114–128).

Kiehl, K. A. (2007) 'Without Morals: The Cognitive Neuroscience of Psychopathy', in W. Sinnott-Armstrong (ed.) *Moral Psychology, 3, The Neuroscience of Morality: Emotion, Brain Disorders, and Development*, pp. 114–128, NY: Bradford Books.

Koenigs, M., L. Young, R. Adolphs, D. Tranel, F. Cushman, M. Hauser, and A. Damasio (2007) 'Damage to the Prefrontal Cortex Increases Utilitarian Moral Judgements', *Nature*, 446, 7138, pp. 908–911.

Krajbich, I., C. Armel, and A. Rangel (2010) 'Visual Fixations and the Computation and Comparison of Value in Simple Choice', *Nature Neuroscience*, 13, 10, pp. 1292–1298.

Leder, H., P. P. Tinio, I. M. Fuchs, and I. Bohrn (2010) 'When Attractiveness Demands Longer Looks: The Effects of Situation and Gender', *The Quarterly Journal of Experimental Psychology*, 63, 9, pp. 1858–1871.

Lee, T. M., A. Raine, and C. C. Chan (2010) 'Lying About the Valence of Affective Pictures: An fMRI Study', *PloS One*, 5, 8, e12291.

Little, T. D., O. Lindenberger, and J. R. Nesselroade (1999) 'On Selecting Indicators for Multivariate Measurement and Modeling with Latent Variables: When "Good" Indicators Are Bad and "Bad" Indicators Are Good', *Psychological Methods*, 4, 2, p. 192.

Luo, Q., M. Nakic, T. Wheatley, R. Richell, A. Martin, and R. J. R. Blair (2006) 'The Neural Basis of Implicit Moral Attitude – An IAT Study Using Event-related fMRI', *Neuroimage*, 30, 4, pp. 1449–1457.

Luria, S. M. and M. S. Strauss (1978) 'Comparison of Eye Movements Over Faces in Photographic Positives and Negatives', *Perception*, 7, pp. 349–358.

Mameli, F., S. Mrakic-Sposta, M. Vergari, M, Fumagalli, M. Macis, R. Ferrucci, and A. Priori (2010) 'Dorsolateral Prefrontal Cortex Specifically Processes General – But Not Personal – Knowledge Deception: Multiple Brain Networks for Lying', *Behavioural Brain Research*, 211, 2, pp. 164–168.

Maner, J. K., C. N. DeWall, and M. T. Gailliot (2008) 'Selective Attention to Signs of Success: Social Dominance and Early Stage Interpersonal Perception', *Personality and Social Psychology Bulletin*, 34, 4, pp. 488–501.

Maner, J. K., D. T. Kenrick, D. V. Becker, A. W. Delton, B. Hofer, C. J. Wilbur, and S. L. Neuberg (2003) 'Sexually Selective Cognition: Beauty Captures the Mind of the Beholder', *Journal of Personality and Social Psychology*, 85, 6, p. 1107.

Marquardt, N. and R. Hoeger (2009) 'The Effect of Implicit Moral Attitudes on Managerial Decision-making: An Implicit Social Cognition Approach', *Journal of Business Ethics*, 85, 2, pp. 157–171.

Masuda, T., P. C. Ellsworth, B. Mesquita, J. Leu, S. Tanida, and E. Van de Veerdonk (2008) 'Placing the Face in Context: Cultural Differences in the Perception of Facial Emotion', *Journal of Personality and Social Psychology*, 94, 3, p. 365.

Masuda, T. and R. E. Nisbett (2001) 'Attending Holistically versus Analytically: Comparing the Context Sensitivity of Japanese and Americans', *Journal of Personality and Social Psychology*, 81, 5, p. 922.

Meier, B. P., M. Sellbom, and D. B. Wygant (2007) 'Failing to Take the Moral High Ground: Psychopathy and the Vertical Representation of Morality', *Personality and Individual Differences*, 43, 4, pp. 757–767.

Mele, M. and S. Federici (2013) 'Believing Is Seeing: Ocular-sensorymotor Embodiment of Implicit Associations', paper presented at *The 1st World Conference on Personality*, Stellenbosch, ZA.

Monteleone, G. T., K. L. Phan, H. C. Nusbaum, D. Fitzgerald, J.-S. Irick, S. E. Fienberg, and J. T. Cacioppo (2009) 'Detection of Deception Using fMRI: Better Than Chance, but Well Below Perfection', *Social Neuroscience*, 4, 6, pp. 528–538.

Nisbett, R. E. and T. D. Wilson (1977) 'Telling More Than We Can Know: Verbal Reports on Mental Processes', *Psychological Review*, 84, 3, p. 231.

Nittono, H. and Y. Wada (2009) 'Gaze Shifts Do Not Affect Preference Judgments of Graphic Patterns', *Perceptual and Motor Skills*, 109, 1, pp. 79–94.

Nosek, B. A., F. L. Smyth, J. J. Hansen, T. Devos, N. M. Lindner, K. A. Ranganath, and A. G. Greenwald (2007) 'Pervasiveness and Correlates of Implicit Attitudes and Stereotypes', *European Review of Social Psychology*, 18, 1, pp. 36–88.

Nummenmaa, L., J. Hyönä, and M. G. Calvo (2006) 'Eye Movement Assessment of Selective Attentional Capture by Emotional Pictures', *Emotion*, 6, 2, p. 257.

Paxton, J. M. and J. D. Greene (2010) 'Moral Reasoning: Hints and Allegations', *Topics in Cognitive Science*, 2, 3, pp. 511–527.

Payne, B. K. (2001) 'Prejudice and Perception: The Role of Automatic and Controlled Processes in Misperceiving a Weapon', *Journal of Personality and Social Psychology*, 81, 2, p. 181.

Payne, B. K. (2005) 'Conceptualizing Control in Social Cognition: How Executive Functioning Modulates the Expression of Automatic Stereotyping', *Journal of Personality and Social Psychology*, 89, 4, p. 488.

Payne, B. K. (2008) 'What Mistakes Disclose: A Process Dissociation Approach to Automatic and Controlled Processes in Social Psychology', *Social and Personality Psychology Compass*, 2, 2, pp. 1073–1092.

Payne, B. K. and Cameron, C. D. (2014). Dual-process theory from a process dissociation perspective. In Sherman, J. W., Gawronski, B., and Trope, Y. (eds.), *Dual-Process Theories of the Social Mind*, pages 107–120. Guilford Publications, New York, NY.

Payne, B. K., C. M. Cheng, O. Govorun, and B. D. Stewart (2005) 'An Inkblot for Attitudes: Affect Misattribution as Implicit Measurement', *Journal of Personality and Social Psychology*, 89, 3, p. 277.

Payne, B. K., O. Govorun, and N. L. Arbuckle (2008) 'Automatic Attitudes and Alcohol: Does Implicit Liking Predict Drinking?', *Cognition and Emotion*, 22, pp. 238–271.

Payne, B. K., J. A. Krosnick, J. Pasek, Y. Lelkes, O. Akhtar, and T. Tompson (2010) 'Implicit and Explicit Prejudice in the 2008 American Presidential Election', *Journal of Experimental Social Psychology*, 46, 2, pp. 367–374.

Payne, B. K., J. F. McClernon, and I. G. Dobbins (2007) 'Automatic Affective Responses to Smoking Cues', *Experimental and Clinical Psychopharmacology*, 15, pp. 400–409.

Pelphrey, K. A., N. J. Sasson, J. S. Reznick, G. Paul, B. D. Goldman, and J. Piven (2002) 'Visual Scanning of Faces in Autism', *Journal of Autism and Developmental Disorders*, 32, 4, pp. 249–261.

Phelps, E. A., K. J. O'Connor, W. A. Cunningham, E. S. Funayama, J. C. Gatenby, J. C. Gore, and M. R. Banaji (2000) 'Performance on Indirect Measures of Race Evaluation Predicts Amygdala Activation', *Journal of Cognitive Neuroscience*, 12, 5, pp. 729–738.

Plumhoff, J. E. and J. A. Schirillo (2009) 'Mondrian, Eye Movements, and the Oblique Effect', *Perception*, 38, 5, p. 719.

Pochon, J., J. Riis, A. G. Sanfey, L. E. Nystrom, and J. D. Cohen (2008) 'Functional Imaging of Decision Conflict', *The Journal of Neuroscience*, 28, 13, pp. 3468–3473.

Polaschek, D. L., R. K. Bell, S. W. Calvert, and M. K. Takarangi (2010) 'Cognitive-behavioural Rehabilitation of High-risk Violent Offenders: Investigating Treatment Change With Explicit and Implicit Measures of Cognition', *Applied Cognitive Psychology*, 24, 3, pp. 437–449.

Priori, A., F. Mameli, F. Cogiamanian, S. Marceglia, M. Tiriticco, S. Mrakic-Sposta, and G. Sartori (2008) 'Lie-specific Involvement of Dorsolateral Prefrontal Cortex in Deception', *Cerebral Cortex*, 18, 2, pp. 451–455.

Quaschning, S., M. Pandelaere, and I. Vermeir (2013) *Easy on the Mind: Rankings and Consumer Product Evaluations,* unpublished manuscript.

Rameson, L. T., A. B. Satpute, and M. D. Lieberman (2010) 'The Neural Correlates of Implicit and Explicit Self-relevant Processing', *Neuroimage,* 50, 2, pp. 701–708.

Rayner, K. (1998) 'Eye Movements in Reading and Information Processing: 20 Years of Research', *Psychological Bulletin,* 124, 3, p. 372.

Reutskaja, E., R. Nagel, C. F. Camerer, and A. Rangel (2011) 'Search Dynamics in Consumer Choice Under Time Pressure: An Eye-tracking Study', *The American Economic Review,* 101, 2, pp. 900–926.

Schaich Borg, J., C. Hynes, J. Van Horn, S. Grafton, and W. Sinnott-Armstrong (2006) 'Consequences, Action, and Intention as Factors in Moral Judgments: An fMRI Investigation', *Journal of Cognitive Neuroscience,* 18, 5, pp. 803–817.

Schaich Borg, J. and W. Sinnott-Armstrong (2013) 'Do Psychopaths Make Moral Judgments?', in K. Kiehl and W. Sinnott-Armstrong (eds) *Handbook of Psychopathy and Law,* New York: Oxford University Press, pp. 107–130.

Schotter, E. R., R. W. Berry, C. R. McKenzie, and K. Rayner (2010) 'Gaze Bias: Selective Encoding and Liking Effects', *Visual Cognition,* 18, 8, pp. 1113–1132.

Shimojo, S., C. Simion, E. Shimojo, and C. Scheier (2003) 'Gaze Bias Both Reflects and Influences Preference', *Nature Neuroscience,* 6, 12, pp. 1317–1322.

Singer, T., S. J. Kiebel, J. S. Winston, R. J. Dolan, and C. D. Frith (2004) 'Brain Responses to the Acquired Moral Status of Faces', *Neuron,* 41, 4, pp. 653–662.

Snowden, R., N. Gray, J. Smith, M. Morris, and M. MacCulloch (2004) 'Implicit Affective Associations to Violence in Psychopathic Murderers', *Journal of Forensic Psychiatry & Psychology,* 15, 4, pp. 620–641.

Spezio, M. L., P.-S. Huang, F. Castelli, and R. Adolphs (2007) 'Amygdala Damage Impairs Eye Contact During Conversations With Real People', *The Journal of Neuroscience,* 27, 15, pp. 3994–3997.

Sriram, N. and A. G. Greenwald (2009) 'The Brief Implicit Association Test', *Experimental Psychology (Formerly Zeitschrift Für Experimentelle Psychologie),* 56, 4, pp. 283–294.

Strack, F. and R. Deutsch (2004) 'Reflective and Impulsive Determinants of Social Behavior', *Personality and Social Psychology Review,* 8, 3, pp. 220–247.

Strohminger, N., F. de Brigard, and W. Sinnott-Armstrong (2014) 'Does Moral Deliberation Reflect Moral Judgment?', unpublished manuscript.

Venkatraman, V., J. Payne, and S. Huettel (2012) *An Overall Probability of Winning Heuristic for Complex Risky Decisions: Choice and Eye Fixation Evidence,* unpublished manuscript.

Walker-Smith, G., A. Gale, and J. Findlay (1977) 'Eye Movement Strategies Involved in Face Perception', *Perception,* 6, 3, pp. 313–326.

Wang, J. T. Y. (2011) 'Pupil Dilation and Eye Tracking', in M. Schulte-Mecklenbeck, A. Kühberger, and R. Ranyard (eds) *A Handbook of Process Tracing Methods for Decision Research: A Critical Review and User's Guide,* pp. 185–204, NY: Psychology Press.

Wang, J. T. Y., M. Spezio, and C. F. Camerer (2010) 'Pinocchio's Pupil: Using Eyetracking and Pupil Dilation to Understand Truth Telling and Deception in Sender-receiver Games', *The American Economic Review,* 100, 3, pp. 984–1007.

Weierich, M. R., T. A. Treat, and A. Hollingworth (2008) 'Theories and Measurement of Visual Attentional Processing in Anxiety', *Cognition and Emotion*, 22, 6, pp. 985–1018.

Wu, E. X. W., B. Laeng, and S. Magnussen (2012) 'Through the Eyes of the Own-race Bias: Eye-tracking and Pupillometry During Face Recognition', *Social Neuroscience*, 7, 2, pp. 202–216.

Yang, Y., A. Raine, T. Lencz, S. Bihrle, L. LaCasse, and P. Colletti (2005) 'Prefrontal White Matter in Pathological Liars', *The British Journal of Psychiatry*, 187, 4, pp. 320–325.

Yang, Y., A. Raine, K. L. Narr, T. Lencz, L. LaCasse P. Colletti, and A. W. Toga (2007) 'Localisation of Increased Prefrontal White Matter in Pathological Liars', *The British Journal of Psychiatry*, 190, 2, pp. 174–175.

11
How to Gauge Moral Intuitions? Prospects for a New Methodology
Martin Bruder and Attila Tanyi

11.1 The role and significance of intuitions

The concept of moral intuitions reflects the idea that there are moral truths and that people arrive at these truths not primarily by a process of reflection and reasoning but rather by a more immediate process somewhat akin to perception.[1] This is crucial from a philosophical point of view: Intuitions matter for a philosopher because they are taken to have *evidential value*. Alvin Goldman's (2007, p. 2, italics in original) remark on Gettier's challenge to the account of knowledge as justified true belief well illustrates the point:

> It wasn't the mere publication of Gettier's two examples, or what he said about them. It was the fact that almost everybody who read Gettier's examples shared the *intuition* that these were not instances of knowing. Had their intuitions been different, there would have been no discovery.

Although Goldman's remark is about epistemology, moral theory appears to be no different when it comes to the relevance and significance of moral intuitions. Like observations in science, intuitions are the raw data that competing moral theories should at least try to accommodate: If an intuition counts in favor of a theory, this is good for the theory; if an intuition counts against a theory, this is bad for the theory. All this goes only *prima facie*, of course. There can be grounds to discount intuitions, or even not to take them into consideration; and there can be other mental states – hunches, premonitions, gut feelings, guesses – that may appear at first to be intuitions but are not. It is also possible that, on balance and compared to other theories, a moral theory turns out to be the best available even though it has counterintuitive implications. Nevertheless, intuitions have initial credibility for (most) philosophers; this is why intuitions have always been important in philosophy.

More recently, the investigation of intuitions has also moved into focus of research in moral psychology, a field that arguably is importantly relevant for experimental moral philosophy. But in contrast to moral philosophy, moral psychology had long neglected moral intuitions. During most of the 20th century, psychologists' treatment of morality has focused on the development of reflective and consciously accessible moral reasoning capacities in children. In particular, Jean Piaget (1999/1932) and Lawrence Kohlberg (1984) have introduced influential stage models of moral-cognitive development. However, in the course of the so-called 'affective revolution' and under the influence of a new focus on non-conscious processes, the last 25 years have seen a revival of the role of intuitions in theorizing in moral psychology (Haidt and Kesebir, 2010).

Although moral intuitions therefore have met with strong and growing interest in both philosophy and psychology, in philosophy at least, there is a range of opposing voices questioning whether this interest is justified. One can be skeptical about the supposed generality of intuitions, both concerning their content (whether they are about specific cases or general principles as well; see, e.g., Hintikka, 1999) and also concerning the scope of their holders (whether they are held by everyone or nearly everyone; see, e.g., Appiah, 2008; Banerjee, Huebner, and Hauser, 2011). There is also the separate but connected debate about whose intuitions count: everyone's, only the experts', or any idiosyncratic intuition could qualify as evidence (Alexander and Weinberg, 2007; Ryberg, 2013). Finally, there is a significant literature discussing whether intuitions can have an evidential role in the first place (Sosa, 2006; Hales, 2000; Singer, 2005).

In this paper, however, our aim is a different one. We are concerned with two problems that, although related to the concerns mentioned above, are more directly relevant for conducting experimental research in philosophy. The first concerns the question of *what intuitions are*; the problem being that in the absence of a proper characterization intuitions appear to be strange, a priori, Platonic entities that philosophers, especially those with naturalistic inclinations, have trouble accepting (Goldman, 2007; Hales, 2000; Hintikka, 1999). The second objection to using intuitions as evidence is more epistemological. The idea is that given what intuitions are (that is, given an answer to the first problem), there are insurmountable problems concerning their empirical investigation.

In other words, the challenge is *how to find intuitions*, even if we know what they are (Kauppinen, 2007; Podsakoff et al., 2003; Nagel, 2012).

In what follows, we will propose responses to both challenges. In the next Section 11.2, we will put forward an account of intuitions that singles out three essential characteristics for a mental state to count as an intuition: immediacy, lack of inferential relations to other mental states, and stability.[2] Building on this account, the same section will outline the basics of a new methodology for experimental philosophy. Next, in Section 11.3, we sketch possible studies implementing the proposed methodology. The context will be a particular objection to consequentialism: the so-called overdemandingness objection. Since these studies have not yet been carried out, in Section 11.4 we present the results of a completed experiment attempting to implement some new methodological features. Section 11.5 summarizes the discussion and concludes.

11.2   The new methodology

A possible definition of moral intuitions reflecting their evidential, perception-like role is the following:[3]

> When we refer to *moral intuitions*, we mean strong, stable, immediate moral beliefs. These moral beliefs are *strong* insofar as they are held with confidence and resist counter-evidence (although strong enough counter-evidence can sometimes overturn them). They are *stable* in that they are not just temporary whims but last a long time (although there will be times when a person who has a moral intuition does not focus attention on it). They are *immediate* because they do not arise from any process that goes through intermediate steps of conscious reasoning (although the believer is conscious of the resulting moral belief). (Sinnott-Armstrong, Young, and Cushman, 2010, p. 247, italics in original)

In what follows we will take on board the above proposal as giving us *two* characteristics of intuitions: immediacy and stability (which, in our account, also includes what is called 'strength' above). The social psychologist Jonathan Haidt further elaborates on the first characteristic – *immediacy* – by stating that 'intuition occurs quickly, effortlessly, and automatically, such that the outcome but not the process is accessible to consciousness' (2001, p. 818). The immediacy of intuitions, however, is only important for philosophers insofar as it increases the likelihood of them being *non-inferential*: The moral judgments upon which they are based are not accepted on the ground that they follow from some moral theory or principle that the agent subscribes to (Tersman, 2008). This is essential if they are to function as evidence that can, at least prima facie, resolve conflict among competing moral theories: they could not support or count against a moral theory were they only to be inferred from that or any other theory. Strangely, this characteristic of intuitions is not mentioned in the above quote, and hence it constitutes an additional aspect in our account. Besides immediacy and lack of inference, philosophers (often in contrast to psychologists) emphasize stability as a further critical characteristic of intuitions. This is because it is difficult to see how intuitions should have evidential value if they were not stable over time. Thus, this condition matters because it helps to elevate intuitions to the level of considered judgments, or, as they were recently called, robust intuitions (as opposed to immediate surface intuitions) (Kauppinen, 2007). Robust intuitions are those immediate of the agent that have, so to speak, withstood the test of reflection: They are those immediate reactions that a competent speaker would retain under sufficiently ideal conditions, such as when the speaker is not biased (Sidgwick, 1907; Liao, 2008). As mentioned, we take this third characteristic to cover both what is called strength and what is called stability in the quotation we began with. That intuitions withstand the test of reflection we take to be the same as the requirement that intuitions 'are held with confidence and resist counter-evidence'. And we also regard intuitions that withstand the test of reflection to be lasting opinions of the agent and not mere temporary whims.

This is, then, our answer to the first question: what are intuitions? Once this account of intuitions is at hand, the next step is to find empirical methods to examine the three core characteristics of intuitions that we have outlined. This will answer the second question of how to find intuitions. The first proposed characteristic poses the least challenge, perhaps. The *immediacy* of intuitions is a central focus of psychological research on intuitive processes (Glöckner and Witteman, 2010). Much of this research is based on dual-process models of reasoning and social behavior (e.g., Epstein et al., 1996; Evans, 2008). These models propose a distinction between rational, controlled processes (which, in line with Epstein et al., 1996, we will call 'analytical-rational'), on the one hand, and automatic, associative, affect-based processes (which we will call 'intuitive-experiential'), on the other. Intuitive-experiential processes are supposed to operate quickly and with low levels of mental effort and conscious awareness. They therefore capture the immediacy characteristic of intuitions. Standard experimental paradigms are available to test the role of intuitive-experiential processes in judgment and decision-making. These include, in particular, placing participants under severe time constraints (Horstmann, Hausmann, and Ryf, 2010) or adding cognitive load (i.e., a second task that has to be completed in parallel to the focal task; Gilbert and Hixon, 1991). Both methods rely on inhibiting analytical-rational processes. The underlying rationale is that once conscious reasoning is precluded from operating, what remains are intuitive-experiential processes that generate immediate intuitions concerning the object of the judgment.

In terms of experimental methodology, the supposed *non-inferential character* of intuitions is particularly challenging. Although immediacy of reaction in the course of an associative, effortless, and non-conscious (i.e., intuitive-experiential) process renders it unlikely that complex inferences made on the basis of a moral theory occur, the speed of a reaction may not by itself be sufficient to demonstrate the lack of inference. We therefore propose a complementary method to address this challenge.

In recent years cognitive theories of emotion have become influential in the philosophy of emotion. In a related development, cognitive appraisal theories of emotion have become the dominant family of theories in psychological emotion research (Moors, 2009). Both families of theories claim that emotions are mental states that have affective, conative, and cognitive aspects at the same time: they are motivating affective states that involve evaluative representations of their objects (Solomon, 1993; Goldie, 2007; Slaby, Stephan, and Walter, 2011). For us it is this latter characteristic that is most important. There are two main interpretations. The more robustly cognitive line has it that the representational intentional content of an emotion is that of a *belief or judgment*, and the phenomenal – which is also the motivating – aspect is merely added on, without explanation, and without any attempt at synthesis with the emotion's cognitive aspect (e.g., Solomon, 1993). The other, less robustly cognitive, line has it that emotions purport to be *perceptions* of properties such as being funny, shameful, pitiable, enviable, and so forth: their intentional (representational) content is understood by analogy to sense perception. In this way, since perception, arguably, possesses phenomenology, the intentional (representational) and the affective – thus also the motivational – aspects of emotion are not unrelated, as on the first reading; on the contrary, the former is part of the latter. Emotions are, as Sabine Döring calls them, *affective perceptions*: they involve a distinct cognition that is distinct exactly because of its phenomenology (Döring, 2003, 2007; Cf. de Sousa, 1987; Roberts,

1988). This thought gives rise to several important ideas that are directly relevant for the proposed methodology.

First, if emotions are indeed states akin to perceptions, they can be correct and incorrect, depending on how well they track the properties of which they are purportedly representations. It is in this sense that philosophers, as well as non-philosophers, speak of the fittingness of emotions: whether it makes sense to feel an emotion in the given situation. In other words, something like a *rationalism* of emotions is true (de Sousa, 1987; Peacocke, 1992). Second, if emotions are analogous to perceptions, then this suggests that, like sense perceptions, their content is not inferentially related to the contents of other states. That is, it is possible for an agent to have an emotion the content of which conflicts with the content of the agent's judgment (belief), without any contradiction being involved. There are thus *no inferential constraints* on emotions, just as there are none on sense perceptions (Döring, 2003). Third, the non-inferential character of emotions opens up the possibility that 'the occurrence of an emotion can, in suitable circumstances, entitle a thinker to judge, and possibly to know, its content simply by taking its representational content at face value. In the case of moral emotions, the possibility emerges that those emotions may give the thinker a non-inferential way of coming to know moral propositions' (Döring, 2003, p. 229). In fact, going one step further, it could be argued that the content of emotions is *gestalt*-like: coming to know, via the emotion, a moral proposition is like suddenly coming to see how the dots together form Marilyn Monroe's face in a pointillist painting. There are no inferential relations between seeing the dots (morally salient features of the situation), and seeing Monroe's face (moral proposition; cf. Döring, 2003; Little, 1997; Roeser, 2011; Hookway, 2002). Finally, depending on one's views of moral properties, emotions can either be facilitative or constitutive of the process of gaining moral knowledge: in the former case one can, in principle, get to know the moral proposition without the requisite emotion, in the latter case one cannot (cf. D'Arms and Jacobson, 2000).

These ideas are relevant for the new methodology because they suggest that there might be an intimate connection between intuitions and emotions; in fact, some have gone as far as to claim that intuitions *are* emotions: that something like an *affectual intuitionism* is true (Roeser, 2011). Assuming for now that an intimate connection (of some sort) exists, it seems that we can begin to address the difficulties surrounding the empirical testability of the non-inferential character of intuitions by focusing on participants' emotional responses to the situation. Insofar as these responses are in line with participants' judgments in the situation, we may conclude that those judgments are indeed intuitive. Were it to turn out that there is no correspondence between participants' emotional responses and their moral judgments, we could conclude that participants' judgments are not intuitions. This could happen, we might further hypothesize, because the participant did not endorse, upon reflection, her original immediate judgment. Checking this hypothesis would then take us to the investigation of the third proposed characteristic of intuition, namely, their stability.

Before this happens, however, some further specification of the proposed method to test the non-inferential aspect of intuitions is needed. In particular, endorsing the link between intuitions and emotions requires that experimental at this point focus on testing with which emotions, and how intensively, participants react to experimental situations. This puts a constraint on the new methodology insofar as, of course, it requires that we have better knowledge of and better ways to assess the emotions that correspond to the relevant judgments than knowledge of and ways to assess the intuitions directly. This seems to be the case though, as we can focus on assessing a number of *moral emotions*, the connections of which to moral properties and judgments are well documented.[4] Although, in philosophy, moral emotions are typically related to so-called 'thick' properties, such as being pitiable, enviable, etc., some argue for a strong, even constitutive connection between the 'thin' property of wrongness and a moral emotion. Thus, for instance, Allan Gibbard (1990, p. 42) holds that '[w]hat a person does is morally wrong if and only if it is rational for him to feel guilty for doing it, and for others to resent him.' And John Skorupski (2010) analyzes wrongness in terms of blameworthiness, that is, whether it makes sense to feel blame toward a person. (Neuro-)psychological research supports this reasoning. Greene et al. (2001) have shown that there are systematic variations in the engagement of emotion-related brain areas in moral judgments. One emotion that has received substantial empirical attention in moral psychology is disgust. Schnall et al. (2008) demonstrated that disgust can render moral judgments more severe. Focusing on moral emotions may therefore help us, in the way proposed above, to investigate people's moral intuitions concerning wrongness and rightness in the experimental situations.

Lastly, let us turn to the investigation of the *stability* of intuitions. Similar to research addressing the immediacy of moral intuitions, studies examining their stability will also attempt to elicit spontaneous moral judgments. However, in a second step, these studies will engage conscious, analytical-rational mental processes to further examine whether the spontaneous judgments stand the 'test of reflection' and therefore acquire the status of considered judgments.

We believe that the methodological approach proposed here to assessing intuitions positively transcends the strong reliance of research in experimental moral philosophy on unquestioned self-reports of moral judgments. Huebner (2011) has recently argued that such experiments alone cannot establish the intuitive nature of moral judgments. Although no single empirical study that we propose would achieve this goal either (and it can be doubted whether such a study is even a possibility), we believe that our multi-method approach will increase understanding of the intuitive processes involved in making moral judgments. Specifically, the proposed methodology involves investigating whether results are consistent across the different proposed characteristics of moral intuitions. Both stabilities and possible instabilities would be informative in understanding what moral intuitions can and cannot tell us about moral truths.

11.3   Implementing the new methodology: a project design

The previous section sketched our proposal for a new methodology. But while more work on the theoretical background of the new methodology is undoubtedly needed, what would even be more useful at this point is to see how the different methods and ideas proposed above would be implemented in practice. In the remainder of the paper, we will therefore present two instances of implementation. Both concern a particular problematic – the so-called overdemand-ingness objection to consequentialism – and both connect to our previous work on the subject. The first, to be discussed in the present section, outlines our plans for the experimental investigation of the objection by using the entire proposed methodology. The second, to be presented in the next section, presents the results of a study that was already carried out which tested some of our methodological proposals.

Let us begin with the philosophical problematic. Proponents of act-consequentialism hold that the right course of action is the one that produces the best results as judged from an impartial perspective. However, it is often claimed that this requirement is so demanding that it is intuitively unacceptable for anyone to follow it (Hooker, 2009, p. 162, footnote 4; Carter, 2009, pp. 163–185). This is because, to take one example, it would require foregoing most, if not all, non-moral personal projects and devoting one's life almost exclusively to alleviating the suffering of those in need. The so-called *Overdemandingness Objection* (OD) attempts to use this supposedly common intuition concerning the inadmissibility of extreme demands as a starting point for rejecting consequentialism. Unlike other discussions of the Objection, in our previous work we aimed to test whether the proposed intuition indeed exists (Bruder and Tanyi, 2014 and forthcoming). We examined what we consider to be the strongest version of the Objection, which is based on the presumed inescapability of consequentialist reasons. According to this reading, consequentialism requires the agent with decisive force to do things that, intuitively, she has not decisive reasons to do.[5]

To test whether people indeed have this intuition, we conducted two studies: one survey study that used imaginary decision scenarios, and one experimental game developed in behavioral economics that allowed us to assess the relevant intuition in a decision situation with real consequences. Based on the philosophical literature discussing the Objection, we initially expected that (a) *Hypothesis 1*: increasing demands would be associated with higher levels of rejection of the consequentialist course of action and (b) *Hypothesis 2*: that at least in some cases the consequentialist course of action would be perceived as overly demanding by most if not all participants. Surprisingly, we found that, while Hypotheses 1 was indeed confirmed, Hypothesis 2 was not confirmed, thus casting doubt on the plausibility of the Overdemandingness Objection or, at least, on the philosophical relevance of situations that indeed call forth the intuition.

These studies were, however, in many ways constrained, not least in the methods they used to detect intuitions. Hence it appears sensible to see how the proposed new methodology could be implemented to test the two hypotheses above. In what follows we will give a brief outline of three closely related empirical studies (Studies 1–3), each of which focusing on one of the aforementioned characteristics of intuitions. These studies have not yet been carried out, but serve as illustration as to how the proposed methodology may be applied to the Overdemandingness Objection as well as other challenging problems.

Study 1 builds on our previous work and tests whether the intuition underlying OD is immediate. To this end, the study examines whether moral intuitions are stable across processing modes within a given individual. Participants will respond to scenarios similar to those used in our previous work.[6] Before they do so, the study will manipulate the degree to which individuals engage in analytical-rational versus intuitive-experiential processing and examine the effects of this manipulation on moral judgments. The underlying assumption is that participants will engage in analytical-rational processing if they have (a) time and (b) cognitive capacity to do so. Using methods borrowed from social-cognitive psychology, two independent manipulations will attempt to put constraints on both of these factors, thereby increasing participants' reliance on more highly automatized (and thus quicker) intuitive-experiential processes. This is done (a) by limiting the time participants have to respond to the scenarios and (b) by asking them to perform a second task (i.e., memorizing numbers) in parallel to their moral judgment task. Although such manipulations are common in psychological decision-making research, applications to the moral judgment domain are rare.[7] Thus, this study will provide evidence as to whether the pattern of results observed in our previous work occurs in an immediate and relatively effortless manner. If it does, this will support the idea that those judgments were made on the basis of intuitions.

Study 2 will draw on cognitive theories of emotion to provide some insight into whether the intuition underlying OD is non-inferential. It will employ a novel unobtrusive test targeting the nonverbal behavior associated with moral emotions. Emotions marking individual moral transgressions – such as shame and some forms of embarrassment – are reliably related to (a) decreased body expansion, (b) averted gaze, and (c) downward head tilt (e.g., Tracy and Matsumoto, 2008). The study will make use of the novel tool of automated face and posture video analysis to assess the degree to which participants experience such emotions while making moral decisions. This assessment largely avoids response biases that may influence self-reports of emotion while retaining the ability to make inferences concerning relatively specific emotions (which is often not possible with physiological measures of emotions). Because emotions in response to fictitious scenarios may differ from emotions experienced in real decision situations (Parkinson and Manstead, 1993), the study is designed to investigate whether the intuition underlying OD can be observed in the emotions experienced in decisions with real-world consequences. Evidently, these decisions cannot involve equally serious implications as those described in the scenarios. However, economic games provide an established framework to investigate decision making with real monetary outcomes. Although rarely the case, some studies have used such games to explicitly investigate moral decision-making (e.g., Aguiar, Branas-Garza, and Miller, 2008). Building on a design used in our previous work, participants will distribute an amount of money between themselves and a charitable organization that alleviates suffering in the developing world (e.g., UNICEF). As our independent variable, we will manipulate demand levels by either having participants first 'earn' the money that they later distribute or giving it to them with no effort from their side involved (as a so-called 'windfall endowment'; Cherry, Frykblom, and Shogren, 2002). We will observe both participants' explicit moral judgments and their nonverbal emotional behavior. If expressed emotions were strong indicators of the intuition underlying OD – ideally fully mediating the effect of our manipulation on moral judgments – this would lend increased credibility to the idea that this intuition is indeed non-inferential. As a follow-up study, a more direct test of the role of emotions in generating intuitions would be to experimentally dampen the emotional experience. Seminal work by Strack, Martin, and Stepper (1988) demonstrated that this can be achieved by inhibiting expressive behavior. Thus, if people donated more money when they are able to freely express their emotions than when they are constrained in their expressive behavior (e.g., because they need to stand upright disallowing them to decrease their body expansion congruent with shame), this would be a further indication that the experience of relevant emotions is part of or, at least, a necessary precondition of having the respective moral intuition.

Study 3 will address whether the moral intuition underlying OD is stable. To do so, the study will use an adapted think-aloud procedure to identify participants' reasoning processes while they are making moral judgments (Van Someren, Barnard, and Sandberg, 1994). Participants will be trained to continuously verbalize their thoughts while responding to morally challenging scenarios similar to those used in the pilot work. We will also manipulate whether or not participants are encouraged to reflect in detail on their immediate responses. Thus, some participants will be led to subject their initial responses to a thorough 'test of reflection'. The study therefore focuses on robust intuitions or considered judgments and examines whether the opinion postulated by OD, if found, belongs to this group. If it does, then this would suggest that participants' immediate responses were not only surface intuitions but qualify as robust intuitions, that is, intuitions proper on our account.

11.4   Implementing the new methodology: a case study

As mentioned above, in our previous work we have carried out a scenario study in which participants were asked to make a choice in ethically demanding situations. The sample of this study was representative of the German population in several key characteristics such as age, gender, and education. In one scenario, participants were, for example, asked to imagine that they had a choice between starting work as a civil engineer building an orphanage in Africa (the consequentialist choice option) or taking up a position in their own country (the non-consequentialist choice option). Given the specific circumstances of the aid project, taking up the alternative offer would mean that the orphanage would not be built. The nature of the alternative job offer varied: It was either objectively attractive (i.e., very lucrative; high objective demands) or not (low objective demands) and either subjectively appealing (i.e., the position one had always dreamed of; high subjective demands) or not (low subjective demands).[8] Participants were then asked three questions. First, they indicated what they would do in such a situation. Second, they answered the question 'Overall, what is the thing to do?' Third, they indicated what they believed morality demanded them to do.

As reported above, our original interest was to test two hypotheses in the context of the overdemandingness problematic. However, our results also included the interesting finding that increasing consequentialist demands led to a change in some participants' moral assessment of the situation: when demands were high they took the nonconsequentialist action to be the morally right one, whereas when demands were low they claimed it not to be demanded by morality (Bruder and Tanyi, 2014).

To see whether these moral judgments were intuitive, we tested, in line with the new methodology, participants' anticipated emotional reactions to increasing consequentialist demands. In particular, participants were asked about their anticipated emotional reactions were they not to take the consequentialist option. For example, in the Africa scenario described above, we asked participants how much they would expect to experience negative emotions if they chose to take the job and not go to Africa. Participants were 1,001 adults (511 female) with a mean age of 47.6 years and a standard deviation of 18 years. The vast majority of the participants were native German speakers (n = 932) with another 66 reporting *good/very good* German skills and only 3 reporting German language skills of *fair* or worse.

We expected that (a) *Hypothesis 1*: increasing consequentialist demands lead to the anticipation of less negative moral emotions when supposing that one acts against consequentialist demands and that (b) *Hypothesis 2*: less negative anticipated moral emotions would correspond to increasing dissent with consequentialism.

Hypothesis 1 was indeed confirmed (see Figure 11.1). Higher demands (both objective and subjective) led participants to anticipate less negative moral emotions when acting against consequentialist moral demands.[9]

Hypothesis 2 also found support: In each of the six scenarios, the probability of holding that the consequentialist course of action was not demanded by consequentialism (i.e., dissent with consequentialism) was strongly associated with a lower intensity of self-reported anticipated negative emotions when acting against consequentialism. Spearman correlation coefficients between dissent with consequentialism and emotional intensity in the six scenarios ranged from −0.42 to −0.57 (all significant at $p < 0.001$).

As long as one accepts that emotions are non-inferential, the fact that both hypotheses were confirmed lends credibility to the idea that the moral judgments made by participants were intuitive in the sense of being non-inferential as well.

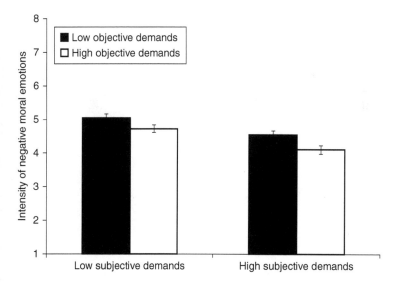

Figure 11.1 Intensity of negative moral emotions under the supposition of acting against consequentialist demands averaged across the six scenarios for each level of objective and subjective demands

11.5 Summary

Examining folk intuitions about philosophical questions lies at the core of experimental philosophy. This requires both a good account of what intuitions are and methods allowing assess to them. In this paper we have proposed to combine philosophical and psychological conceptualizations of intuitions by focusing on three of their features: immediacy, lack of inference, and stability. With this account at hand, we have moved on to develop a methodology that can test all three characteristics without eliminating any of them. In the final part of the paper, we have then proposed implementations of the new methodology as applied to the experimental investigation of the so-called overdemandingness objection to consequentialism. Given constraints of space, our discussion, concerning all these points, was necessarily short and somewhat sketchy, requiring important details to be filled in. Nevertheless, we believe that there is sufficient ground to claim that there are (good) prospects for a new and more adequate methodology in experimental moral philosophy.

Acknowledgments

We would like to thank audiences in Konstanz, the Hague, Nottingham, Bayreuth, and Lucca, as well as all those who have commented on prior versions of the manuscript. This particularly applies to the editors of the present volume, Christoph Luetge, Hannes Rusch, and Matthias Uhl. The research reported in this paper was funded by several grants from the Zukunftskolleg at the University of Konstanz. It was also supported by a grant to Attila Tanyi from the German Research Foundation (Grant number: TA 820/1–1).

Notes

1. By speaking of 'moral truth' we are not intending to take sides in the meta-ethical debate whether there are such truths. As far as we are concerned, what we say in the paper should also be compatible with a minimalist account of truth that most moral anti-realists appear to favor (if they are willing to speak of moral truth at all).
2. We propose these characteristics as necessary and sufficient conditions for a mental state to qualify as an intuition. However, we are open to discussion on this point.
3. We do not, at this point, make a distinction between moral intuitions and intuitions in general, but use the terms interchangeably. When the difference becomes important, we will make a note of that.

4. See Tangney, Stuewig, and Mashek (2007) for a review on psychological research on moral emotions; for utilitarianism and the moral emotions, see Fehige and Frank (2010).
5. That this is the best version of OD is argued for in Tanyi (2012).
6. In our scenarios participants were asked to imagine themselves in a situation of a choice with a clear consequentialist alternative, such as donating one's inheritance to charity, and a non-consequentialist option, such as keeping the money to buy a new house. The basic situations were then so manipulated that the demand created by choosing the consequentialist option continuously increased until it reached a high demand level. In each version of each scenario, participants were asked three questions: what they would do, what is overall the thing to do, and what morality demands them to do. For more details on this study see the next section.
7. For recent exceptions demonstrating the promise of the methodology see Suter and Hertwig (2011).
8. The distinction between objective and subjective demands is one we introduced for purposes that is not relevant for the presentation in what follows. Briefly, we claim one's choice to be more *objectively* attractive than an alternative choice if it is reasonable to assume that there is a (near) consensus concerning a quantitative grading of its attractiveness in the sense of 'the more, the better'. With the notion of *subjective* demandingness, on the other hand, we aim to capture the phenomenon that different people often perceive the very same thing as differently attractive. A good example are monetary rewards: losing a lot of money is more objectively demanding than losing little and therefore constitutes a difference in objective demandingness; losing a certain amount of money, however, can be very demanding of some (e.g., because they are poor), but relatively less demanding of others (e.g., because they are affluent), thereby constituting a difference in subjective demandingness.
9. Objective demands: $F(1, 993) = 11.17$, $p = 0.001$, $\eta^2_p = 0.011$; subjective demands: $F(1, 993) = 23.44$, $p < 0.001$, $\eta^2_p = 0.023$.

References

Aguiar, F., P. Branas-Garza, and L. M. Miller (2008) 'Moral Distance in Dictator Games', *Judgment and Decision Making Journal*, 3, pp. 344–354.

Alexander, J. and J. M. Weinberg (2007) 'Analytic Epistemology and Experimental Philosophy', *Philosophy Compass*, 2, pp. 56–80.

Appiah, K. A. (2008) *Experiments in Ethics* (Cambridge, MA: Harvard University Press).

Banerjee, K., B. Huebner, and M. Hauser (2011) 'Intuitive Moral Judgments Are Robust across Demographic Variation in Gender, Education, Politics, and Religion: A Large-scale Web-based Study', *Journal of Cognition and Culture*, 10, pp. 253–281.

Bruder, M. and A. Tanyi (2014) 'Consequentialism and Its Demands: A Representative Study', *Journal of Value Inquiry*, 48 (2), pp. 293–314, a special issue edited by S. Roeser and J. Rickard.

Bruder, M. and A. Tanyi (forthcoming) 'Overdemanding Consequentialism? An Experimental Approach', *Utilitas*.

Carter, A. (2009) 'Is Utilitarian Morality Necessarily Too Demanding?', in T. Chappell (ed.) *The Problem of Moral Demandingness: New Philosophical Essays* (London: Palgrave MacMillan), pp. 163–85.

Cherry, T. L., P. Frykblom, and J. F. Shogren (2002) 'Hardnose the Dictator', *American Economic Review*, 92, pp. 1218–1221.

D'Arms, J. and D. Jacobson (2000) 'The Moralistic Fallacy: On the "Appropriateness" of Emotions', *Philosophy and Phenomenological Research*, 61, pp. 65–90.

de Sousa, R. (1987) *The Rationality of Emotion* (Cambridge, MA: MIT Press).

Döring, S. A. (2003) 'Explaining Action by Emotion', *Philosophical Quarterly*, 53, pp. 214–230.

Döring, S. A. (2007) 'Seeing What to Do: Affective Perception and Rational Motivation', *Dialectica*, 61, pp. 363–394.

Epstein, S., R. Pacini, V. Denes-Raj, and H. Heier (1996) 'Individual Differences in Intuitive-experiential and Analytical-rational Thinking Styles', *Journal of Personality and Social Psychology*, 71, pp. 390–405.

Evans, J. (2008) 'Dual-processing Accounts of Reasoning, Judgment, and Social Cognition', *Annual Review of Psychology*, 59, pp. 255–278.

Fehige, C. and R. H. Frank (2010) 'Feeling Our Way to the Common Good: Utilitarianism and the Moral Sentiments', *The Monist*, 93, pp. 141–164.

Gibbard, A. (1990) *Wise Choices, Apt Feelings: A Theory of Normative Judgement* (Cambridge, MA: Harvard University Press).

Gilbert, D. T. and J. G. Hixon (1991) 'The Trouble of Thinking: Activation and Application of Stereotypic Beliefs', *Journal of Personality and Social Psychology*, 60, pp. 509–517.

Glöckner, A. and C. Witteman (eds.) (2010) *Foundations for Tracing Intuition: Challenges and Methods* (New York, NY: Psychology Press).

Goldie, P. (2007) *The Emotions: A Philosophical Exploration* (Oxford, UK: Oxford University Press).

Goldman, A. I. (2007) 'Philosophical Intuitions: Their Target, Their Source, and Their Epistemic Status', *Grazer Philosophische Studien*, 74, pp. 1–26.

Greene, J. D., R. B. Sommerville, L. E. Nystrom, J. M. Darley, and J. D. Cohen (2001) 'An fMRI Investigation of Emotional Engagement in Moral Judgment', *Science*, 293, pp. 2105–2108.

Haidt, J. (2001) 'The Emotional Dog and Its Rational Tail: A Social Intuitionist Approach to Moral Judgment', *Psychological Review*, 108, pp. 814–834.

Haidt, J. and S. Kesebir (2010) 'Morality', in S. Fiske and D. Gilbert (eds), *Handbook of Social Psychology* (Hobeken, NJ: Wiley), pp. 797–832.

Hales, S. D. (2000) 'The Problem of Intuition', *American Philosophical Quarterly*, 37, pp. 135–147.

Hintikka, J. (1999) 'The Emperor's New Intuitions', *Journal of Philosophy*, 96, pp. 127–147.

Hooker, H. (2009) 'The Demandingness Objection', in T. Chappell (ed.), *The Problem of Moral Demandingness: New Philosophical Essays* (London: MacMillan), pp. 148–162.

Hookway, C. (2002) 'Emotions and Epistemic Evaluation', in P. Carruthers (ed.), *The Cognitive Basis of Science* (Cambridge, UK: Cambridge University Press), pp. 251–262.

Horstmann, N., D. Hausmann, and S. Ryf (2010) 'Methods for Inducing Intuitive and Deliberate Processing Modes', in A. Glöckner and C. Witteman (eds), *Foundations for Tracing Intuition: Challenges and Methods* (New York, NY: Psychology Press), pp. 219–237.

Huebner, B. (2011) 'Critiquing Empirical Moral Psychology', *Philosophy of the Social Sciences*, 41, pp. 50–83.

Kauppinen, A. (2007) 'The Rise and Fall of Experimental Philosophy', *Philosophical Explorations*, 10, pp. 95–118.

Kohlberg, L. (1984) *The Psychology of Moral Development: The Nature and Validity of Moral Stages* (San Francisco: Harper & Row).

Liao, S. M. (2008) 'A Defense of Intuitions', *Philosophical Studies*, 140, pp. 247–262.

Little, M. O. (1997) 'Virtue as Knowledge: Objections from the Philosophy of Mind', *Noûs*, 31, pp. 59–79.

Moors, A. (2009) 'Theories of Emotion Causation: A Review', *Cognition & Emotion*, 23, pp. 625–662.

Nagel, J. (2012) 'Intuitions and Experiments: A Defense of the Case Method in Epistemology', *Philosophy and Phenomenological Research*, 85, pp. 495–527.

Parkinson, B. and A. S. R. Manstead (1993) 'Making Sense of Emotion in Stories and Social Life', *Cognition & Emotion*, 7, pp. 295–323.

Peacocke, C. (1992) *A Study of Concepts* (Cambridge, MA: MIT Press).

Piaget, J. (1999/1932) *The Moral Judgment of the Child* (Oxon: Routledge).

Podsakoff, P. M., S. B. MacKenzie, J. Y. Lee, and N. P. Podsakoff (2003) 'Common Method Biases in Behavioral Research: A Critical Review of the Literature and Recommended Remedies', *Journal of Applied Psychology*, 88, pp. 879–903.

Roberts, R. C. (1988) 'What an Emotion Is: A Sketch', *Philosophical Review*, 97, pp. 183–209.

Roeser, S. (2011) *Moral Emotions and Intuitions* (Basingstoke, UK: Palgrave Macmillan).

Ryberg, J. (2013) 'Moral Intuitions and the Expertise Defence', *Analysis*, 73, pp. 3–9.

Schnall, S., J. Haidt, G. L. Clore, and A. H. Jordan (2008) 'Disgust as Embodied Moral Judgment', *Personality and Social Psychology Bulletin*, 34, pp. 1096–1109.

Sidgwick, H. (1907) *The Methods of Ethics*, 7th edn (London, UK: Macmillan).

Singer, P. (2005) 'Ethics and Intuitions', *Journal of Ethics*, 9, pp. 331–352.

Sinnott-Armstrong, W., L. Young, and F. Cushman (2010) 'Moral Intuitions', in J. M. Doris (ed.), *The Moral Psychology Handbook* (New York, NY: Oxford University Press), pp. 246–272.

Skorupski, J. (2010) *The Domain of Reason* (Oxford, UK: Oxford University Press).

Slaby, J., A. Stephan, and H. Walter (eds) (2011) *Affektive Intentionalität. Beiträge zur welterschließenden Funktion der menschlichen Gefühle* (Paderborn, Germany: Mentis).

Solomon, R. (1993) *The Passions: Emotions and the Meaning of Life* (Indianapolis, IN: Hackett).

Sosa, E. (2006) 'Intuitions and Truth', in P. Greenough and M. P. Lynch (eds), *Truth and Realism* (Oxford, UK: Clarendon Press), pp. 208–226.

Strack, F., L. L. Martin, and S. Stepper (1988) 'Inhibiting and Facilitating Conditions of the Human Smile: A Nonobtrusive Test of the Facial Feedback Hypothesis', *Journal of Personality and Social Psychology*, 54, p. 768–777.

Suter, R. S. and R. Hertwig (2011) 'Time and Moral Judgment', *Cognition*, 119, pp. 454–458.

Tangney, J. P., J. Stuewig, and D. J. Mashek (2007) 'Moral Emotions and Moral Behavior', *Annual Review of Psychology*, 58, pp. 345–372.

Tanyi, A. (2012) 'The Case for Authority', in S. Schleidgen (ed.), *Should We Always Act Morally? Essays on Overridingness* (Marburg, Germany: Tectum), pp. 159–189.

Tersman, F. (2008) 'The Reliability of Moral Intuitions: A Challenge from Neuroscience', *Australasian Journal of Philosophy*, 86, pp. 389–405.

Tracy, J. L. and D. Matsumoto (2008) 'The Spontaneous Expression of Pride and Shame: Evidence for Biologically Innate Nonverbal Displays', *Proceedings of the National Academy of Sciences of the United States of America*, 105, pp. 11655–11660.

Van Someren, M. W., Y. F. Barnard, and J. A. C. Sandberg (1994) *The Think Aloud Method* (London, UK: Academic Press).

12

Descriptive and Pragmatic Levels of Empirical Ethics: Utilizing the Situated Character of Moral Concepts, Judgment, and Decision-Making

Andreas Bunge and Alexander Skulmowski

12.1 Introduction

Empirical ethics, understood as comprising all empirical research on morality, is commonly conceived as being a purely descriptive endeavor. Research in this field can be broken into two interrelated methodological approaches. The first approach is to merely record subjects' moral intuitions, judgments, decisions, and behavior. For instance, researchers might be interested in whether people sacrifice one person in order to save five in versions of the trolley dilemma (see Di Nucci, this volume). We call this approach *experimental recording*. However, empirical ethicists usually are not satisfied just recording responses, but rather also want to provide explanations for them. That is, they trace subjects' responses back to their causes – an approach we refer to as *experimental retracing*.[1] The provided explanations can stem from various fields of research such as psychology, neurobiology, or even evolutionary biology. For instance, neuroimaging has been used to examine which cognitive mechanisms bring about different judgments with regard to dilemmas like the famous trolley dilemma (Greene et al., 2001; 2004).

Normative accounts, which prescribe what people ought to do, are generally seen as clearly separate from the descriptive domain. Which option subjects actually choose in the trolley dilemma does not inform us about what people should opt for in such situations. In this article, we will not argue for specific normative claims, as this is not within the scope of empirical ethics. In the following section, we instead present a possible interface between the descriptive and the normative domain: the pragmatic level of empirical ethics. Given certain normative standards, empirical ethics research can provide hints on how to encourage people to comply with these standards. Moreover, research in this field can provide insight into how we might design more humane organizations and societal institutions. In the second part of this article, we point out which research methods are needed by empirical ethics to properly fulfill the pragmatic function outlined above. It is stressed that the methodology should take into account the fact that judgments, decisions, and behaviors are the result of interplay between individual traits or states of the agent and contextual factors. By examining only one blade of a pair of scissors, one will not understand how scissors cut. Similarly, by focusing on the mind and ignoring the environment one will not fully understand the causes of moral behavior. The corresponding research program investigating morality as a function of mind and environment has been dubbed 'ecological morality' (Gigerenzer, 2010).

12.2   The pragmatic level of empirical ethics

Within the framework of ecological morality, an important question to ask is how we can encourage people to behave in a morally decent way. As already indicated, we will not attempt to develop a prescriptive account. However, it is a matter of fact that there are generally accepted moral norms in every society and that people sometimes fail to meet these norms, leading to regret on the part of the agent and disapproval by others. A better understanding of why people often fail to behave in a way that they should, attained through experimental retracing, will help us in finding instruments to promote moral behavior. Heinzelmann, Ugazio, and Tobler (2012) have identified two principle problems that keep people from acting and judging in a morally appropriate way: first, they sometimes make mistakes in moral reasoning which lead them to hold false beliefs about what they ought to do; and second, even when they know what they should do, they sometimes fail to act accordingly due to personal weaknesses. In the following, we first elaborate on features of the mind and thereafter on features of the environment that are potential causes of these problems and sketch how empirical ethics research can provide remedy.

Obviously, mental disorders can be a cause of the first problem, that is, for making mistakes in moral reasoning. However, even a non-pathological restriction of a single mental capacity may make people blind to what they ought to do (Heinzelmann Ugazio, and Tobler, 2012). Such a capacity may be as basic as memory. For instance, a person might simply forget her promise to help a friend moving into a new apartment and therefore be unaware that her reluctance to assist is rude. However, the cognitive capacity presumably most frequently linked to morality is empathy (Goldman, 1992). A person who is not able to put herself in others' shoes is more likely to overlook the misery of people who could potentially be supported. Considerable psychological evidence supports the link between empathy and prosocial behavior (see Hein and Singer, 2010, for a review). Efforts to train empathy, however, have exhibited mixed results. An extensive research review (Lam, Kolomitro, and Alamparambil, 2011) suggests it is feasible to enhance one's knowledge about empathy and the skills required to 'act' empathically with a variety of training methods, but finds no sound evidence that people can transfer their learning in order to change their empathic behaviors in natural environments. Hence, empirical ethicists are well advised to continue research into the trainability of empathy with a particular focus on the environments in which empathic behavior might unfold.

Besides a lack of cognitive capacities, people may also fail to grasp what they ought to do because they apply problem-solving heuristics and decision-making strategies that are not optimally tuned to today's moral requirements (Gigerenzer, 2010). Following heuristics may have been advantageous during our evolutionary history and indeed still proves beneficial, as heuristics reduce computational demands and help us navigate in complex environments. However, the function of these heuristics is not to help us meet the requirements of a normative moral theory. For instance, people generally prefer helping a single identifiable person in need over helping an anonymous group of people. As a consequence, when donating to charitable causes, money is often concentrated on a single victim even though more people would be helped if resources were dispersed. This has been called the identifiable victim effect and has been extensively studied in social psychology (Small, Loewenstein, and Slovic, 2007). Usually, the effect is explained by evidence that identifiable targets stimulate a more powerful emotional response than do statistical targets. Reliance on such feelings can be described as an affect heuristic (Slovic et al., 2007). However, from a moral perspective, a bias toward helping identifiable victims is dubious, as there is no reason to assume that identifiability of a person constitutes a morally relevant property. Thus, empirical research should be aimed at detecting such biases and finding strategies to overcome them.

We now turn to the problem that people fail to act morally although they know what should be done. Heinzelmann, Ugazio, and Tobler (2012) identify weakness of will, usually called *akrasia* by philosophers, as a main cause of this issue. According to a common view, an agent's will is weak if she acts against her own best judgment. In such cases, we sometimes say that the agent lacks the willpower to do what she knows or believes would be better (Davidson, 1980). Within the moral realm, a standard example for this is pursuing the temptation to spend one's extra money on luxury goods, despite one's knowledge that it would be better to donate it for charitable purposes. As this example shows, promoting empathy could once again offer a solution. The more a person empathizes with others, the more likely she is to prioritize helping others over pursuing her self-interest. However, a more promising strategy in this context might be to enhance peoples' self-control. According to a common view in psychology, self-control entails the effortful inhibition of temptation impulses. Others define self-control more broadly as 'the general process by which people advance abstract, distal over concrete, proximal motives in judgment, decisions, and behavior' (Fujita, 2011). Following this view, self-control dilemmas are fundamentally dual-motive conflicts. The proximity and salience of the smaller, more concrete reward (for example, buying luxury goods), renders it challenging to follow the motive that presses for the larger, more abstract and distal reward (for example, donating to a charitable organization). Baumeister and Exline (1999) construe self-control as a 'moral muscle' and a 'master virtue'. On their view, virtue involves putting the collective interests ahead of the selfish interest of the individual, which in turn requires self-control. Hence, virtues are based on the positive exercise of self-control, whereas sin and vice revolve around failures of self-control. Much research has been done on the link between the deficiency of self-control and anti-social behavior (Piquero, Jennings, and Farrington, 2010), but the relationship between pro-social behavior and self-control has been largely neglected. Empirical ethicists might test whether self-control indeed constitutes the groundwork of moral virtues, as proposed by Baumeister and Exline (1999). Should this be true, it would also be promising to investigate whether training self-control could facilitate the execution of actions thought to be morally desirable.

So far we have focused on traits of the mind that either lead to mistakes in moral reasoning or keep people from behaving morally although they know what would be required to do. However, it is not necessarily the case that people lack certain cognitive capacities, apply poor decision-making strategies, or are particularly weak-willed if they fail to do the right thing. It is also possible that they find themselves in external circumstances that make it extraordinarily difficult both to understand what is morally required and to act accordingly. This point can be illustrated by research carried out in behavioral business ethics showing that organizational contexts have a strong impact on the degree to which employees behave morally (see Schminke and Priesemuth, 2012, for a review). Business ethicists employ two strongly related constructs to describe the contextual factors that influence the moral attitudes and behavior of organization members. The first, ethical climate, characterizes organizations in terms of broad normative characteristics that tell people what kind of organization they are in – especially what the organization values. The second construct, ethical culture, can be understood as characterizing the organization in terms of formal and informal structures and systems like rules, reward systems, and norms (Treviño, Butterfield, and McCabe, 1998). Research has shown that various aspects of ethical climates and cultures may promote immoral behavior. For instance, Treviño, Butterfield, and McCabe (1998) found a climate focused on self-interest to be associated with unethical behavior, especially in organizations that have not adopted a formal code of ethics. Furthermore, they identified a strong focus on obedience to authority to be a good predictor of unethical conduct. The investigation of those contextual factors that influence ethical behavior is thus a further promising line of research for empirical ethicists.

In fact, changing environments is often a more efficient way of promoting moral behavior than changing minds. This can be illustrated by differences in organ donation policies between countries (Gigerenzer, 2010; Johnson and Goldstein, 2003). Every year, several thousand Americans die waiting for a suitable donor organ. Although most Americans say that they approve of postmortem organ donation, only about 28 percent have granted permission by signing a donor card. A similar pattern can be observed in the United Kingdom and Germany. In these countries, an explicit consent is required in order to register as an organ donor. In contrast, other countries have adopted a policy according to which citizens are organ donors unless they opt out. In these presumed-consent countries like France, Portugal, or Austria, the rate of potential donors is close to 100 percent. It has been shown experimentally that even if no effort is required for overriding the default option, 82 percent ended up as potential donors when consent was presumed, compared to only 42 percent when explicit consent was needed (Johnson and Goldstein, 2003). This indicates that people rely on a simple heuristic: if there is a default, do nothing about it (Gigerenzer, 2010). Peoples' readiness to donate organs is to a large extent a function of the provided default option (opt-in or opt-out) and only to a much lesser degree influenced by reasoning, knowledge, or personal opinion. Knowing this, it is no wonder that organ donation information campaigns in explicit-consent countries have been largely ineffective. Consequently, if saving lives is the goal, creating a donation-friendly environment by introducing a proper default should have priority over attempts to change peoples' minds by information campaigns or related means. Altering the organ donation default from explicit-consent to presumed-consent is an example of what has become known as 'nudging'. A nudge is defined as 'any aspect of the choice architecture that alters peoples' behavior in a predictable way without forbidding any options or significantly changing their economic incentives' (Thaler and Sunstein, 2008). In our example, changing the default option would change an aspect of the choice architecture that is presumed to have a positive influence on peoples' organ donation readiness, without coercing people to comply. Nudges have the potential to improve life within societies, but due to their covert nature they need to be investigated and implemented responsibly.

As of yet, we have focused on how research in empirical ethics could help us in finding ways to promote moral conduct. We have seen that carefully designed organizations and societal institutions can provide environments that enhance peoples' moral behavior. Now we turn to a different but closely related question: what do people perceive to be good institutions? Depending on how this question is answered, empirical ethicists can make suggestions for adjusting institutional designs accordingly. This is exemplified by research on organizational justice (see Colquitt et al., 2001, for a review). Justice has been described by organizational psychologists in terms of at least three subjective perceptions: the fairness of outcome distributions or allocations (distributive justice), the fairness of the processes determining these outcomes (procedural justice), and the fairness of interpersonal interactions (interactional justice). Interactional justice comprises the manner both in which employees are treated by those with authority over them and in which they are informed about the reasons for certain procedures or outcome allocations. Justice perceptions have been shown to exhibit a positive impact on constructs like job satisfaction, organizational citizenship behavior, job performance, and commitment. Moreover, favorable justice evaluations are supposed to reduce counterproductive work behaviors, turnover intentions, workplace hostility, revenge, and retaliation (Rupp, 2011). This vast array of positive effects on employees' attitudes and behavior underlines the importance of designing organizations that are perceived as just. The role of the empirical ethicist is to investigate which kinds of processes, outcome distributions, and interpersonal interactions contribute to the perception of justice. Rather than being restricted to organizations, this investigation can also be directed at markets and societies. This is exemplified by Wolf and Lenger's study (this volume), in which they examine to what extent social mobility affects the acceptance of market-based income inequality.

Further evidence for the relevance of empirical ethics research for social engineering stems from investigations on the psychology of moral dilemmas. Cushman and Young (2009) argue that moral dilemmas arise when distinct psychological mechanisms for moral judgment yield conflicting judgments of individual cases. Consider, for instance, the question whether it is appropriate for a mother to smother her crying baby in order to prevent the discovery of her hidden family by enemy soldiers who have orders to kill all civilians. People struggle to find a satisfying answer to this question. Accumulated evidence suggests that two distinct psychological processes of moral judgment are in conflict when people evaluate dilemmas such as these: a cognitive response favors the welfare-maximizing choice, but an affective process prevents actions involving direct physical harm to specific individuals (Greene et al., 2001; 2004; 2008). Greene and colleagues associate the former response with the philosophical theory of utilitarianism and the latter with deontology. Accordingly, a dilemma is not a moral question for which we have no answer; rather, it is a moral question for which we have multiple answers (Cushman and Young, 2009). Thus, confronting a dilemma can be psychologically distressing and may lead to interpersonal conflict if people disagree on how to resolve it. One way of dealing with this is to reduce the rate at which people have to face dilemmas. Carefully constructed institutions avoid creating conflicts between multiple psychological systems of moral judgments. Cushman and Young (2009) mention affirmative action in higher education as an example. One possible admission policy is to rank all applicants without regard to personal characteristics like race and then to demote individuals from overrepresented groups while in turn promoting individuals from underrepresented groups. Such a procedure is likely to trigger conflicting evaluations both within and between individuals. Admitting underprivileged persons at the cost of rejecting privileged persons might be judged as appropriate on utilitarian grounds, but witnessing a particular individual personally suffer the loss of admission to college violates deontological intuitions. An alternative institutional design would be to raise scholarship money for extra admissions and select only candidates from underrepresented groups for these extra slots. Such a policy is welfare maximizing, not subject to deontological concerns as no particular candidate loses her admission, and most likely perceived as fair in terms of procedural and distributive justice.

12.3   Methodological suggestions for the descriptive level of empirical ethics

After having discussed the pragmatic aspects, we can now turn to the descriptive level of empirical ethics. As we have already seen, both our minds and our environment influence our behavior and shape our actions. Based on the aforementioned examples, we now discuss the methods that enable us to study moral behavior in a holistic manner. In order to understand why a holistic perspective is necessary and which factors need to be considered, we examine several components involved in moral cognition and discuss alternatives to those methods that fail to sufficiently take into account the properties of our cognitive system. Since empirical ethics is primarily concerned with moral concepts, judgment, and decision-making, we focus on methodological issues with regard to these three research areas.

Gigerenzer (2010) introduced the research program of ecological morality in response to the shortcomings of current empirical research on moral cognition. In order to improve empirical ethics, Gigerenzer calls for (1) studying social groups rather than just isolated individuals, (2) examining behavior in natural environments rather than in laboratory experiments, and (3) the analysis of moral behavior in addition to verbal reports. In the remainder of this article, we expand on these criticisms from a mainly cognitive perspective and point out concrete methods that can be used to achieve better insight into the interaction between the individual and the environment in moral contexts.

Many studies in empirical ethics revolve around the contents and applications of specific moral concepts. For instance, as we have shown above, researchers are interested in what people perceive as just. Thus, they investigate the circumstances under which people employ their concept of justice. In the following, we introduce empirically informed theories of concepts and highlight the difficulties as well as opportunities stemming from the properties of concepts' cognitive representations. As individuals, we have representations of both concrete and abstract concepts. Generally, concrete concepts are assumed to be mental representations of concrete (groups of) objects that can be generated from perceptual data. Cognitive psychologists and psycholinguists have amassed an impressive amount of evidence that suggests concepts are not represented using an amodal mental code devoid of perceptual information, a hypothesis most famously defended by Fodor (1975), but instead rely on a wide variety of sensorimotor data (Barsalou, 1999). However, moral concepts such as 'justice' and 'virtue' are prime examples for abstract concepts that at first glance appear to be unrelated to perceptual data. Recent research has shown that this common notion is wrong: abstract concepts are the result of several concrete experiences (Barsalou, 1999; 2005), such as situations in which we learn how to distribute goods evenly as children in the case of 'justice'. Such situations may involve the perception of quantities and relations, movements and bodily states, and emotions (Carey, 2009). This work presents a much more vivid sense of mental representation than suggested by earlier theories. Similarly, current research in social psychology has downplayed the importance of abstract, rational pathways of moral reasoning by showing how emotions and actions influence moral judgments (Schnall, Benton, and Harvey, 2008; Schnall et al., 2008).

As a consequence of the situated nature of abstract concepts, it has been established that the study of such concepts should involve concrete situations (Barsalou and Wiemer-Hastings, 2005). One standard method in empirical ethics is the use of scenario study designs in which participants are assigned one of a number of vignettes that differ in a single aspect. For example, in Knobe's (2003) famous scenario, a chairman of a company welcomes the profits that a new program will generate while expressing his indifference toward the fact that the program will harm the environment. In the second version of this scenario, the situation remains the same with the sole exception that the environment will be helped instead of harmed. In order to find out whether the variation of this aspect causes different judgments, participants were then asked whether the chairman intentionally helps or harms the environment. In fact, while a majority indicated that the chairman intentionally harmed the environment in the first scenario, only a minority attributed the intention of helping the environment in the second. A range of doubts have been raised regarding the validity of these kinds of studies. Methodological research by Auspurg, Hinz, and Liebig (2009) has pointed to the fact that vignette studies featuring rare or implausible scenarios distort subjects' responses: excessive cognitive demands and the resulting use of oversimplified decision-making strategies can lead to unnatural judgments. The complexity and plausibility of scenarios, as well as learning effects, have been shown to influence judgments. The authors explain that artificial or implausible scenarios lead participants to disregard or fully exclude the aspects causing the implausibility from their decision-making process. In light of this criticism, many scenarios used in empirical ethics appear to be invalid research tools. Even the well-known Knobe cases (2003) lack a certain sense of plausibility or at least familiarity, as we are not accustomed to people openly dismissing helping the environment anymore. Furthermore, the idea that changing a few phrases in a scenario manipulates only the desired dimensions cannot be taken for granted in the case of more complex vignettes. As a useful addition to check for any unwanted side-effects, we propose the use of qualitative items in survey studies. Questionnaires should, if possible, always include open questions that enable study participants to explain their judgments (Bunge et al., in preparation). In the case of the Knobe scenario, one should ask participants why they think that the chairman acted intentionally or unintentionally and analyze the responses. Such an analysis could reveal criteria that people use when determining the intentionality status of an action. By including such items, it becomes apparent if a judgment is based on the intended manipulation or if unforeseen contextual factors, such as stereotypes or ambiguous language pragmatics have distorted the responses.

In general, it should be noted how little resemblance filling out a survey form involving more or less contrived scenarios bears to making a moral judgment in everyday life. When people judge a chairman's misbehavior, they usually already know something about her and the company or will be given at least some context by the reporting media. In the case of a scenario study, participants usually only receive a basic description of the agent, the action, and the outcome. In the Knobe scenarios, for example, there is no information regarding the type or history of the company and no details about the chairman are mentioned. As Sripada (2010) pointed out, people need to extrapolate a lot of information from the underspecified scenario in order to make a judgment. They do so by using stereotypes as a fallback method. Such decision heuristics and biases are hard to detect without asking participants for their reasons. Although some judgment processes lend themselves better to explicit justifications than others (Cushman, Young, and Hauser, 2006), justifications can still be used as guides when devising follow-up studies and as further evidence for a hypothesis. The use of open questions that invite participants to explain their responses helps in grounding their choice by giving the survey a discursive element and by providing the impression of actually explaining and justifying their judgment to the researchers, much like we justify our moral judgments in everyday life. This component of surveys helps to address methodological criticisms such as those raised by Kauppinen (2007). On his view, survey studies are only able to record 'surface intuitions', while we should rather be interested in 'robust intuitions' that are elicited when failures of competence, failures of performance, and the influence of irrelevant factors are ruled out. He argues that these requirements are only met in philosophical dialogues. We acknowledge that there is some truth to Kauppinen's position and believe that studies on conceptual intuitions will benefit from including dialogical elements that can be subjected to qualitative analysis.

More directly than by conceptual knowledge, human behavior is driven by attitudes and desires that are either conscious or unconscious and can thus be investigated using explicit or implicit methods. Attitudes and reactions toward moral issues can be measured using surveys and compared both cross-culturally or between social groups such as in Jonathan Haidt's highly influential study, which showed that moral judgments are variable across cultural background and socioeconomic status (Haidt, Koller, and Dias, 1993). On the basis of decision-making architectures present in all humans, our social environment shapes our mental states by prescribing social norms, thereby calibrating our decision-making strategies around social expectations. Therefore, it is important to differentiate between variant and invariant aspects of moral judgments and attitudes. Those aspects that vary cross-culturally or between social groups are usually researched by social and personality psychologists. In contrast, invariant aspects of ethical decision-making processes are present in all humans and are usually investigated by cognitive psychologists or neuroscientists. When combined, these two approaches can be used to describe and explain moral judgments, as well as to improve moral behavior. For instance, the aforementioned research on moral conduct in business organizations can benefit from the realization that different societies may require different organizational contexts in order to trigger moral behavior. Presumably, some aspects of organizational contexts invariantly foster moral behavior, whereas the success of other aspects depends on the cultural background of the employees.

A shining example showcasing the benefits of combining behavioral and neural levels of description is the dual-process model of moral judgment put forth by Greene and colleagues (2001; 2004; 2008). By investigating the activity of brain regions during reflection on dilemmas using fMRI, it was found that utilitarian judgments are most strongly associated with the activity of regions involved in cognitive control, while deontological judgments are predominantly associated with regions active in emotion and social cognition. As shown above, results such as these can be used to predict what kind of institutional designs are likely to create dilemmas. Just like moral judgments, decisions can either be based on quick, automatic but error-prone heuristics or on more time-consuming reasoning processes. Which decision route becomes active depends on several variables, for example, on how often a similar situation has been encountered, how important the decision is, and how much time is available. In line with our previous criticism regarding the use of decontextualized, contrived scenarios in surveys, we highlight the importance of situational factors as well as affective and motivational states when investigating decision-making strategies. Returning to an example from the beginning of this article, this means one should investigate not only the states of the agent but also the contextual factors that determine whether helping a single identifiable victim or helping an anonymous group of people is preferred in a given situation.

In response to Gigerenzer's (2010) criticism regarding simplified laboratory experiments that are unable to map the complexity of real-life events, holistic research methods that emulate concrete situations should be introduced. An emerging trend in social and moral psychology is to conduct experiments using immersive virtual environment technology (IVET). Virtual reality experiments are likely to have a greater ecological validity than the questionnaires ordinarily used in moral dilemma studies. In virtual reality, a person can actually experience a scenario, and the types of thoughts and emotions that would be evoked in real life are likely to be generated (Rovira et al., 2009). At the same time, IVET allows conducting experiments that would be ethically unacceptable to execute in non-virtual environments. Of course, one might object that these experiments cannot reveal something about real-world behavior, as participants are aware of being in an artificial environment and know that their actions have no legal, reputational, physical, or long-term emotional consequences (Navarrete et al., 2012). However, several studies have shown that participants' behavior and experience in virtual reality settings map their behavior and experience in real world settings. For example, Slater and colleagues (2006) found that participants in a virtual reality replication of Milgram's (1963) obedience experiment responded almost in the same way as in the original study. Although all participants knew that neither the stranger nor the electrical shocks administered to the stranger were real, they tended to react to the situation at the subjective, behavioral, and physiological levels as if it were real. Furthermore, it seems that the degree of realism of the virtual environment is only marginally important for the participant's feeling of being immersed and present in the virtual world (Sanchez-Vives and Slater, 2005). It is reasonable to expect that IVET can minimize the trade-off between ecological and internal validity because it offers the opportunity to create settings that both mirror real-life situations and are under the complete control of the experimenter (Rovira et al., 2009). Using additional equipment, physiological parameters such as eye movements, pupil diameter, heart frequency, or skin conductance can be recorded while participants are immersed in the virtual world. These data can be analyzed to understand the physiological correlates of moral behavior, judgments, and decisions. Accordingly, IVET provides an outstanding groundwork for investigating capacities like empathy and self-control, which we have identified as being related to moral behavior.

12.4 Conclusion

As we have seen, the pragmatic and descriptive levels of empirical ethics are deeply intertwined. A thorough analysis of the roots of morality is required if we intend to promote peoples' understanding of and compliance with moral requirements. Morality is to be characterized as the result of an interaction between mind and environment. Similarly, the design of humane institutions is in need of a holistic perspective that takes into account both individual and situational aspects. Accordingly, we conclude with the most important demand for future empirical research on morality: it is only through the use of more dialogical surveys, context-sensitive study designs, and innovative methods such as the use of virtual reality technology that the situated character of moral concepts, judgment, and decision-making can be fully appreciated. In order for empirical ethics to successfully fulfill its potential to become an influential part of the social sciences, researchers must fully embrace the complexities of morality.

Note

1. Experimental recording and experimental retracing bear some resemblance to what Nadelhoffer and Nahmias (2007) have called 'experimental analysis' and 'experimental descriptivism'. We chose the word 'recording' instead of 'analysis' in order to make clear that work in empirical ethics is more than just an advancement of conceptual analysis. That is, empirical ethicists are not just interested in conceptual intuitions, but in decisions, behavior, etc. Moreover, we think that 'experimental descriptivism' is better used as an umbrella term for both 'experimental recording' and 'experimental retracing' than as a synonym for the latter.

References

Auspurg, K., T. Hinz, and S. Liebig (2009) 'Komplexität von Vignetten, Lerneffekte und Plausibilität im Faktoriellen Survey', *Methoden, Daten, Analysen*, 3, 1, pp. 59–96.

Barsalou, L. W. (1999) 'Perceptual Symbol Systems', *Behavioral and Brain Sciences*, 22, 4, pp. 577–660.

Barsalou, L. W. (2005) 'Abstraction as Dynamic Interpretation in Perceptual Symbol Systems', in L. Gershkoff-Stowe and D. H. Rakison (eds), *Building Object Categories in Developmental Time*, pp. 389–431, Majwah: Erlbaum.

Barsalou, L. W. and K. Wiemer-Hastings (2005). 'Situating Abstract Concepts', in D. Pecher and R. A. Zwaan (eds), *Grounding Cognition: The Role of Perception and Action in Memory, Language, and Thought*, pp. 129–163, New York: Cambridge University Press.

Baumeister, R. F. and J. J. Exline (1999) 'Virtue, Personality, and Social Relations: Self-control as the Moral Muscle', *Journal of Personality and Social Psychology*, 67, 6, pp. 1165–1194.

Bunge, A., A. Skulmowski, B. R. Cohen, B. Kreilkamp, and N. Troxler (in preparation) 'A Situated Approach for Investigating Conceptual Contents: Testing Theoretical Models of Intentional Action by Analysing Participant-Generated Scenarios'.

Carey, S. (2009) *The Origin of Concepts* (Oxford: Oxford University Press).

Colquitt, J. A., D. E. Conlon, M. J. Wesson, C. O. L. H. Porter, and K. Y. Ng (2001) 'Justice at the Millennium: A Meta-analytic Review of 25 Years of Organizational Justice Research', *Journal of Applied Psychology*, 86, 3, pp. 425–445.

Cushman, F. A., L. Young, and M. D. Hauser (2006) 'The Role of Reasoning and Intuition in Moral Judgments: Testing Three Principles of Harm', *Psychological Science*, 17, 12, pp. 1082–1089.

Cushman, F. and L. Young (2009) 'The Psychology of Dilemmas and the Philosophy of Morality', *Ethical Theory and Moral Practice*, 12, 1, pp. 9–24.

Davidson, D. (1980) 'How Is Weakness of the Will Possible?', in *Essays on Actions and Events*, pp. 21–42, Oxford: Clarendon Press.

Fodor, J. A. (1975) *The Language of Thought* (Cambridge, MA: Harvard University Press).

Fujita, K. (2011) 'On Conceptualizing Self-control as More Than the Effortful Inhibition of Impulses', *Personality and Social Psychology Review*, 15, 4, pp. 352–366.

Gigerenzer, G. (2010) 'Moral Satisficing: Rethinking Moral Behavior as Bounded Rationality', *Topics in Cognitive Science*, 2, 3, pp. 528–554.

Goldman, A. I. (1992) 'Empathy, Mind, and Morals', *Proceedings and Addresses of the American Philosophical Association*, 66, 3, pp. 17–41.

Greene, J. D., S. A. Morelli, K. Lowenberg, L. E. Nystrom, and J. D. Cohen (2008) 'Cognitive Load Selectively Interferes with Utilitarian Moral Judgment', *Cognition*, 107, 3, pp. 1144–1154.

Greene, J. D., L. E. Nystrom, A. D. Engell, J. M. Darley, and J. D. Cohen (2004) 'The Neural Bases of Cognitive Conflict and Control in Moral Judgment', *Neuron*, 44, 2, pp. 389–400.

Greene, J. D., R. B. Sommerville, L. E. Nystrom, J. M. Darley, and J. D. Cohen (2001) 'An fMRI Investigation of Emotional Engagement in Moral Judgment', *Science*, 293, 5537, pp. 2105–2108.

Haidt, J., S. H. Koller, and M. G. Dias (1993) 'Affect, Culture, and Morality, or Is It Wrong to Eat Your Dog?', *Journal of Personality and Social Psychology*, 65, 4, pp. 613–628.

Hein, G. and T. Singer (2010) 'Neuroscience Meets Social Psychology: An Integrative Approach to Human Empathy and Prosocial Behavior', in M. Mikulincer and P. R. Shaver (eds), *Prosocial Motives, Emotions, and Behavior: The Better Angels of Our Nature*, pp. 109–125, Washington: American Psychological Association.

Heinzelmann, N., G. Ugazio, and P. N. Tobler (2012) 'Practical Implications of Empirically Studying Moral Decision-making', *Frontiers in Neuroscience*, 6, 94, doi: 10.3389/fnins.2012.00094.

Johnson, E. J. and D. Goldstein (2003) 'Do Defaults Save Lives?', *Science*, 302, pp. 1338–1339.

Kauppinen, A. (2007) 'The Rise and Fall of Experimental Philosophy', *Philosophical Explorations*, 10, 2, pp. 95–118.

Knobe, J. (2003) 'Intentional Action and Side Effects in Ordinary Language', *Analysis*, 63, 3, pp. 190–194.

Lam, T. C. M., K. Kolomitro, and F. C. Alamparambil (2011) 'Empathy Training: Methods, Evaluation Practices, and Validity', *Journal of MultiDisciplinary Evaluation*, 7, 16, pp. 162–200.

Milgram, S. (1963) 'Behavioral Study of Obedience', *Journal of Abnormal and Social Psychology*, 67, 4, pp. 371–378.

Nadelhoffer, T. and E. Nahmias (2007) 'The Past and Future of Experimental Philosophy', *Philosophical Explorations*, 10, 2, pp. 123–149.

Navarrete, C. D., M. M. McDonald, M. L. Mott, and B. Asher (2012) 'Virtual Morality: Emotion and Action in a Simulated Three-dimensional "Trolley Problem"', *Emotion*, 12, 2, pp. 364–370.

Piquero, A. R., W. G. Jennings, and D. P. Farrington (2010) 'On the Malleability of Self-control: Theoretical and Policy Implications Regarding a General Theory of Crime', *Justice Quarterly*, 27, 6, pp. 803–834.

Rovira, A., D. Swapp, B. Spanlang, and M. Slater (2009) 'The Use of Virtual Reality in the Study of People's Responses to Violent Incidents', *Frontiers in Behavioral Neuroscience*, 3, 59, pp. 1–10.

Rupp, D. E. (2011) 'An Employee-centered Model of Organizational Justice and Social Responsibility', *Organizational Psychology Review*, 1, 1, pp. 72–94.

Sanchez-Vives, M. V. and M. Slater (2005) 'From Presence to Consciousness Through Virtual Reality', *Nature Reviews Neuroscience*, 6, 4, pp. 332–339.

Schminke, M. and M. Priesemuth (2012) 'Behavioral Business Ethics: Taking Context Seriously', in D. De Cremer and A. E. Tenbrunsel (eds), *Behavioral Business Ethics: Shaping an Emerging Field*, pp. 47–79, New York: Routledge.

Schnall, S., J. Benton, and S. Harvey (2008) 'With a Clean Conscience: Cleanliness Reduces the Severity of Moral Judgments', *Psychological Science*, 19, 12, pp. 1219–1222.

Schnall, S., J. Haidt, G. L. Clore, and A. H. Jordan (2008) 'Disgust as Embodied Moral Judgment', *Personality and Social Psychology Bulletin*, 34, 8, pp. 1096–1109.

Slater, M., A. Antley, A. Davison, D. Swapp, C. Guger, C. Barker, N. Pistrang, and M. V. Sanchez-Vives (2006) 'A Virtual Reprise of the Stanley Milgram Obedience Experiments', *PLoSONE*, 1, 1, e39.

Small, D. A., G. Loewenstein, and P. Slovic (2007) 'Sympathy and Callousness: The Impact of Deliberative Thought on Donations to Identifiable and Statistical Victims', *Organizational Behavior and Human Decision Processes*, 102, 2, pp. 143–153.

Slovic, P., M. L. Finucane, E. Peters, and D. G. MacGregor (2007) 'The Affect Heuristic', *European Journal of Operational Research*, 177, 3, pp. 1333–1352.

Sripada, C. S. (2010) 'The Deep Self Model and Asymmetries in Folk Judgments About Intentional Action', *Philosophical Studies*, 151, 2, pp. 159–176.

Thaler, R. H. and C. R. Sunstein (2008) *Nudge: Improving Decisions About Health, Wealth, and Happiness* (New Haven: Yale University Press).

Treviño, L. K., K. D. Butterfield, and D. L. McCabe (1998) 'The Ethical Context in Organizations: Influences on Employee Attitudes and Behaviors', *Business Ethics Quarterly*, 8, 3, pp. 447–476.

13
Robust Intuitions, Experimental Ethics, and Experimental Economics: Bringing Reflective Equilibrium into the Lab

Fernando Aguiar, Antonio Gaitán, and Blanca Rodríguez-López

13.1 Introduction

Among the recent proposals for philosophical reform, none has generated as much controversy as experimental philosophy. Despite its originality and the suggestiveness of some of its results, experimental philosophy has been criticized almost from its very beginnings. In this chapter, we focus on a methodological objection due to Antti Kauppinen (Kauppinen, 2007). According to Kauppinen, experimental philosophy (in any of its possible formulations) would not be able to identify the robust conceptual intuitions of speakers. In this chapter, we counter Kauppinen's criticism by highlighting the relevance of experimental economics to identify the behavioral dimension of our conceptual competence. To the extent that experimental economics is particularly well equipped to identify the behavioral aspect of our conceptual competence, experimental ethics would do well in enriching its methodology (based on questionnaires and vignettes, and an overly linguistic bias) with behaviorally-oriented experiments. This would permit us to more clearly define the contours of our conceptual competence in the contexts that are relevant for our discussion – attribution of moral responsibility, fairness, etc. Importantly, experimental work on this behavioral dimension of our conceptual competence will also contribute to experimentally modeling processes of reflective equilibrium that would justify our principles and normative standards.

The message of this chapter is therefore twofold: Firstly, we will defend that an experimental philosophy which is methodologically sensitive to the dual nature of our conceptual competence (linguistic responses and behavioral manifestations) should look at itself in the mirror of experimental economics. Secondly, we will argue that moving experimental ethics closer to the methodology of experimental economics is the first step to experimentally examine actual choice processes, processes that can be described in terms of reflective equilibrium. The framework offered by reflective equilibrium, we will argue, is more faithful to the complex nature of our real decisions than the simple intuitions of the hypothetical scenarios used by philosophers or the responses to questionnaires and vignettes that are common in experimental philosophy.

13.2   Reflective equilibrium and experimental philosophy

The activity of moral philosophers is very diverse. Many are engaged in practical discussions aimed at guiding the way we organize our institutions. Others are interested in more abstract aspects that have to do with the evaluative component of our agency or with the meaning of our moral terms. But still the primary activity of moral philosophers today is to establish principles that justify our actions and guide us in our daily choices (Kahane, 2013, p. 422).

To establish these principles, most moral philosophers appeal to what is known as *reflective equilibrium* (Rawls, 1971; Daniels, 1996). According to this methodological ideal, the plausibility of any moral principle depends on the degree of 'fit' or equilibrium between that principle and agents' intuitions about particular cases. This reflective equilibrium is considered a method for revising or refining intuitions and justifying general principles.

In the *narrow* version of reflective equilibrium, the plausibility of a principle P depends on a process of mutual adjustment between P and our judgments about particular cases (those intuitions that are not the result of prejudice, misinformation, or clear defects in reasoning). In this version the aim of moral philosophers would be to find the sufficient conditions so that case X is an instance of the concept they are analyzing (justice, belief, knowledge, etc.). In the *wide* version of reflective equilibrium, the plausibility of any principle P depends on a process of mutual adjustment between P, the refined intuitions about a particular case, and *a set of background theories* that, depending on the case, may be physical, psychological, sociological, economic, or others. The wide equilibrium would therefore imply seeking the sufficient and necessary conditions so that case X is an instance of the concept being analyzed.

Although reflective equilibrium is often described as a *method of theoretical justification*, it may also be understood as a *decision procedure* (Hauser, 2007). But how reliable are the intuitions that support reflective equilibrium in both its normative and descriptive variant? The epistemic status of intuitions has undoubtedly been the focus of a recent and intense methodological debate (Sosa, 2008; Appiah, 2008; Cappelen, 2012) at the center of which lies experimental philosophy. Most experimental philosophers understand its proposal as a reaction to the Standard Program of Conceptual Analysis (SPCA hereafter). Though there are nuances and differences, for any version of SPCA, speakers' intuitions, which are *modeled on the intuitions of philosophers about imaginary cases and hypothetical scenarios*, are essential when analyzing a particular concept C (Jackson, 2000). According to experimental philosophers, however, it is not clear that the philosopher's intuitions about C are representative of what speakers understand as C.

For some of its practitioners, the aim of experimental philosophy fails to break radically with the methodology of SPCA. Experimental philosophy would, in essence, be a more effective way of operationalizing the use of intuitions typical of conceptual analysis (Nadelhoffer and Nahmias, 2007). Understood therefore as *experimental analysis*, the so-called *positive program* would overlap with conceptual analysis when taking the intuitions of speakers as a starting point (Alexander, 2012). Unlike classical conceptual analysis, however, experimental analysis would insist on the need for quantitative and systematic methods to access these intuitions and not (only) thought experiments (Weinberg, 2007; Alexander, 2012). Experimental analysis, therefore, would question those appeals to reflective equilibrium which assume that the intuitions of philosophers regarding thought experiments and scenarios are reliable data. In short, reflective equilibrium would only be a valid method of theoretical justification if it relies on intuitions obtained by experimental procedures.

On the other hand, the so-called *experimental restrictionism* or *negative program* considers that the results of experimental philosophy and psychology must rule out the intuitions of philosophers and much of the intuitions of speakers when analyzing a particular concept (Nichols,

Stich, and Weinberg, 2003; Alexander, 2012, pp. 82–84). Since many of the intuitions of speakers about a given concept C are subject to variation and cultural biases (Weinberg, Nichols, and Stich, 2001), irrelevant contextual determinants (Petrinovic and O'Neill, 1996; Swain, Alexander, and Weinberg, 2008), framing effects, or gender bias, proponents of this interpretation understand that these intuitions provide material of questionable relevance for the construction of a theory about the content of C. According to this perspective, it makes no sense to seek equilibrium between our intuitions and those principles centered on C when justifying theoretical principles: the equilibrium is flawed by the same biases that affect the intuitions about C.

The negative program questions the nature of moral intuitions as evidence, and hence rejects the reliability of the reflective equilibrium as a method to justify general principles. Proponents of the negative program appear to be supported by many experimental results in which there exists little agreement among moral subjects regarding what their intuitions dictate to them in specific cases.

However, while it is true that the moral intuitions of speakers are unreliable in many cases, experimental results do not permit us to fully reject the reliability of intuitions, thus leaving the door open for the positive program, and hence the experimental use of reflective equilibrium. Based on the regularity of responses by experimental subjects to the two most widely-studied cases of the trolley problem, sidetrack, and footbridge, Guy Kahane (2013) recently defended a kind of narrow reflective equilibrium in experimental ethics, which he summarizes in a five-step argument:

1. Our moral intuitions about particular cases give us defeasible reason to believe in their contents. [...]
2. Our moral intuitions about particular cases *track* certain moral principles. [...].
3. Evidence about what moral principles our intuitions track gives us defeasible reason to believe in these moral principles. [*From 1, 2*]

But

4. Facts about what principles our intuitions track are *empirical* facts, and are therefore discoverable using the methods of empirical psychology.

   More specifically, facts about what our intuitions track are *exactly* the kind of functional facts psychologists seek to discover.

Therefore

5. Psychological evidence about the principles our intuitions track gives us defeasible reasons to endorse these moral principles. [*From 3, 4*] (Kahane, 2013, pp. 428–429)

The narrow reflective equilibrium or, as Kahane prefers to call it, the local coherence between concrete principles and intuitions (point 3), is reached due to the capacity of intuitions to provide clues about principles that are supported by facts obtained using the methods of experimental psychology (4 and 5).

Kahane ascribes a prominent epistemic role to moral intuitions. According to him, this is because intuitions give us strong reasons to believe in their propositional content. The experimental contribution, which appears in steps 4 and 5, has a threefold function: to confirm, by inductive generalizations, that most subjects have intuitions that are similar to those of most philosophers (it is morally wrong to push the fat man from the bridge to stop the trolley, for example); to ensure that the insights obtained are not accidental; and to provide evidence about the mechanisms underlying the principles that our intuitions track.

Through this process, however, a reflective equilibrium cannot be reached because moral subjects do not reflect on their intuitions or on the consequences of making decisions based on them, where 'reflect' is understood as the process of revising one's own intuitions, which leads to their being accepted or rejected so that we can say that they are not accidental (Eggleston, 2010). Reflective equilibrium is a process that the moral subjects themselves must engage in; it is not a simple external attribution of a philosopher that engages in this process in the comfort of his or her armchair. What would be of interest then, is that it occurs in the *laboratory itself* and that it could be reproduced in multiple experiments. If this is achieved, we can speak of a true experimental ethics and not just an ethics supplemented with laboratory data.

In light of the foregoing, it could be argued, therefore, that experimental philosophy has two basic and distinct variants. However, it is evident that both routes share a common methodological assumption. This assumption highlights the relevance of quantitative empirical methods when addressing philosophical questions of a conceptual nature; questions that have to do with the intuitions of speakers on a particular concept. The importance of the quantitative dimension for the practice of moral theory is evident. The quantitative dimension would enrich those processes of reflective equilibrium by which the moral philosopher justifies the moral principles that guide our evaluative responses to certain situations. Similarly, the quantitative information gained from any variant of experimental philosophy could contribute to better illustrating the nature of the decision process engaged in by the moral agent in some contexts and shedding light on the factors that influence their decisions (Bicchieri 2006). Now, is this common methodological minimum incontrovertible? Hardly. In the recent literature, the reliance of experimental philosophy on quantitative empirical methods has been attacked on several fronts (Weinberg, 2007, p. 69; Knobe and Nichols, 2008, p. 9; Alexander, 2012, pp. 110–113). In the next section we deal with the particular version of this criticism formulated by Antti Kauppinen (Kauppinen, 2007).

13.3 Experimental philosophy and robust intuitions

To access the intuitions of speakers in relation to a particular concept, experimental ethics frequently relies on the use of questionnaires and vignettes. This methodological choice, however, is highly controversial. Leaving aside the fact that these questionnaires are one of the least frequent methodological options in experimental psychology, a general problem threatens those who use them. The problem is that due to their inability to control a number of factors that could distort the subjects' responses, the questionnaires and vignettes typical of experimental ethics do not guarantee access to the robust intuitions of speakers on a particular concept: 'yes/no' answers, Likert scales, the irrelevant or bizarre stories sometimes presented to experimental subjects, and conversational implicatures arouse reasonable doubts about the actual access to robust intuitions with these techniques (Cullen, 2010).

In line with this general methodological objection, Antti Kauppinen pointed out that the intuitions of interest to the SPCA are those that *competent* speakers would express in *ideal* conditions without being influenced by *pragmatic* factors (Kauppinen, 2007, p. 101). This subset of intuitions would establish the *robust* conceptual competence of speakers. The problem with experimental philosophy, according to Kauppinen, is that once we assume this, it would be a complicated task to access the level of competence of interest to SPCA using the methods of experimental ethics (questionnaires, vignettes, etc.).

This methodological incapacity would affect any of the variants of experimental philosophy. But Kauppinen not only criticizes the methodological component common to all experimental philosophy. He also puts forward a positive proposal aimed at addressing the methodological incapacity of experimental philosophy. Kauppinen's solution explores some assumptions central to SPCA in order to accommodate a robust level of conceptual competence, one that does not always coincide with the goals of experimental philosophy.

According to Kauppinen the canonical form by which analytic philosophy appeals to conceptual intuitions is as follows:

(I) S; In S we would (not) say that X is C

Where S is a description of a particular case, imaginary or real, X is an element of that case, and C is the concept that applies (or fails to apply) to X. In Kauppinen's view, what experimental philosophy does is transform (I) to (E):

(E) (I) predicts what most people will (not) say about C if X is presented to them.

But according to Kauppinen, (E) is unaccurate. Kauppinen presents some arguments to support this claim. Surveys conducted by experimental philosophers ignore the fact that speakers express their intuitions in an *elliptical* manner. Moreover, as already noted, the typical methods of experimental ethics cannot control the pragmatic aspects that affect the correctness or appropriateness of the statements made by the people involved in philosophical experiments (Petrinovic and O'Neill, 1996; Swain, Alexander, and Weinberg, 2008). Because of these problems, Kauppinen argues that it is necessary to rephrase (E) as follows:

(A) "In S, we would say that X is C" is a hypothesis about how (1) *competent users* of the concepts in question would respond if (2) they *considered the case in sufficiently ideal conditions* and (3) their answer was *influenced only by semantic considerations*. (Kauppinen, 2007, p. 101)

Kauppinen argues that the conditions in (A) do not interpret the practice of conceptual analysis as an empirical prediction about the conceptual intuitions of speakers based on their willingness to respond to a survey, a vignette or a questionnaire – as (E) does. The conditions stated in (A) must be understood rather as a *hypothesis* about the use of the concepts by competent users. According to Kauppinen, this hypothesis can only be tested by engaging in dialogue with the test subjects using the Socratic method, thus violating the spirit and letter of the quasi-observations of experimentalists (Kauppinen, 2007, pp. 96 and 106).

Although this is a poignant criticism, it does not imply that we should abandon experimental philosophy. Against this extreme interpretation of Kauppinen's objection, we believe that the plurality of methodological proposals in the social sciences should prompt us to supplement experimental philosophy with alternative experimental methods that are not relying only on questionnaires and surveys (Nadelhoffer and Nahmias, 2007 p. 132). In the next section we explore one of these methodological programs.

13.4   A question of method

If questionnaires and vignettes do not provide access to robust intuitions and hence invalidate any process of reflective equilibrium constructed from them, what experimental methods could help us to overcome this problem? We believe the answer lies in experimental economics. In other words, experimental ethics could reveal the robust intuitions of speakers if its experiments were modeled on a few basic methodological principles taken from experimental economics.

When we inquire into the influence that experimental economics could have on experimental ethics, two options seem obvious at the meta-methodological level. If we were to take an extreme position, we should wholly renounce vignettes and questionnaires. A more ecumenical stance, however, suggests that although questionnaires and vignettes continue to be used in experimental ethics to access the intuitions of speakers, this methodology could be enriched with the experimental methods of experimental economics (Konow, 2003). In this paper, we defend that this second option is the best way to enrich the methods of experimental ethics. For our proposal to make sense, we must answer two general questions:

> [M] To what extent do the methodological features that define experimental economics differ substantially from the methods used in experimental ethics?
>
> [IR] To what extent can experimental economics (as defined by these features) help to accommodate the *conceptual competence* of agents?

As regards [M], Ralph Hertwig and Andreas Ortmann (Hertwig and Ortmann, 2001, H&O hereafter) have recently systematized the methodological features that separate experimental economics from experimental psychology (primarily on those branches dealing with issues such as decision making, social cognition, problem solving, and reasoning, in both their individual and social variants). H&O have proposed a number of features that distinguish experiments conducted by experimental economists from experiments in experimental psychology. From among the features they propose, we highlight the following three (Hertwig and Ortmann, 2001, pp. 384–390):

13.4.1 Enacting a script versus 'ad-libbing'

In the typical experiment run in experimental economics, subjects are provided a detailed script which specifies the role of each participant, the type of task that the experimenter wants each participant to perform, the action choices associated to each role, and the possible gains or losses arising from each choice. In psychological experiments, however, participants are not usually provided such detailed scripts. The absence of a script forces participants to ad-lib, thus legitimizing the kind of pragmatic inferences that can distort their responses (Hertwig and Ortmann, 2001, p. 385).

13.4.2 Repeated trials versus snapshot studies

Experimental economists repeat experiments to allow subjects to become familiar with the task and adapt to the experimental setting. But repeating experiments also helps to gain insight into the influence of learning on the subjects' responses and decisions (Hertwig and Ortmann, 2001, p. 387). Rather than repeating tasks, experimental psychology tends to test subject's competence in a discreet manner, thus minimizing the role of learning and the responses of other experimental subjects.

13.4.3 Financial incentives versus no incentives

In both economic and psychological experiments, subjects are paid for participating, but few psychological experiments provide incentives according to how the task is performed during the experiment itself (*task-related incentives*). The justification for such incentives is threefold (Guala, 2005). Task-related incentives permit distinguishing between the extrinsic and intrinsic motivation of subjects, which in turn permits controlling unobservable variables and hence the internal validity of the experiment. Task-related incentives also foster cognitive effort, thus ensuring that experimental subjects will pay more attention to the task they have to perform. Finally, economic incentives reduce performance variability. For example, if individuals are presented a set of principles of justice and the choice of one or another depends on the reward they will receive (they or other subjects), these rewards will decrease the likelihood that the subjects will make random choices and therefore minimize the arbitrary variation of responses (Guala, 2005, p. 240).

It seems clear, therefore, that these features are not consistent in the experimental designs typical of experimental psychology. Of course, to the extent that experimental ethics looks in the mirror of psychology, such inconsistencies may be transferred to experimental ethics itself. The consequences of such an extrapolation will be the focus of the next section where we will attempt to determine the extent to which the methodological features enumerated above can help identify the 'robust intuitions' of speakers at the conceptual level.

13.5   Experimental ethics and experimental economics: reflective equilibrium in the lab

As we noted above, our methodological proposal should, in addition to highlighting the positive aspects of the methods of experimental economics, answer the following question:

> [IR] To what extent can experimental economics (as defined by these features) help to accommodate the *conceptual competence* of agents?

In order to respond to [IR], it is necessary to emphasize the complex nature of our conceptual competence. Being competent with regard to a given concept C implies exemplifying, at various levels, certain dispositions. Conceptual competence involves discriminative dispositions: dispositions that are related to the role C plays in agent's reasoning and dispositions to produce certain answers (Margolis and Lawrence, 1999; Pettit, 1993, pp. 54–106). Philip Pettit summarizes this distinction as follows:

> The practices that commit us to practical presumptions – that is, shared practical presumptions – are, in the first place, practices of a discursive and inferential kind (...) the practices involved also have a decisive role in the way we conduct toward the world, toward other people and toward ourselves. It would be a great mistake to miss this, for it would lead us to think, quite wrongly, that philosophy is exclusively focused on matters of language. (Pettit, 2004, p. 313)

It is important to highlight that this behavioral aspect of our conceptual competence as described by Pettit does not exclude that, in many cases, it remains true that being competent in exemplifying C means being able to *say* something that falls under the domain of C. What the behavioral component stresses, rather, is that being competent in relation to C also involves *behaving* in such a way that our conduct is subject to the rules governing the use of C. And this applies regardless of when we are able to say something that falls under the domain of C. It is sufficient for us to be able to behave toward X as if it were a case of C so that someone can ascribe us the possession of C. In an admirable manner, Alfano and Loeb emphasized the importance of the distinction between discursive conceptual competence and behavioral conceptual competence to experimental ethics:

> [M]orality is not just a matter of what people would say, but also a matter of what they would *notice, do,* and *feel*, as well as how they think they would reason and respond. Surveys provide only minimal and indirect evidence about these latter activities, and so it would behoove experimental philosophers to employ or devise further outcome measures that would more reliably and directly capture these features of morality. (Alfano and Loeb, 2014)

When we take account of this behavioral or practical aspect of our conceptual competence, the relevance of experimental economics methods for studying our conceptual competence becomes clear. Indeed, much of the typical methodology of experimental economics rests precisely on a behavioral assumption; an assumption that assigns a large weight to the agent's conduct in certain contexts governed by economic incentives, beyond their linguistic responses. It could be argued that in contrast to the excessive emphasis experimental ethics places on the linguistic responses of experimental subjects – subjects who are provided vignettes and questionnaires – experimental economics primarily seeks to isolate the *behavioral manifestations* associated with certain moral concepts such as altruism, reciprocity, fairness, trust, etc.

These behavioral manifestations, although hypothetical, play an important role in Rawls's model of reflective equilibrium, albeit they have been obscured by the linguistic analogy. To use the verb 'sing' correctly in a sentence is not the same as singing: if someone says in perfect English 'I sing very well' and when asked to sing instead begins to dance, we would not say he or she knows what it means to 'sing'. While it is true that in Rawls's model an adjustment is needed between refined intuitions or considered moral judgments, principles, and background theories, this adjustment implies that the moral subject must make a decision: the adjustment forces the subject to choose, in a context of uncertainty, a principle of justice that governs the distribution of scarce resources. Rawls's model rests in part on a decision model: moral subjects not only have to *say* what is fair, but they have to *choose* a principle and *use it*. What experimental economics does is to transform the hypothetical context of reflection into one of actual decision making, be it parametric (as in the original position) or strategic. In this real context, individuals' decisions on trust, altruism, reciprocity, fairness, etc. have real consequences in moral terms. But for this to be so, individuals have to play a real moral role in the laboratory, and that role must be clearly set out in scripts and have costs and benefits. Unlike hypothetical decisions in the first person and judgments about what others should do in the hypothetical scenarios of experimental ethics, real moral decisions must be brought to the laboratory. If these decisions are repeated at different stages of the same experiment in which subjects try to adjust their intuitions to principles or to principles and background theories, a reflective equilibrium can be reached in the laboratory.

In their pioneering work *Choosing Justice*, Frohlich and Oppenheimer designed a three-part experiment to reach a reflective equilibrium in the laboratory (Frohlich and Oppenheimer, 1992, pp. 42–43; for a recent discussion of the methodological relevance of this program, see Hauser, 2007, chapter 2). In the first part of the experiment, the subjects are presented four principles of justice (floor constraint, difference principle, maximum income, and range constraint), provided a brief explanation of the four principles and asked to make a preliminary ranking of the principles. The authors then discuss with the subjects the principles in greater depth, their implications and how the subjects' task relates to the principles. Following this step, the subjects take a test to ensure that they understood the principles and rank the principles a second time. Thus, they are given

> [a] set of four choice situations, where the subjects' choices of particular principles of justice had financial consequences for them personally. These situations involved more than reading and writing; in them the subjects randomly selected a chit that assigned them to an income class. (Frohlich and Oppenheimer, 1992, p. 42)

When they are faced with the decision problem and after being assigned an income class, subjects then rank the principles a third time and move on to the second part of the experiment in which they discuss and decide in groups which principle to choose in order to solve four distribution problems. While it is true that Rawls's veil of ignorance cannot be fully simulated, this does not preclude subjects from making impartial decisions in the experimental setting because they do not know their particular interests (Frohlich and Oppenheimer, 1992, p. 55; Aguiar, Becker, and Miller, 2013). In the third part of the experiment, subjects are given a questionnaire on their beliefs and attitudes and asked for a final ranking of the principles.

The behavioral and linguistic aspects of the concept of justice are well reflected in this experiment, whose express purpose, according to the authors, is to reach a reflective equilibrium in the laboratory (Frohlich and Oppenheimer, 1992, p. 100, p. 104, p. 112). The detailed explanation of the principles, their implications and background theories, reflection by the experimental subjects – who are moral subjects – on how to rank the principles, and the real consequences of their decisions allow transferring the reflective equilibrium to the lab, and thus obtaining more robust intuitions. In this sense, an experimental ethics that (without renouncing vignettes) addresses such processes of experimental reflective equilibrium will be closer to Kauppinen's proposal as the Socratic model is transferred to the laboratory and enriched with real moral decisions that also have real consequences.

This is demonstrated not only in *Choosing Justice*, but also in later studies in which subjects must engage in complex processes of reflection in the laboratory. As several authors have shown in experiments related to moral decisions and justice, faster, less thoughtful decisions are more purely selfish in nature than those that are influenced by other-regarding concerns, which require more time for reflection (Úbeda, 2013). Similarly, in classic games such as the ultimatum game or the dictator game, repetition, learning, incentives (economic or otherwise) and the use of precise scripts allow individuals to reflect on moral decisions and lead to very stable and robust results 'across (developed) cultures, levels of stakes [...] and changes in experimental methodology' (Camerer and Fehr, 2004, p. 59).

Therefore, once we consider the dual nature of our conceptual competence – at least in terms of producing responses within a particular domain – experimental economics seems to be well-equipped methodologically to *at least* isolate the behavioral aspect of our conceptual competence in relation to a given concept C. Many of the features listed above may in fact be interpreted as specific methodological 'recipes' which aid in achieving that goal. The use of economic incentives and the repetition of tasks also contribute to improving the reliability of behavioral responses to complex concepts, as well as determining to what extent the mastering of such concepts varies with learning. But where the interest of experimental economics in isolating the behavioral component of our conceptual competence is most evident is in its constant appeal to scenarios or scripts. These tools detail the type of action to be studied (a monetary proposal, punishment for a given distribution made by others, etc.), the alternatives available to the agent, and the economic costs associated with each alternative. Each of these elements helps to focalize the type of response of interest to the experimenter, beyond the simple reports of subjects.

Obviously, from what we have said it does not follow that the linguistic manifestations linked to our conceptual competence are irrelevant to experimental ethics. Rather, experimental economics could enrich the experimental methods used in experimental philosophy, though without completely substituting them. Thus, for example, where we find a variety of *linguistic* responses by subjects about C, we could also find consistency in their *behavioral* responses. However, these tensions between behavioral experimental findings and linguistic experimental findings in relation to our conceptual competence within a certain domain should not be a concern at the methodological level. Indeed, the opposite seems to be the case, as some of these tensions can be tremendously informative. Such situations 'of conflict' would allow us to identify in a more detailed and complex manner cases in which language – a tool that is highly permeable to distorting influences – perverts our conceptual competence at the behavioral level as well as the function associated with certain concepts (Haidt, 2012; Nichols, 2004). Nonetheless, on other occasions – when, for example, the linguistic responses of subjects are highly consistent – a significant divergence between our *behavioral* conceptual competence and our *linguistic* conceptual competence might suggest that what experimental economists tend to call biases in the application of C may be a constitutive component of our global competence in relation to C. That is, there may be cases in which economists identify an apparent language bias (due to the divergence between these responses and their behavioral findings), but in reality this variation provides highly valuable clues about the constitutive nature of conceptual competence due to the high consistency of the linguistic response (Alexander, 2012, pp. 110–113).

Therefore, it is not simply a matter of inquiring as to whether experimental economics can isolate the robust intuitions of agents on a given concept. We must first be aware of the dual nature of these intuitions. If we understand that these intuitions are manifested only at a linguistic level (an assumption shared by proponents of classical conceptual analysis, experimental philosophers and Kauppinen), then experimental economics alone cannot provide reliable methodological tools to identify such intuitions. However, if we assume, as we should, that our conceptual competence is of a dual nature, experimental economics can provide a more methodologically reliable way to access at least some level of our conceptual competence, enriching in this way the method of experimental philosophy.

13.6   Conclusion

Experimental ethics assumes that our responses to hypothetical questions formulated by questionnaires and vignettes provide a reliable means of access to our moral intuitions. According to this recent approach, these moral intuitions serve as empirical data that effectively delineate the principles governing our conceptual competence. Although this methodological procedure is a firm step forward in providing empirical content to proposals aimed at clarifying concepts, the use of questionnaires and vignettes in experimental ethics blurs the difference between robust conceptual intuitions and apparent conceptual intuitions, that is, those which are extremely sensitive to bias or prejudice caused by irrelevant factors related to the experimental design itself.

To correct this shortcoming, which is motivated in part by a too narrow view of our conceptual competence, in this chapter we have recommended adopting some general methodological principles from experimental economics. What we have proposed is simple: experimental ethics would do well in enriching its methodology (based on questionnaires and vignettes, and an overly linguistic bias) with behaviorally-oriented experiments. This would allow us to identify more clearly the contours of our conceptual competence in those contexts that are relevant for normative discussions – attribution of moral responsibility, fairness, etc.

Enriching experimental ethics in the manner that we suggest could certainly give rise to tensions, but immediate benefits as well. An obvious benefit would be the possibility of having a framework that allows us to judge whether certain biases in our responses are constitutive of our conceptual competence in relation to a given concept C and whether other biases (especially divergent in relation to the behavioral manifestation of our conceptual competence on C) are the result of illusions, ideological mechanisms, or prejudices: aspects that have little to do with the function linked to C.

In addition to making a general methodological recommendation, in this chapter we have also discussed what types of experiments could contribute to identifying our robust conceptual competence. According to our proposal, Rawls's reflective equilibrium would provide a good framework for designing experiments aimed at identifying the behavioral aspects of our robust conceptual competence. Implementing reflective equilibrium in experimental settings would respect the inherent complexity of situations in which agents decide according to a normative principle, the interactive nature of these situations, and the important role of learning in these decision-making contexts. The use of the conventional methods of experimental economics would ensure that individuals involved in complex decision-making processes will reflect on different moral principles and make quasi-real decisions based on the principles they consider to be the most solid. In short, Rawls's framework would provide us a way to test the actual choices of agents in experimental settings.

Acknowledgements

We acknowledge financial support by the Spanish Government through the Research Projects *Agency, Identity, and Normativity,* FF2011–25131 (Fernando Aguiar and Antonio Gaitán) and *Second-Order Concepts. An Expressivist Account,* FFI2010-15704 (Antonio Gaitán).

References

Aguiar, F., A. Becker, and L. Miller (2013) 'Whose Impartiality: An Experimental Study of Veiled Stakeholders, Involved Spectators and Detached Observers', *Economics and Philosophy*, 29, pp. 155–174.

Alexander, J. (2012) *Experimental Philosophy: An Introduction* (London: Polity Press).

Alfano, M. and D. Loeb (2014) `Experimental Moral Philosophy´, *The Stanford Encyclopedia of Philosophy* (Summer 2014 Edition), Edward N. Zalta (ed.), URL = <http://plato.stanford.edu/archives/sum2014/entries/experimental-moral/>. Retrieved 8 July 2014.

Appiah, K. A. (2008) *Experiments in Ethics* (Harvard: Harvard University Press).

Bicchieri, C. (2006) *The Grammar of Society: The Nature and Dynamics of Social Norms* (Cambridge: Cambridge University Press).

Camerer, C. and E. Fehr (2004) 'Measuring Social Norms and Preferences Using Experimental Games: A Guide for Social Scientist', in J. Heinrich, R. Boyd, S.

Bowles, C. Camerer, and E. Fehr (eds) *Foundations of Human Sociality: Economics Experiments and Ethnographic Evidence from Fifteen Small-Scale Societies* (Oxford: Oxford University Press), pp. 55–95.

Cappelen, H. (2012) *Philosophy without Intuitions* (Oxford: Oxford University Press).

Cullen, S. (2010) 'Survey-Driven Romanticism', *Review of Philosophy and Psychology*, 1, pp. 275–296.

Daniels, N. (1996) *Justice and Justification: Reflective Equilibrium in Theory and Practice* (Cambridge: Cambridge University Press).

Eggleston, B. (2010) 'Practical Equilibrium: A Way of Deciding What to Think about Morality', *Mind*, 119, pp. 549–584.

Frohlich, N. and J. Oppenheimer (1993) *Choosing Justice: An Experimental Approach to Ethical Theory* (California: California University Press).

Guala, F. (2005) *The Methodology of Experimental Economics* (Cambridge: Cambridge University Press).

Haidt, J. (2012) *The Righteous Mind* (New York: Allen Lane).

Hauser, M. (2007) *Moral Minds: The Nature of Right and Wrong* (New York: Harper & Collins).

Hertwig, R. and A. Ortmann (2001) 'Experimental Practices in Economics: A Methodological Challenger for Psychologists?' *Behavioural and Brain Sciences*, 24, pp. 383–451

Jackson, F. (2000) *From Metaphysics to Ethics: A Defence of Conceptual Analysis* (Oxford: Oxford University Press).

Kahane, G. (2013) 'The Armchair and the Trolley: An Argument for Experimental Ethics', *Philosophical Studies*, 162, pp. 421–445.

Kauppinen, A. (2007) 'The Rise and Fall of Experimental Philosophy', *Philosophical Explorations*, 10, pp. 95–108.

Knobe, J. and S. Nichols (eds) (2008) *Experimental Philosophy* (Oxford: Oxford University Press).

Konow, J. (2003) 'Which Is the Fairest One of All?: A Positive Analysis of Justice Theories', *Journal of Economic Literature*, 41, pp. 1186–1237.

Margolis, E. and S. Lawrence (eds) (1999) *Concepts: Core Readings* (Cambridge, Mass.: MIT Press).

Nadelhoffer, T. and E. Nahmias (2007) 'The Past and Future of Experimental Philosophy', *Philosophical Explorations*, 10, pp. 123–149.

Nichols, S. (2004) *Sentimental Rules* (Oxford: Oxford University Press).

Nichols, S., S. Stich, and J. Weinberg (2003) 'Metaskepticism: Meditations in Ethno-epistemology', in S. Luper (ed.) *The Skeptics* (Burlington: Ashgate), pp. 227–232.

Petrinovich, L. and P. O'Neill, (1996) 'Influence of Wording and Framing Effects on Moral Intuitions', *Ethology and Sociobiology*, 17, pp. 145–171.

Pettit, P. (1993) *The Common Mind* (Oxford: Oxford University Press).

Pettit, P. (2004) 'Existentialism, Quietism and the Role of Philosophy' in Brian Leiter, ed., *The Future for Philosophy*, Oxford: Oxford University Press, pp. 304–327.

Rawls, J. (1971) *A Theory of Justice* (Cambridge, Mass.: The Belknap Press).

Sosa, E. (2008) 'Experimental Philosophy and Philosophical Intuition', in J. Knobe and S. Nichols (eds) (2008) *Experimental Philosophy* (Oxford: Oxford University Press), pp. 231–240.

Swain, S., J. Alexander, and J. Weinberg (2008) 'The Instability of Philosophical Intuitions: Running Hot and Cold on Truetemp', *Philosophy and Phenomenological Research*, 6, pp. 138–155.

Úbeda, P. (2013) 'The Consistency of Fairness Rules: An Experimental Study', *Journal of Economic Psychology*, http://dx.doi.org/10.1016/j.joep.2012.12.007.

Weinberg, J. (2007) 'How to Challenge Intuitions Empirically Without Risking Skepticism', *Midwest Studies in Philosophy*, 31, pp. 318–343.

Weinberg, J., S. Nichols, and S. Stich (2001) 'Normativity and Epistemic Intuitions', *Philosophical Topics*, 29, pp. 429–460.

Part IV
Critical Reflections

Introduction to Part IV

After parts II and III of this volume have presented selected examples of empirical work in the field of Experimental Ethics and ideas on how to improve its methodology, it is now time to take a step back. The following two chapters in Part IV are both concerned with the general question of how empirical findings in Experimental Ethics relate to the enterprise of systematic philosophical ethics.

In his chapter Jacob Rosenthal skeptically reflects on the general value of survey results for philosophical questions. He claims that surveys of laypersons' philosophical intuitions have no specific bearing on the systematic debates in philosophy, as the questioning of laypersons typically does not yield anything like clear-cut 'folk intuitions' on the matters in question. Instead, intuitions seem to be divided, and Rosenthal argues that it is hardly possible to dismiss minority opinions as mere 'performance errors'. Therefore, in his view, the philosophical options and pros and cons are about the same and as weighty as before. What remains as an achievement, Rosenthal concludes, is that no party can easily claim to represent the 'common sense', thereby saddling the opponents with the burden of argument.

Ultimately arriving at more optimistic conclusions about the role of experiments in ethics, in the following chapter, Nikil Mukerji examines the implications of the observed divergence of lay and expert opinions, or 'intuitions', on issues in moral philosophy. He presents a rejection of three common arguments for the position that we should give no weight to low-level intuitions about cases. All three arguments themselves, he argues, have an empirical basis. The first is the argument from disagreement. Here, Mukerji directly tackles the problem which brought

Rosenthal to his skeptical conclusions about the value of surveys in philosophy. The second argument draws on framing effects. And the third employs debunking explanations. Mukerji aims to make a substantive methodological point about ethical inquiry, namely that low-level intuitions are not to be shunned. Above that, however, he tries to illuminate, by way of illustration, the relation between empirical findings and normative conclusions – a link that is rather intricate and, as Mukerji argues, can only be explored through armchair reflection.

14
Experimental Philosophy Is Useful – But not in a Specific Way

Jacob Rosenthal

In this contribution I try to tentatively assess the relevance of experimental philosophy for systematic philosophy. Imagine that some philosophical claim is debated. Pros and cons are exchanged, thought experiments brought forth; implications are asserted, disputed, and evaluated; specifications and distinctions introduced; etc. – and now the disputants receive information on how ordinary people assess certain scenarios associated with the claim. That is, they learn about 'folk intuitions' on the topic. (In rare cases they may also learn about behavioral data in the narrower sense, or about associated patterns of brain activity. But I will put this aside, as it raises different issues.) How should such findings affect the discussion? This is the question I am going to pursue here. The significance of experimental-philosophical results for philosophical debates could well depend on the debate in question, but as it happens, this is largely not the case – or so it seems to me. To my mind, a general diagnosis can be argued for.

14.1 Introduction: What is behind experimental philosophy?

In its methodological aspects, experimental philosophy is a branch of psychology. Thus, the question concerning its relevance for philosophy could be understood as simply being a case of asking if empirical findings of such-and-such kind are relevant to this-and-that philosophical claim. There is more to it, however.

First, as its designation indicates, experimental philosophy is also a kind of philosophy. It could not be pursued largely independent of it, like other branches of empirical science. The surveys are connected to specific philosophical problems, and thus presuppose familiarity with theories and ongoing debates in philosophy on the side of the investigator. The scenarios and questions could not be framed, nor would the survey results mean much, without intimate knowledge of these debates. Thus, the experimenters not only need philosophical along with psychological expertise, but there is an asymmetry between these: The latter concerns the methodological aspects of the investigation, whereas the former supplies its aim and motivation.

Second, the test subjects are confronted with questions directly concerning (certain aspects of) the philosophical topic, framed in a comprehensible way. Surveys aim at finding out whether ordinary people tend to a causal or rather to a descriptive theory of reference, whether their notion of knowledge is internalistic or externalistic, whether they tend to a deontological or to a consequentialist mode of moral reasoning, or whether they are compatibilists or libertarians concerning free will and determinism. It is not as if their behavior in certain situations was observed in order to draw, for example, conclusions for moral psychology potentially relevant to moral philosophy, but rather the subjects are simply *asked* certain questions that concern moral philosophy. This cannot be done in a straightforward way, to be sure, as people might not understand, but by confronting them with concrete scenarios described without technical vocabulary. It is as if, for example, experimental economics did not investigate into the actions of subjects in experimental settings in order to test the empirical adequacy of certain behavioral models, but rather simply asked test subjects what *they* think how people behave under the relevant circumstances. The results could well be psychologically illuminating, but would have no bearing on the question of the adequacy of the models under consideration.

These peculiarities make experimental philosophy a truly unique enterprise and the question of its philosophical significance especially pressing. Its source is relatively plain, however. It is that in philosophical argument there is much (explicit or implicit) appeal to so-called *intuitions*. If one is not going to be content with implications, captured by conditionals like 'if your concept of moral responsibility is such-and-such, then the person in this-or-that scenario is responsible for what she does', at some point one has to flatly assert or deny that a certain case is a case of moral responsibility. The same goes for any other philosophical topic. The term 'intuition' does not matter here – in this sense, its widespread use is a relatively recent phenomenon. The point is a systematic one: In order to make progress toward a definite stance on a philosophical question, you need some anchoring in assertions that are not conditional in kind.

But how does one know that a certain carefully described case is or is not a case of knowledge, or reference, or morally required behavior, or free will? Well, it is just apparent that the respective predicate applies or does not apply to the case at hand. This, at least, would often be the claim. Such intuitions (whatever they are exactly – a bit more on this later) provide a basis for philosophical reasoning. Consequently, they are not supposed to be mere subjective inclinations, but assumed to be *shared*, and not only by experts, still less by philosophers of a certain provenance (in which case the appeal to them in argument would be pointless), but rather by any reasonable person.

Thus, the role of intuitions in philosophy is sometimes compared to that of perceptions in the empirical sciences. They provide the data on which the theory is built, and if people did not agree on the data, the whole enterprise of empirical science or philosophy would collapse. I cannot investigate into this analogy further here, however. It is not easily assessable, for there are also clear differences: Unlike perceptions, philosophical intuitions may have abstract, general contents, they also arise in connection with purely hypothetical cases, and they probably cannot be calibrated in anything like the way our faculties of perception can. It may well turn out that there is no useful analogy after all.

Anyway, the intuitions in question are supposed to be common-sense- or everyday-intuitions. They concern 'what we would say' about the case at hand. The tacit idea is that our concept of reference or knowledge or moral obligation or free will commits us to certain judgments, so that everybody who masters the respective concept is bound to apply it to a clearly described scenario in the same way. There may be performance errors, to be sure, but by and large the conceptual competence should prevail (more on this later). Properly analyzed, the answers of the subjects reveal theoretical commitments implicit in our everyday ascriptions, and so contribute to the correct philosophical account of reference, knowledge, moral obligation, free will, etc.

If this is the tacit assumption behind appeals to intuition in philosophical debates, it is evident that experimental philosophy is of great importance. Do ordinary people really make the assessments ascribed to them by philosophers who argue for a certain claim and back it up by appeals to intuition? How can we find out without actually conducting surveys? Psychological investigations are required. And they have to be done by people with philosophical expertise. It is of little use, for example, to put forward questions concerning the compatibility of free will and determinism to ordinary people if one has never thought about the different possibilities for explicating 'determinism', or if one simply takes it for granted that determinism precludes the ability to do otherwise than one actually does. If you do not know the respective philosophical debates, you are not sensitive to certain important distinctions and will most likely lump together different issues, so that you can neither formulate the questions properly, nor assess the answers given by the test subjects. The point of experimental philosophy stands.

14.2   Appeal to intuition in philosophical argument and everyday intuitions

Before reviewing actual accomplishments of experimental philosophy, I elaborate on the fundamental matters a bit further. Three remarks are in order.

First, the sketched justification for experimental philosophy is tied to the idea that it is really common-sense-intuitions that are to be given argumentative weight in philosophical discourse, and thus, that the appeal to intuition (whether or not it is called by that name) is meant to refer to *these*. I should not like to claim that this is always the case, still less, that it must be so. What is in the background here is the view that philosophical issues concern – *inter alia* at least – the proper understanding of everyday concepts and their ordinary modes of application. It is not my business here to argue in favor of this understanding of philosophy; I just note that it is widespread. Along with it goes the tacit idea that philosophy cannot easily be revisionary. A philosopher like Plato, on the contrary, who distinguished 'true happiness' or 'true knowledge' from what the man in the street thought about happiness or knowledge, would have little use for surveys. In the Socratic dialogues everyday intuitions are raised all the same, but with the consequence or even the purpose of questioning them and dumbfounding the dialogue partner in order to make him reconsider. *This* kind of eliciting and dealing with ordinary people's answers to philosophical questions is very different from what experimental philosophy does, and this difference reflects a diverging understanding of philosophy.

Second, the talk about intuitions is somewhat misleading, as it suggests a special source, mode, or content of the judgments in question. There is a broad discussion about what philosophical intuitions, properly speaking, are, how much authority can be claimed for them, and how they are to be distinguished from other mental states (see, e.g., the volumes DePaul and Ramsey, 1998; Horvath and Grundmann, 2012; or Booth and Rowbottom, 2014). For reasons of space I do not enter this debate here, but note a dilemma. If 'philosophical intuition' is given a distinctive sense, on the one hand, it is quite improbable that it covers all or most (explicit or implicit) appeals to intuition in philosophical discourse. The greater the extent to which it achieves that, on the other hand, the more open and vague it has to be. Whatever merits a clear-cut concept of intuition may have, whatever epistemological function intuitions in some distinctive sense might fulfill, it is not intuitions in any such sense that are elicited by experimental philosophy. At the very least, there is no reason to think so. Presumably, no interesting kind of mental states is captured by the term 'intuition' in its encompassing sense (see Williamson, 2004; 2007, chapter 7).

When laypersons are asked about certain scenarios, they probably answer quite spontaneously, and without doing much explicit theorizing, the background for which they lack anyway. This does not mean, however, that they do not make inferences, or conscious inferences – after all, they are supposed to make the case at hand clear to themselves, so there is plenty of time for episodes of reasoning. Moreover, nothing is known about a specific conceptual or modal content of people's assessments, or the modal force people would be inclined to ascribe to their answers. We also do not know whether they provide mere guesses or firm convictions, whether or not their answers are based on persistent 'intellectual seemings', or anything of this kind. Thus, it is opinions in the broadest sense of the term the surveys may be said to deliver, and no more. Most importantly perhaps, there is no reason to think that what people say is pre-theoretical in any fundamental sense. There can be little doubt that the philosophical, religious, and scientific disputes of bygone ages as well as our own time and the various theories emerging from them have partly shaped what all of us, and philosophically untrained subjects in particular, think.

So, the 'folk intuitions' experimental philosophy surveys are nothing else than ordinary people's assessments of certain cases, made after not too long a thought. If intuitions of this kind provide a basis for philosophical theory, it is a basis in the sense that we just happen to take certain things as preliminary and defeasible starting points. It is at best an open question whether the answers given by test subjects mirror intuitions in any epistemologically distinctive sense. This, however, does not diminish the relevance of the investigations. When an alleged common sense has a role to play in philosophical argument, it is simply a good idea to test whether the opinion in question is in fact widely shared by ordinary people. Whether you are prepared to call it 'intuition' or not, experimental philosophy cashes out what is otherwise merely assumed. There are no fundamental objections against experimental philosophy that would not also count against the very appeal to intuition in philosophical debates – *if* only this appeal is indeed meant to refer to what 'we' or 'one' or 'any reasonable person' would say.

It is understandable that several worries I can barely mention arise in connection with such surveys. The test subjects may misconstrue the issues at hand or misinterpret central notions. Their answers may depend on irrelevant features of the presentation or its context. Different scenarios may evoke inconsistent responses, in which case it is not clear which should be given priority. The answers people give might be influenced by doubtful pieces of theory or ideology. In short, people's responses may depend on all sorts of distorting influences . Thus, one may feel that they have to be debunked rather than given argumentative weight.

The answer to objections of this sort is the same as before. Even if it was granted that philosophers' judgments are considerably less subject to distorting influences of certain kinds, it would not matter. If you *really* distrust the 'common sense' – and there may be plenty of reason to do so – then you may not appeal to common-sense-intuition or -usage in philosophical argument. Conversely, if you rely on it, you should respect what ordinary people in fact say when asked – unless they are somehow led astray. But again, this leading them astray must not be too easy. If there is such a thing as ordinary people's intuitions, they should be displayed quite consistently and robustly.

For the same reason, one should not be too quick in detecting distorting influences and performance errors. When it is really everyday intuitions and (implicit) theories that are at stake, the task is precisely to find out which features of a situation are considered to be relevant by ordinary people, and in what respect. This is achieved inter alia by varying scenarios. Claiming that people are misled by irrelevant features of the presentation or give inconsistent answers when the scenario is changed is often blatantly circular, simply assuming one's own assessments and distinctions in view of the matter.

To sum up, it is no use to claim that everyday intuitions are such-and-such, but that people, when actually asked, often answer differently. If the appeal to 'what we would say' is meant to carry argumentative weight, it has to introduce an independent element to the debate. Everyday intuitions may not be just hypothetical assessments, made by idealized reasoners or under counterfactual circumstances. There is no point in claiming that *if* people only thought long and hard enough about the issue at hand, they would share one's own opinions. To know the actual judgments of people, one has to conduct surveys. This is the only way to seriously check the validity of appeals to 'what we would say', in contrast to 'what we *should* say'.

Third, not all, but many experimental-philosophical studies seek to find out about the assessments of laypersons by asking several students that have not (yet) taken a course in philosophy. The students volunteer for participation; they are not selected in a way that is liable to yield a representative sample of the student sub-population, let alone of the population as a whole. Moreover, the total numbers of test subjects are rather small: Often just a few dozens, at most a few hundreds. This constitutes a serious methodological objection to experimental philosophy. In the introductory book by Alexander (2012), this embarrassment displays itself in an omission pattern: There are no exact data reported in the main text; the reader is informed about the experimental parameters only in the endnotes. But not about the total numbers of participating subjects! This information is left out altogether. Readers have to estimate those numbers from the reported proportions and significance levels.

Accordingly, most experimental-philosophical results have to be treated with caution. There is no reason to be particularly confident that the results would generalize when more representative surveys were conducted. This problem has to be mentioned, but I am not going to dwell on it. Large and representative surveys are costly and laborious. What experimental philosophers do is not too far away from the general practice in psychology, the social sciences, or experimental economics. Even here, test subjects are very often simply taken from data bases of student volunteers, and in comparable numbers. For the sake of argument I assume that the results we deal with would generalize.

14.3   Actual achievements of experimental philosophy – a case study

The surveys done by experimental philosophy have so far yielded a variety of interesting phenomena. Just to recall some examples (which are all contained in the volume Knobe and Nichols, 2008): The side-effect effect (or Knobe effect) shows that opinions about the intentionality of some behavior strongly depend upon the moral assessment of the agent and the context of the behavior in question. Sensitivity to Gettier cases seems to vary with cultural context, so that it would be considerably more difficult to convince East Asian people that the traditional account of knowledge is defective than Westerners. Also, East Asians seem to favor a descriptive account of the reference of names over a causal one, contrary to what Westerners do. Several studies were conducted on the question of the compatibility of free will or moral responsibility and determinism, with different scenarios and varying explications of determinism. These will serve as my prime example.

One of the most discussed philosophical questions concerning free will and moral responsibility is whether or not they are compatible with determinism (perhaps depending on the *kind* of determinism). The debate is very complex, of course, and several different positions are taken within each camp, but both sides draw to some extent on (alleged) everyday intuitions. Incompatibilists claim that free will and moral responsibility are tied to possible alternative courses of action, that these are precluded when everything that happens is fully determined in advance, and that compatibilists therefore have to dream up surrogate senses of 'can do otherwise' that may look as if they could do the trick for them but are ultimately pieces of sophistry. Compatibilists, on the other hand, feel that the question as to whether or not determinism is true is primarily one of natural science, that no matter what its results and theories are we would and should go on with our usual practices of praising, blaming, and holding responsible, as well as uphold the corresponding judgments, and that it is muddle-headed to suppose that social practices and reactive attitudes toward one another should depend on what we think is going on on some fundamental level in the constitution of matter. This rough-and-ready sketch should do for our purposes. It is fair to say that both sides in some way try to connect to an assumed common sense.

Thus, it is a good idea to investigate into the intuitions of laypersons on the matter. In the surveys of Nahmias et al., varying majorities gave compatibilist answers. In several scenarios, the idea of determinism was spelled out in different ways, and actions of different kinds taking place under deterministic circumstances were depicted. Test subjects were asked whether the described agents were morally responsible for what they did and whether they acted of their own free will. Across the board, most subjects affirmed both of these, with majorities varying between around 60 percent and around 90 percent, depending on the case at hand (see Nahmias et al., 2005; 2006).

Other studies on the same matter had diverging results, however. Nichols and Knobe found that if the question of the compatibility of moral responsibility and determinism is asked in an abstract way, most people answer negatively (around 85 percent). When specific cases are given, there are up to 70 percent compatibilist answers – but only with scenarios that are liable to provoke intense emotions, like a case of cold-blooded murder. When it is about cheating on one's taxes, most people give incompatibilist assessments (see Nichols, 2004; Nichols, 2006a; Nichols and Knobe, 2007).

Only the last result mentioned is in direct conflict with what Nahmias et al. found, but also the general tendency displayed in the studies of the two research groups undoubtedly points in different directions. How could one explain the diverging results? First, different characterizations of determinism may come to mind. In all of the mentioned investigations, 'determinism' and related terms were not explicitly used because apparently laypersons either do not understand them or think that they rule out free will by definition (see Nahmias et al., 2006, section 3). While one could take this as evidence that the common sense favors incompatibilism, Nahmias et al. rather conclude that one has to circumscribe determinism. They have different ideas how to do this, but in all of them not only 'determinism' is avoided, but also, to a large extent, modal phrases like 'is necessary', 'has to happen', 'inevitably', etc. Instead, they prefer to talk about predictability or causation or production or implications of initial conditions and laws of nature, whereas Nichols and Knobe make free use of phrases openly connected to necessity.

Second, there may be performance errors. According to Nichols and Knobe a majority of laypersons has incompatibilist intuitions, but these may give way to the desire to hold the agent responsible in emotionally charged cases. While this nicely fits the results of their own surveys, it does not explain why in the studies of Nahmias et al. people favored the compatibilist answer even in neutral cases. Using the idea of performance errors in quite another way, Nahmias and Murray (2011) have argued that people give incompatibilist answers to certain scenarios because they confuse determinism with epiphenomenalism or fatalism, specifically with the claim that what a person does is not causally or counterfactually dependent on episodes of practical reasoning, volitions, or intentions (see also Nahmias, 2006).

Third, part of the difference between the findings may correspond to general differences in reply to abstract questions and concrete scenarios. That this is a phenomenon occurring in several domains was suspected and preliminarily investigated by Sinnott-Armstrong (2008) (see also Knobe and Doris, 2010). Many people are attracted to general principles regarding a certain concept that do not fit several of its standard applications, presumably because they are too demanding. General principles often set high standards that are partly ignored in practice, so that the concept can be applied without much ado. One may think of ascriptions of intentionality, responsibility, or knowledge. While this may not be particularly surprising, I take it that it is a philosophically relevant topic not yet sufficiently explored.

Let's now put aside speculation about the sources of divergence between survey results and turn to an overall assessment of these. Although there is more material to be reviewed, it would only confirm the fact that there simply are no definite results as to whether or in which respects our everyday notions of free will or moral responsibility are compatibilist or incompatibilist. Still, the widely shared assumption is that they must be one of these, and that appearances to the contrary have to be explained away by reference to distortions of various kinds (for an exception, see Feltz, Cokely, and Nadelhoffer, 2009). Nichols (2006a) as well as Knobe and Doris (2010) envisage varying criteria for free will or moral responsibility, but for different contexts. They still hold that, given a certain context, there is a shared folk intuition on the matter.

It is, however, this very assumption that severe doubt is cast upon by the data. The most straightforward explanation of these is that there is no clear-cut everyday notion of free will or moral responsibility that allows an unambiguous answer to compatibility questions. The majorities vary greatly, and there are always considerable dissenting minorities. Diverging judgments may be traced back to performance errors, to different notions of free will or moral responsibility, or to vagueness in these notions. Or maybe the disagreement is not of a conceptual kind at all. It seems not unlikely that we face some hardly resolvable mix of these factors.

Even so, one can investigate further into these matters. Also, the very fact that there seems to be no unambiguous everyday belief on the compatibility of free will or moral responsibility and determinism may be surprising and was worth eliciting. That said, the philosophical discussion can largely go on as before, as the questioning of laypersons has not even remotely yielded anything like 'what we would say' about the matter. The philosophical problems and options, and pros and cons, are just the same and also as weighty as before. The only achievement of experimental-philosophical investigations concerning the systematic debate is that no one can claim to represent the 'common sense', thereby saddling his opponents with the burden of argument. This can be important indeed, and I will say a bit more about it in the Conclusion. It is an unspecific benefit, restoring or providing the parties with starting points that are symmetrical in this respect. But no position taken in the debate is particularly supported or undermined by the survey results.

Interestingly, one may attempt to use such a standoff in favor of one's own position. Nahmias et al. (2005, 2006) argue that incompatibilism needs to be more intuitive to laypersons than compatibilism to be taken seriously because it is the more demanding position. Why unnecessarily burden our concepts of free will or moral accountability with an implication of ontological indeterminism? It is, however, not at all clear that it is unnecessary to explicate and defend a position that does justice to several people's intuitions, even if these are not the majority. (I grant this contentious claim of Nahmias et al. (2005, 2006) for the sake of argument here.) They are certainly too many to put their assessments aside as 'performance errors'.

14.4 Actual achievements of experimental philosophy – a tentative general assessment

The picture sketched in the last section generalizes. When one takes a closer look at any of the sub-enterprises of experimental philosophy, one has hardly the impression that the corresponding systematic debates within philosophy can or should be influenced by the empirical results to any considerable extent. The surveys yield nothing like a uniform or clear-cut picture. Very often, there is a majority's opinion, but the dissenting minorities are typically quite large. Thus, whatever question is asked, for each possible answer – in most cases there are just two alternatives – there are many people in favor of it.

This is somewhat concealed by phrases like 'people (strongly) tend to' or 'subjects are (much) more inclined to' or 'are (very) likely to say this-and-that' which are often used to report findings of experimental philosophy. Officially, they are just shorthand for what is actually going on, but in fact they are not that innocent. They are liable to give the wrong impression that (almost) everybody tends to or is more inclined to or is likely to make a certain judgment. They suggest truths about each individual, and thus uniformity where none is to be found. Sometimes, qualifications are entirely dropped to yield statements like "In some contexts, people treat agency as indeterminist; in other contexts, they treat agency as determinist" (Nichols, 2006a), which are misleading to a high degree. It would be much better to avoid such phrases throughout and instead talk about what 'many' or 'more' or 'most' test subjects said.

It is the quantitative distributions of survey results, not a problem one could detect from the outset, that deprives experimental philosophy of most of its potential influence on philosophical debates. You simply do not *learn* anything from those figures, as far as the systematic topic under discussion is concerned. Certainly a philosopher should not be bothered when her position is shared by 'only' 20 percent or 30 percent of the laypersons, even if these numbers appear more robustly than in our paradigm case. She knows anyway that several trained and intelligent people disagree with her among her colleagues, but also that many of them hold similar opinions. If she learns that the same is true for untrained subjects, what is she going to make of that? The question becomes all the more pressing if majorities are shaky, depending on wording, context, and scenario, but this seems to be more of an additional problem. The core problem is that it is not at all evident that the numbers elicited by experimental philosophers tell a philosopher more than that there are several laypersons seemingly agreeing, but also several ones apparently disagreeing with her.

A general, but unspecific benefit remains: The results of experimental philosophy remind us of something important that is all too easily forgotten in philosophical disputes, namely, that many philosophical questions, as well as most of the possible answers, have their roots in everyday thinking. They are not far-fetched inventions cooked up in response to hair-splitting problems the common person does not see. The plain truth is that ordinary people are as divided on the appropriate answers to these questions as are philosophers. The exact proportions do not matter much as far as the systematic problem is concerned, nor even on which side the majority falls. Only a large and robust majority would indicate a common sense, but suchlike seems to be lacking in all disputed philosophical topics. I do not pretend to be able to answer the tricky questions as to how large a majority would have to be and what kind of robustness it would have to display in order to count as expression of a shared folk opinion. But that clear criteria are very hard to come by does not mean that there could not be clear cases.

Attempts to show, contrary to appearance, that there is a common sense, but that many people are misled by certain features of some of the scenarios at hand, are liable to make things even more complicated, like in our paradigm example. There is plenty of room for interpretation as to which applications of a concept are genuine and which constitute performance errors, as well as concerning the question whether different people apply different concepts (i.e., associate different concepts with the same verbal expression), or different folk theories tied to a shared concept, or concepts that are vague or open in crucial respects. It is far from clear that it is possible to unravel this, if only in principle.

A philosopher arguing for a certain position *already* has to confront the nagging problem why so many of his colleagues disagree with him. It may easily be as difficult to assess what exactly is going on when laypersons are divided on an issue. That was not clear from the start.

There *could* have been a gain, that is, a clear-cut picture of how laypersons think about the topic at hand might have emerged, but as a matter of fact, it has not happened. Asking laypersons thus proves to be just an epicycle of asking professional philosophers, with the additional disadvantage that it is not clear how many of them misunderstand the issue, are liable to make inconsistent judgments, what justification, if any, they would give for their opinions if they were criticized, how strongly they attach to them, etc.

This obscurity also prevents certain metaphilosophical views from claiming support by experimental philosophy. While the survey results do not speak in favor of particular answers to philosophical questions, they might be taken to confirm a general skeptical or relativistic attitude with regard to those answers. But the problem, sometimes called 'the scandal of philosophy', that there seems to be no consensus among professional philosophers with regard to almost any question of importance, centuries of philosophical enquiry notwithstanding, is already with us. This problem needs to be addressed, and possibly has to teach us important lessons about philosophy, but here, again, the point comes out not more, but considerably less, clear with surveys of folk opinions.

That it is the most straightforward reading of the results that people are simply divided or uncertain with regard to the matter is something experimental philosophers would not easily admit. Alexander, when discussing the 'side effect effect', writes: 'How should we explain these minority responses? Typically, such responses are treated as noise resulting from some kind of performance error' (Alexander, 2012, p. 66). But why are they so treated? There certainly is no in-principle reason to consider the opinion of a minority of 20 percent or 30 percent to be 'noise'. Everyday intuitions should display themselves robustly to deserve the name. As the experimenters did not deliberately try to lead their subjects astray, how could 20 percent or 30 percent of them miss the point? But if it is easy to miss the point – whatever this might mean when "everyday intuitions" are at stake – why can't it be the 70 percent or 80 percent that are in error?

While experimental philosophers are in general reluctant to admit that our everyday intuitions might be non-uniform or undecided, they are happy to discover cultural or socio-economic or gender differences (for an overview, see again Alexander, 2012, chapter 4). This is no surprise, since the former tends to deprive experimental philosophy of its systematic import, whereas the latter indicates that different cultures or socio-economic groups or genders favor different answers to philosophical questions or use crucially diverging concepts in the domain under discussion. It is, however, differences of the very same kind that count as 'performance errors' in the usual context that are supposed to reflect important conceptual or theoretical discrepancies in the latter. Kirk Ludwig, when discussing experimental-philosophical studies on criteria for knowledge ascription, remarks:

> It is not clear, of course, why the variation in responses across groups is to be counted as evidence for variation in norms while the variation within groups is not. If the variation within groups were treated as evidence for variation of norms, then of course the claim that there are different epistemic norms in different cultures or socioeconomic groups would have to be given up. We would get instead the conclusion that the same norms are present in the various groups, but adhered to by different proportions of people. (Ludwig, 2010, p. 161; see also Williamson, 2007, pp. 190–191)

Of course, one may conclude from the fact that even after various investigations nothing like a clear-cut picture as to what 'the folk opinion' on a certain topic might be emerges that further and deeper research has to be done. Perhaps questionnaires have to be supplemented by 'neuroanatomical accounts of the cognitive processes and mechanisms' and 'evolutionary (or other teleological) accounts of the work that our folk concepts are supposed to be doing' (Alexander, 2012, p. 69). Evidently, this opens a rich field for study, but it has no longer to do with experimental philosophy in its particular sense. The case for it shifts ground if survey results are treated as psychological data among others. That results of empirical science can be relevant to philosophy is not in dispute. Information on cognitive processes; on the evolutionary development of certain attitudes, concepts, and practices; and also on what the folk have to say about particular issues can be important in certain respects and for some areas of philosophy. There is no general diagnosis to be made about that. In this respect, however, experimental philosophy does not amount to a new or supplementary methodology of philosophy, but provides just another kind of empirical data that may have to be taken into account by philosophers.

14.5   Conclusion

It seems that there are conflicting tendencies rooted within everyday thought as to what the precise application conditions of certain concepts are. What these tendencies exactly amount to is well worth investigating.

Our concepts might be vague, or undecided in crucial respects, or people might associate different concepts with the same term, or the divergence might not be conceptual at all, but a matter of (implicit) theory. But whatever the right interpretation is, the idea to significantly enrich philosophical disputes by asking the folk is ill-conceived. The assumed 'common sense' apparently does not exist. Rather, the diverging tendencies within everyday thought explain to a good deal *why there are philosophical disputes at all*. Instead of helping to resolve them, the 'everyday intuitions' constitute their background. Experimental philosophy helps to bring this to mind again, and herein lies its utility for philosophical investigations. There is, however, no confirmation or disconfirmation of a particular philosophical account of something by experimental philosophy.

A distinctive achievement, however, is the following: In philosophical argument, there is often the temptation to reduce or even get rid of the effort of bringing forth reasons that speak in favor of one's own position. Instead, the opponents are saddled with the 'burden of proof', because their position is allegedly 'counter-intuitive'. If this maneuver succeeds, the first party can sit back comfortably while the second has to work. The first party declares itself winner by default, so to speak (or, for that matter, in case any serious doubts remain). I cannot assess the merits and drawbacks of such effortless fighting, but observe that at least one effort is required all the same: One has to argue that what the opponents have to say is *in fact* counter-intuitive in some serious sense, in comparison with one's own position.

The results of experimental philosophy accumulated so far show that such a claim should better not rely on a supposed common sense – very likely there is none. It is, on the contrary, quite probable that either party connects to some tendencies inherent in everyday thinking (and consequently also goes against other ones). Either position is intuitive in some respects or to some people, but unintuitive in other respects or to other people. Not that I think that undivided, clear-cut folk intuitions are never to be found – but it seems that very often there are none in philosophically disputed cases.

References

Alexander, J. (2012) *Experimental Philosophy: An Introduction* (Cambridge: Polity Press).

Booth, A. and D. Rowbottom (eds) (2014) *Intuitions* (Oxford: Oxford University Press).

DePaul, M. and W. Ramsey (eds) (1998) *Rethinking Intuition* (Lanham: Rowman & Littlefield).

Feltz, A., E. Cokely and T. Nadelhoffer (2009) 'Natural Compatibilism versus Natural Incompatibilism: Back to the Drawing Board', *Mind and Language*, 24, pp. 1–23.

Horvath, J. and T. Grundmann (eds) (2012) *Experimental Philosophy and Its Critics* (London: Routledge).

Knobe, J. and J. Doris (2010) 'Responsibility', in J. Doris and The Moral Psychology Research Group (eds.), *The Moral Psychology Handbook* (Oxford: Oxford University Press), pp. 321–354.

Knobe, J. and S. Nichols (eds) (2008) *Experimental Philosophy* (Oxford: Oxford University Press).

Ludwig, K. (2010) 'Intuitions and Relativity', *Philosophical Psychology*, 23, pp. 427–445, also in Horvath and Grundmann (eds) (2012), pp. 145–163.

Nahmias, E. (2006) 'Folk Fears about Freedom and Responsibility: Determinism vs. Reductionism', *Journal of Cognition and Culture*, 6, pp. 215–237.

Nahmias, E., S. Morris, T. Nadelhoffer, and J. Turner (2005) 'Surveying Free Will: Folk Intuitions about Free Will and Moral Responsibility', *Philosophical Psychology*, 18, pp. 561–584.

Nahmias, E., S. Morris, T. Nadelhoffer, and J. Turner (2006) 'Is Incompatibilism Intuitive?', *Philosophy and Phenomenological Research*, 73, pp. 28–53, also in Knobe and Nichols (eds) (2008), pp. 81–104.

Nahmias, E. and D. Murray (2011) 'Experimental Philosophy on Free Will: An Error Theory for Incompatibilist Intuitions', in J. Aguilar, A. Buckareff, and K. Frankish (eds), *New Waves in Philosophy of Action* (New York: Palgrave-Macmillan), pp. 189–216.

Nichols, S. (2004) 'The Folk Psychology of Free Will: Fits and Starts', *Mind and Language*, 19, pp. 473–502.

Nichols, S. (2006a) 'Folk Intuitions on Free Will', *Journal of Cognition and Culture*, 6, pp. 57–86.

Nichols, S. (2006b) 'Free Will and the Folk: Responses to Commentators', *Journal of Cognition and Culture*, 6, pp. 305–320.

Nichols, S. and J. Knobe (2007) 'Moral Responsibility and Determinism: The Cognitive Science of Folk Intuitions', *Nous*, 41, pp. 663–685, also in Knobe and Nichols (eds) (2008), pp. 105–126.

Sinnott-Armstrong, W. (2008) 'Abstract + Concrete = Paradox', in Knobe and Nichols (eds), pp. 209–230.

Williamson, T. (2004) 'Philosophical "Intuitions" and Scepticism about Judgement', *Dialectica*, 58, pp. 109–153.

Williamson, T. (2007) *The Philosophy of Philosophy* (Oxford: Blackwell).

15
Intuitions, Experiments, and Armchairs

Nikil Mukerji

Most ethicists agree that moral doctrines should fit our moral intuitions. They disagree, however, about the interpretation of this evaluative criterion. Some predominantly draw on low-level intuitions about cases (e.g., Foot, 1978; Kamm, 2007; Thomson, 1976). Others believe that we should rather trust our high-level intuitions about moral principles (e.g., Hare, 1981; Singer, 1974; Singer, 2005). In this paper, I examine and reject three empirically informed arguments against the former view: the argument from disagreement, the argument from framing effects, and debunking explanations. I will not argue that we are immediately justified to accept our low-level intuitions about cases as moral beliefs. I merely want to dispel doubts about a considerably weaker claim, *viz.* that at least some of our low-level intuitions can count as evidence for (or against) a moral theory.

Though I am critical of certain empirical arguments against the evidential role of low-level intuitions, I am not hostile to an empirically informed approach to ethics. Quite contrarily, I think it holds great promise. However, certain conclusions that have been drawn from experimental research seem to me hasty or flawed. The ulterior motive behind my discussion is to illustrate how empirical findings relate to normative conclusions. This relation deserves close and conscious attention and can only be explored from the armchair. At any rate, so I will argue.

Here is how I shall proceed. I will start by examining John Rawls's ideas about moral epistemology and explain how they make room for empirical investigations. Then, I will offer a general argumentation scheme for empirically informed arguments that attack the moral-epistemological credentials of intuitions. On that basis, I will analyze how these arguments can be criticized. After that, I will examine three empirically informed arguments that seek to discredit low-level intuitions. Finally, I will sum up and conclude with some thoughts on the role of the armchair after the advent of experimental philosophy.

15.1   From reflective equilibrium to experimental ethics

John Rawls's famous idea of 'reflective equilibrium' (RE) can be interpreted in two ways: firstly, as a theory construction device and, secondly, as a theory selection tool. When we use it in the latter way, we compare competing moral theories, A and B, with regard to various evaluative criteria (see, e.g., Mukerji, 2013b, p. 299) before we aggregate the results of this comparison into an overall verdict of the form 'Theory A is to be preferred to Theory B'. One such evaluative criterion within the RE approach is intuitive fit. It says that a moral theory is justified to the extent that is fits our moral intuitions.[1] Let me briefly clarify what this means.

First of all, what is an intuition? There are many different answers to this question. Some authors have characterized intuitions as forms of immediate knowledge (e.g., Russell, 1999, p. 442) or simply as beliefs (e.g., Lewis, 1983, x). In the context of RE, this is not the right way to view them, however. RE presupposes that intuitions can be false (or inadequate) and that we can reject them upon reflection. The best way to do this is, I think, to view them as seeming states. To be sure, seemings are in many respects like knowledge and belief. They have propositional content and they have a 'mind-to-world' direction of fit (Searle, 1983, p. 8; Tolhurst, 1998, p. 293). Unlike knowledge, however, seemings can be false. (I cannot say: 'I know p, but p is false.' But I can say: 'It seems to me that p, but p is false.') And unlike beliefs, I can reject seemings upon reflection. (I cannot say 'I believe p, but I reject p upon reflection.')

Now we can proceed to the idea of intuitive fit. I want to make three points about it.

- Intuitive fit is not an all-or-nothing affair. All moral theories fit our intuitions about individual cases ('low-level intuitions') and our intuitions at the principled level ('high-level intuitions') to higher or lower degrees and are, to that extent, more or less justified.
- Their degree of fit does not depend exclusively on the absolute 'number' of intuitions that it accommodates. What counts is *overall* fit which is also a function of the intuitions' importance. If theory A fits more important intuitions than theory B, intuitive fit may rank A over B, even though B fits more intuitions in absolute terms.

- Not all intuitions count. Intuitive fit merely requires that a moral theory fits those intuitions that possess 'initial credibility'.

These three points can be wrapped up into a concise statement.

Criterion of Intuitive Fit

A moral theory is adequate to the extent that it achieves an overall fit with our *initially credible* moral intuitions.

Note, then, that a definite interpretation of intuitive fit requires a theory of initial credibility that tells us which intuitions are initially credible and which ones are not.[2] This theoretical *desideratum* invites experimental research.

15.2 A general argumentation scheme

As ethicists, we want to avoid including initially incredible intuitions into our moral investigations. Experimental research can provide the data that we need to detect them. But, of course, it cannot do that by itself. Initial (in)credibility is not a property that can be read off straight from the data. We need a philosophical argument for that. In its simplest form, such an argument may be construed as follows.

Argumentation Scheme

(P1) X-intuitions have property P.
(P2) If an intuition has property P, then it lacks initial credibility.
(C) X-intuitions lack initial credibility.[3]

In this paper, I want to examine and reject three experimental arguments against low-level intuitions that I construe as instances of this general argumentation scheme. To this end, I can either reject their empirical premise P1 or their bridging premise P2. Before I do that, however, I should comment on the logic of these arguments.

I asked quite a few philosophers whether the above scheme is logically valid. Almost all of them said 'yes'. But, in fact, there is no telling. The scheme is an instance of what logicians call 'concealed quantification'. That is, P1, P2, and C can each be interpreted as existentially or universally quantified statements. That makes eight interpretations of the above scheme possible, as Table 15.1 shows.

Table 15.1 Possible interpretations of the Argumentation Scheme

P1	P2	C	Inference
Existential	Existential	Existential	*Invalid*
Universal	Existential	Existential	Valid
Existential	Universal	Existential	Valid
Universal	Universal	Existential	Valid
Existential	Existential	Universal	*Invalid*
Universal	Existential	Universal	*Invalid*
Existential	Universal	Universal	*Invalid*
Universal	Universal	Universal	Valid

Note that not all of these interpretations are equally interesting. As I have argued so far, the motivation for putting forward experimental arguments is to arrive at a definite interpretation of the criterion of intuitive fit. We want an evaluative criterion which says: Our moral theories should fit our moral intuitions, while fit with *X*-, *Y*- and *Z*-intuitions is irrelevant, since they *all* lack initial credibility. That is, we are only interested in versions of the argument which warrant the conclusion that *all X*-, *Y*- and *Z*-intuitions lack initial credibility. These are the bottom four. Note, furthermore, that only one out of those four interpretations makes for a logically valid argument. It is the one in which both P1 and P2 are interpreted as universally quantified statements. With this logical note in mind, I will now turn to three stylized arguments against low-level intuitions.

15.3 Moral disagreement

The argument from disagreement[4] begins with an obvious requirement that Henry Sidgwick called the 'criterion of consent' (Sidgwick, 1879, p. 108). Elsewhere, Sidgwick (1907, pp. 341–342) argued that

> the denial by another of a proposition that I have affirmed has a tendency to impair my confidence in its validity. [...] For if I find any of my judgments, intuitive or inferential, in direct conflict with a judgment of some other mind, there must be error somewhere: and if I have no more reason to suspect error in the other mind than in my own, reflective comparison between the two judgments necessarily reduces me temporarily to a state of neutrality.

In other words, if I encounter a reasonable person who disagrees with my intuition about some moral question, this should reasonably decrease my confidence that my intuition is correct. I should consider it initially incredible and should not use it as a premise in moral argument. Based on that reasoning, one can formulate an objection against low-level intuitions using the above argumentation scheme. P1 may be construed as saying that people disagree about low-level intuitions. P2, which employs Sidgwick's point, may be expressed as purporting that, if people disagree on an intuition, then that intuition is not initially credible. From P1 and P2, we would then be able to conclude C, *viz.* that low-level intuitions are not initially credible.

Now remember that for this argument to be formally valid and substantively interesting, both premises have to be interpreted as universally quantified statements. That is, we would have to state the argument as follows:

(P1) People disagree about all low-level intuitions.
(P2) For all intuitions it is true that, if people disagree about them, they are not initially credible.
(C)   All low-level intuitions are not initially credible.

How can the initial credibility of low-level intuitions be defended against this criticism? Let me first say a few words about the 'expertise reply' that has received quite a bit of attention in recent years (e.g., Archard, 2011; Cowley, 2011; Gesang, 2010; Tobia, Buckwalter, and Stich, 2012; Weinberg et al., 2010; Williamson, 2011). It objects that experimental studies usually test lay people's intuitions. If these show widespread disagreement, this does not, by itself, discredit low-level intuitions. What counts are the intuitions of moral philosophers, who are, after all, experts in moral matters. Similarly, we would not dismiss the intuitions of professional physicists because lay physicists disagree with them (Hales, 2006, p. 171).

This response is likely to backfire, as its empirical basis may be questioned. We know that experts often make intuitive mistakes. Experts in statistics, for example, are bad intuitive statisticians (Tversky and Kahneman, 1971). So the fact that moral philosophers are experts does not, in and of itself, get them a pass.

But maybe we should distinguish between various fields of expertise. Perhaps experts in one field, for example statistics, are bad at intuiting their own subject matter, while others are good at it. When statisticians go about their business, they work through complicated formulas. They never rely on intuitions. In contrast, moral philosophers rely heavily on their intuitions when they address moral questions. Therefore, we should expect that they are much better at intuiting moral matters than statisticians are at intuiting statistical problems, such that conclusions that we draw from one case do not necessarily apply to the other.

This is a neat counter-argument. Unfortunately, it fails. If philosophers' intuitions were, in fact, more reliable than lay people's intuitions, we would expect no intuitive disagreements between the former. But moral philosophers disagree about important intuitive questions *all the time*. Jesse Prinz has commented that 'one reason why philosophers seem to have different intuitions about the same cases' is that their 'intuitions are not theory neutral' (Prinz, 2010, p. 387). Rather, they tend to be biased toward their own philosophical position. In fact, this is what we should expect, given what psychologists call the 'confirmation bias' (Nickerson, 1998). It predicts that moral philosophers will tend to respond to moral cases in ways that make them fit with their favored theory.[5] If that is true, the expertise reply is unacceptable.

Here is my answer to the argument from disagreement. I simply think that its first premise is almost certainly false. We may get the impression that intuitive disagreement on moral cases is widespread. But this impression is, I think, caused by the fact that experimentalists have mostly conducted experiments of a particular kind. They have used scenarios that are meant to test a given theory or decide (more or less) conclusively between competing theories.[6] Most of these theories have been around for a while. We should, therefore, expect that they are hard to refute and that any case that aims to do this will elicit significant disagreement. This does not mean, however, that there is disagreement on *all* low-level intuitions, as P1 claims. In fact, there are many cases on which we should reasonably expect no disagreement at all (even among philosophers). As Bernard Gert says, moral questions 'such as whether it is morally acceptable to hurt someone simply because you dislike him are not controversial at all, but because they generate no discussion they tend to be forgotten' (Gert, 2004, p. 14). If that is true, there seems to be no reason why we cannot use at least some low-intuitions to test our moral theories.

Let me add two points to this reply. Firstly, it may be objected that '[t]he universality of moral beliefs about cases like this one [which are uncontroversial] could hardly be used to justify any moral theory or any controversial moral belief' (Sinnott-Armstrong, 2006, p. 349). I doubt that. Uncontroversial intuitions sometimes have surprising and far-reaching logical implications. In fact, social choice theory, which is a branch of inquiry at the intersection of moral philosophy, political theory, economics, and formal logic, is devoted to studying them. Social choice theorists formalize moral principles and examine their implications – often with astonishing results. Amartya Sen, for example, has demonstrated in a well-received theorem that a minimal conception of moral rights, which grants you, say, the right to choose 'whether you should sleep on your back or on your belly' (Sen, 1970, p. 152), is logically incompatible with the weak version of the Pareto Principle. Hence, if you accept the seemingly innocuous idea that all individuals should have at least some moral rights, you have a premise that is logically powerful enough to establish a very controversial moral claim, *viz.* the claim that the Pareto Principle should be rejected. The bottom line is this: As empiricists, we should wait for the evidence to come in. So far, only a small fraction of our low-level intuitions have been tested (Sinnott-Armstrong, Young, and Cushman, 2012, p. 268). So the extent to which people agree on them and what follows from the intuitions they share is still an open question.

Secondly, how intuitions are tested is, of course, a matter of utmost importance. We have to make sure, for example, that people under-stand cases correctly, that they use the concepts as intended, and so on. Experimentalists, I understand, take great care to ensure this (see, e.g., Nadelhoffer and Nahmias, 2007). But we also need to engage in some armchair reflection. We need to determine which kind of evidence would count as (dis)confirming the premises of the argument. In partic-ular, it is important to clarify the notion of disagreement. Suppose one person has a particular intuition about a given case, while 999 persons oppose it. Does that confirm that people disagree on that case? Or does it disconfirm it? Speaking more generally, we need to clarify what P1 actu-ally purports. If we lower the bar for (what counts as) disagreement, we will likely find that people disagree on many things. But note that this would make P2 comparatively less plausible. I, for one, am not willing to regard my intuition that p as initially incredible, merely because one in 1,000 persons intuits that non-p. That means the lower we set the bar for disagreement, the more likely it is that P1 can be supported empirically. But setting the bar low would make P2 rather incredible as a philosoph-ical judgment. Conversely, setting the bar high would make P2 rather acceptable. But it would make P1 comparatively harder to establish. So proponents of the argument from disagreement will have to calibrate it carefully with regard to the argument's central notion. This, I suspect, will be no easy task.

15.4   Framing effects

In an oft-cited paper, Amos Tversky and Daniel Kahneman report that people's intuitions about how one should act in a particular case may change depending on how the choice is verbally framed. Participants were given the following scenario:

> Imagine that the U.S. is preparing for an outbreak of an unusual Asian disease which is expected to kill 600 people. Two alternative programs to fight the disease, A and B, have been proposed. Assume that the exact scientific estimates of the consequences of the programs are as follows: (Tversky and Kahneman, 1981, p. 453)

The first group was presented with this description of A's and B's consequences.

> If program A is adopted, 200 people will be saved. If program B is adopted, there is a 1/3 probability that 600 people will be saved, and a 2/3 probability that no people will be saved. (Tversky and Kahneman, 1981, p. 453)

The second group was given a choice between C and D (instead of A and B). This was the description of their consequences:

> If program C is adopted, 400 people will die. If program D is adopted, there is a 1/3 probability that nobody will die and a 2/3 probability that 600 people will die. (Tversky and Kahneman, 1981, p. 453)

Each group was asked which program they favored. Participants were not asked specifically for their moral intuitions. But it is reasonable to suppose that that is what they reported (Sinnott-Armstrong, 2008, p. 55). In the first group 72 percent favored option A and 28 percent favored option B. In the second group 22 percent favored option C and 78 percent favored option D. Note that the only information participants had about programs A, B, C, and D concerned their effects. Programs A and C and programs B and D, respectively, had the same effects, though these effects were framed differently (i.e., A and B in terms of lives *saved*, C and D in terms of lives *lost*). Such a difference in verbal framing, it seems, should not make a difference in the moral evaluation of the respective options. But, as Tversky and Kahneman (1981) have shown, it does seem to affect people's intuitions.

Not all framing effects depend on the wording of cases.[7] A famous *sequence* framing effect (also called 'order effect') is associated with the work of the philosopher Peter Unger. Unger (1996) observes that in moral thought experiments – most notably the so called 'trolley cases' due to Foot (1978) – there are usually only two choice options. And we tend to have strong intuitions in favor of or against them. Using his 'Method of Several Options' he attempts to show that our intuitions change as further options are added to the choice problem.

Findings like these may give rise to the following argument from framing effects.

(P1) All low-level intuitions are subject to framing effects.

(P2) For all intuitions it is true that, if they are subject to framing effects, they are not initially credible.

(C) All low-level intuitions are not initially credible.

Before I offer my own reply to this argument, I would like to examine whether something like the expertise reply is appropriate in this case. In the previous section, we saw that it cannot plausibly be turned against the argument from disagreement. But perhaps philosophical expertise at least ensures that philosophers' intuitions are less likely to be subject to framing effects. Therefore, one might argue, the fact that lay people's intuitions exhibit these effects is irrelevant because philosophers' intuitions are not affected by them. Note that this is a testable hypothesis, which was, in fact, recently tested and rejected. Schwitzgebel and Cushman (2012) studied the moral intuitions of three groups, *viz.* non-philosophers, philosophers, and ethicists. They found that both low-level and high-level intuitions of philosophers and, in particular, ethicists were affected by the order in which questions were asked. Hence, there is experimental evidence which suggests that the expertise reply cannot reasonably overturn the argument from framing effects.

However, as much as the expertise reply still seems inappropriate, the answer that I gave above still seems appropriate. Until P1 may count as established, more experimental evidence is needed. It is certainly true that many low-level moral intuitions are subject to framing effects. Based on present evidence, however, we should not conclude that all of them are. Not all studies that investigated framing effects in low-level intuitions were able to demonstrate their existence in all the examined cases.[8] But even if they had, the overall number of studies (and the narrow range of cases they have studied) gives us reason to doubt the sweeping conclusion that all our low-level intuitions are subject to framing effects.

In addition, even if it was true that all of our low-intuitions were, in fact, affected by framing effects, this would not mean that we have to dismiss them *tout court*, since P2 seems dubious. At least sometimes, it seems that we can still form an initially credible intuition about a given case, even if our intuitions about that case are subject to framing effects. Here is why. It is not implausible to suppose that framing effects arise because a particular wording (or context) of a case draws our attention to particular features of it. This, in turn, may lead to a problem that is, in fact, well-known to moral philosophers (Cf., e.g., Brink, 1984, p. 117). We tend to neglect other features that may be of equal importance. Since we know that our intuitions are prone to such 'blind spots' (Bazerman and Tenbrunsel, 2011; Sorensen, 1998, p. 273), we should be able to discipline ourselves. We can enrich the description of a given case (or study multiple descriptions of it) in order to ensure that we pay attention to all morally relevant aspects of the choice problem. We can then carefully examine our intuitive verdicts about that problem. To illustrate, take, for example, wording effects of the Tversky-Kahneman type. Let us assume that, in a given case, our intuitions about the preferability of two choice options change as the description of these options changes. That is, we prefer option A over option B when we have to choose between A and B and we prefer option D over option C when we have to choose between C and D, even though A is identical to C and B is identical to D. Once we know that, we should consider both descriptions of the choice problem (and perhaps even further descriptions) and reflect upon them in order to form what we may call an 'all-things-considered' intuition. I do not see why that should not be possible.

15.5   Debunking explanations

A third reason to be skeptical of low-level intuitions is that there might be debunking explanations for them. They might be due to genetically or culturally evolved dispositions for emotional responses to particular cases. Take, for example, our intuitions about killing. Joshua Greene and his colleagues conducted a series of experiments to study when and how strongly people morally (dis)approve of killing innocent persons. In one study, participants were asked to imagine that a runaway trolley was threatening to kill five people working on the tracks of a railway. They could save the five by killing another person. One group was told that they would have to physically push a fat man over the rim of a footbridge and onto the tracks, turning him into a trolley stopper. The second group was told that the fat man was standing on a trap door on the footbridge which they could open by pushing a button. Participants in both groups were asked to report how strongly they (dis)approved of the option to kill on a nine-point scale. Significantly greater approval was found in the second group (Greene et al., 2009).

Greene's explanation for this is that our species developed, as a matter of *contingent* fact, emotional 'point-and-shoot' responses to certain types of cases that our ancestors were frequently exposed to. As Peter Singer comments, '[t]he thought of pushing the stranger off the footbridge elicits these emotionally based responses' (Singer, 2005, p. 348), while the notion of hitting a switch does not. And he goes on to argue that since 'these moral intuitions are the biological residue of our evolutionary history', 'it is not clear why we should regard them as having any normative force' (Singer, 2005, p. 331). (As Greene, 2008, reports, certain judgments about cases are, indeed, associated with increased neural activity in emotion-related areas of the brain, e.g., the posterior cingulate cortex, medial prefrontal cortex, and amygdala.)

Using our general argumentation scheme, the above reasoning can be expressed as follows.

(P1)   All low-level intuitions are caused by emotional responses that evolved throughout our contingent evolutionary history.

(P2)   For all intuitions it is true that, if they are caused by emotional responses that evolved throughout our contingent evolutionary history, they are not initially credible.

(C)   All low-level intuitions are not initially credible.

Much could be said about the empirical and philosophical underpinnings of P1 and P2. Unfortunately, I do not have the space to address them in any detail. Therefore, I will merely make two principled points, which hopefully show that there are reasons to doubt the argument.

Firstly, if our moral intuitions are indeed caused by emotional responses to cases, this seems not, by itself, to be a reason to dismiss them as initially incredible. Contrary to P2, a number of scholars have taken the stance that appropriate emotional involvement is a precondition for reliable moral judgments (e.g., Nussbaum, 2003; Berker, 2009, p. 316, fn. 54). Note, however, that some philosophers, notably Peter Singer, have taken the argument further. They do not object to intuitions merely because they are (allegedly) caused by emotions. Rather, they argue that, since these emotions are the product of our contingent evolutionary history, they are unlikely to pick up on the morally relevant properties. This second argument is fundamentally problematic. Obviously, 'it is necessary to *first* establish which properties are the relevant moral properties' (Ernst, 2007, p. 132, emphasis in the original). Only once that is done can we compare whether our emotions do, in fact, pick up on them. But we can know the morally relevant properties only if we presuppose the correctness of a moral theory. The argument, hence, begs the question against anyone who disbelieves that theory, and it is superfluous for those who already believe it, since the latter can infer the credibility or incredibility of intuitions simply by comparing them with the correct theory.

Secondly, P1 lacks empirical support. Superficially, it seems to be corroborated by the correlation between the occurrence of moral intuitions and emotions. But as Prinz and Nichols (2012, p. 116) point out, currently available data 'are consistent with several different models of how emotions and moral judgment relate'. Whenever variations in some observable phenomenon x (emotion) are associated with variations in y (intuition) and the correlation is statistically unlikely to be accidental, one may hypothesize, for example, that

i. variations in x cause variations in y; or
ii. *vice versa*; or
iii. variations in some other factor, z, cause variations in x and y; or
iv. variations in x cause variations in y whenever some co-factor w is present.

P1 relies on something like hypothesis (i) being correct. According to Huebner, Dwyer, and Hauser (2009, p. 2), however, some of the models of moral judgment that currently 'delimit the most promising avenues for empirical enquiry' are instantiations of hypotheses (ii), (iii), and (iv). For the time being, the debunking explanation for low-level intuitions that I have discussed in this section seems therefore to be empirically unfounded.

15.6   Conclusion

In this paper, I tried to cast doubt on three empirically informed arguments against the evidential status of low-level intuitions in ethics. To this end, I discussed Rawls's RE and showed how it invites experimental research. Its purpose is to determine which intuitions are initially credible and which ones are not. I pointed out that this question cannot be answered purely by observation and proposed a general scheme for philosophical arguments that attack the initial credibility of certain intuitions. After that, I examined three stylized arguments against low-level intuitions. The first holds that they are initially incredible, since people disagree on them. I answered that experiments have so far focused on particularly controversial cases that are meant to test theories. It is hardly surprising that people disagree on them. But this does not suggest that people disagree on *all* low-level intuitions. There are many intuitive matters on which we obviously agree. But since they are so obvious, we tend not to see the forest for the trees and simply ignore them. The second argument I addressed purports that intuitions are not initially credible since they are subject to framing effects. I replied, firstly, that it would be premature to conclude that all low-level intuitions are affected by them and, secondly, that the presence of framing effects should not, by itself, give us reason for concern, as there may be ways to deal with them. The third argument I looked at invokes debunking explanations for low-level intuitions. I rejected it because it relies on an empirical assumption that is not unrivalled and pointed out that it is not clear what its philosophical point is, since it seems either question-begging or superfluous. In conclusion, then, I see no reason to mistrust low-level intuitions based on the arguments I have examined. Of course, that conclusion is not final, most importantly because it rests on certain assumptions that can only be corroborated through an empirical investigation.

At the beginning, I announced that I wanted to make a more general point, *viz.* that we should engage in conscious armchair reflection about the way we draw normative conclusions from empirical research. This, in fact, should be obvious from the general argumentation scheme that I introduced in the second section. Its second premise, P2, bridges the logical gap between the empirical data reported by P1 and the normative conclusion in C. P2 obviously relies for its plausibility on careful philosophical judgments which can only be the product of armchair investigation. But my point has also been made, I think, by the way in which I discussed the three arguments. My answers to them did not consist solely in reviewing empirical data. In the context of the argument from disagreement I remarked that the central notion, *viz.* that of disagreement, needs to be carefully calibrated in order to make the argument work. This task obviously involves a great deal of conceptual clarification and careful philosophical assessment of the matter at hand. The same holds in the case of the argument from framing effects. P2 says that all intuitions that are subject to framing effects are initially incredible.

In response, I suggested that framing effects may not be problematic by themselves and that there may be ways of addressing them. Perhaps this is not entirely correct. But it is clear that anything we can say in this context is a matter of philosophical judgment, which – again – is the product of armchair reflection. Finally, when I discussed debunking explanations for low-level intuitions, I raised a general worry, *viz.* that such explanations seem either question-begging or superfluous. Again, perhaps I am wrong here. But that cannot be decided by an experiment. Rather, we need to devote attention to the way the philosophical argument runs. And that was the point I wanted to make.

Since the arguments I discussed were construed as instances of a rather general scheme of argumentation, a more general conclusion suggests itself. I submit that we can *never* decide philosophical issues only based on experiments. Even after the advent of experimental philosophy, philosophical issues are still decided as they always have been, *viz.* by armchair reflection. Of course, to the extent that this reflection relies on factual assumptions, it should be informed by experimental findings. But it is reasonable to suspect, I think, that a great share of ethical investigation will still rely on philosophical judgment as well as on careful reflection about conceptual matters and inferential relations. The articles in this volume are no doubt inspiring. But we should not draw hasty conclusions from them. In any case, we should not burn our armchairs. If we want to do philosophy, we *will* still need them in the future!

Acknowledgment

I would like to thank Johanna Jauernig, Robert Hümmer, Christoph Luetge, Hannes Rusch, Matthias Uhl, and the participants of the GAP.8 workshop 'The Scope and Limits of Experimental Ethics' for their helpful comments on an earlier version of this paper.

Notes

1. As Kappel (2006, p. 132) points out, reflective equilibrium can be factorized into a number of sub-criteria. I have discussed them elsewhere (see Mukerji, 2013a).
2. Rawls has no complete theory of initial credibility. He only gives us a few examples of dubitable intuitions (see Rawls, 1971/1999, p. 42).
3. For certain purposes, this argumentation scheme may be too simple. For a more complex scheme, see, for example, Bengson (2013).

4. This argument should not be confused with two other arguments by the same name, which are directed, respectively, against moral realism (see, e.g., Brink, 1989) and experimental ethics (see Kauppinen, 2007).
5. I suspect that, for the most part, the confirmation bias plays out unconsciously. But some authors seem to be quite aware of it. The consequentialist moral philosopher Alastair Norcross (2008, p. 66), for example, says that he is 'all too aware that non-consequentialists' intuitions diverge radically from [his] own' consequentialist intuitions.
6. For example, Greene et al. (2001) and others have tested trolley cases. Brigard (2010) and others have tested Nozick's 'experience machine' up one way and down the other.
7. Framing effects can be categorized in various ways. Levin, Schneider, and Gaeth (1998), for example, partition them into 'risky choice framing effects', 'attribute framing effects', and 'goal framing effects'.
8. Petrinovich and O'Neill (1996), for example, failed to detect wording-related framing effects in specific trolley-type cases.

References

Archard, D. (2011) 'Why Moral Philosophers Are Not and Should Not Be Moral Experts', *Bioethics*, 25, 3, pp. 119–127.

Bazerman, M. H. and A. E. Tenbrunsel (2011) *Blind Spots: Why We Fail to Do What's Right and What to Do About It* (Princeton: Princeton University Press).

Bengson, J. (2013) 'Experimental Attacks on Intuitions and Answers', *Philosophy and Phenomenological Research*, 86, 3, pp. 496–532.

Berker, S. (2009) 'The Normative Insignificance of Neuroscience', *Philosophy and Public Affairs*, 37, 4, pp. 293–329.

Brigard, F. de (2010) 'If You Like It, Does It Matter If It's Real?', *Philosophical Psychology*, 23, 1, pp. 43–57.

Brink, D. O. (1984) 'Moral Realism and the Sceptical Arguments From Disagreement and Queerness', *Australasian Journal of Philosophy*, 62, 2, pp. 111–125.

Brink, D. O. (1989) *Moral Realism and the Foundations of Ethics*, Cambridge Studies in Philosophy (Cambridge: Cambridge University Press).

Cowley, C. (2011) 'Expertise, Wisdom and Moral Philosophers: A Response to Gesang', *Bioethics*, 26, 6, pp. 337–342.

Ernst, Z. (2007) 'The Liberationists' Attack on Moral Intuitions', *American Philosophical Quarterly*, 44, 2, pp. 129–142.

Foot, P. (1978) *Virtues and Vices and Other Essays in Moral Philosophy* (Berkeley and Los Angeles: University of California Press).

Gert, B. (2004) *Common Morality: Deciding What to Do* (New York: Oxford University Press).

Gesang, B. (2010) 'Are Moral Philosophers Moral Experts?', *Bioethics*, 24, 4, pp. 153–159.

Greene, J. D. (2008) 'The Secret Joke of Kant's Soul', in *Moral Psychology (Volume 3): The Neuroscience of Morality: Emotion, Brain Disorders, and Development*, edited by Walter Sinnott-Armstrong, pp. 35–80 3 (Cambridge, Massachusetts: MIT Press).

Greene, J. D., F. A. Cushman, L. E. Stewart, K. Lowenberg, L. E. Nystrom, and J. D. Cohen (2009) 'Pushing Moral Buttons: The Interaction Between Personal Force and Intention in Moral Judgment', *Cognition*, 111, 3, pp. 364–371.

Greene, J. D., B. R. Sommerville, L. E Nystrom, and J. D. Cohen (2001) 'An fMRI Investigation of Emotional Engagement in Moral Judgment', *Science*, 293, 5537, pp. 2105–2108.

Hales, S. D. (2006) *Relativism and the Foundations of Philosophy* (Cambridge, MA: The MIT Press).

Hare, R. M. (1981) *Moral Thinking: Its Levels, Method and Point* (Oxford: Clarendon Press).

Huebner, B., S. Dwyer, and M. Hauser (2009) 'The Role of Emotion in Moral Psychology', *Trends in Cognitive Sciences*, 13, 1, pp. 1–6.

Kamm, F. M. (2007) *Intricate Ethics: Rights, Responsibilities, and Permissible Harm (Oxford Ethics Series)* (Oxford: Oxford University Press).

Kappel, K. (2006) 'The Meta-Justification of Reflective Equilibrium', *Ethical Theory and Moral Practice*, 9, 2, pp. 131–147, doi: 10.1007/s10677–005–9006–2.

Kauppinen, A. (2007) 'The Rise and Fall of Experimental Philosophy', *Philosophical Explorations*, 10, 2, pp. 95–118.

Levin, I. P., S. L. Schneider, and G. J. Gaeth (1998) 'All Frames Are Not Created Equal: A Typology and Critical Analysis of Framing Effects', *Organisational Behaviour and Human Decision Processes*, 76, 2, pp. 149–188.

Lewis, D. (1983) *Philosophical Papers: Volume I* (New York: Oxford University Press).

Mukerji, N. (2013a) 'The Case Against Consequentialism Reconsidered', PhD Thesis, LMU Munich.

Mukerji, N. (2013b) 'Utilitarianism', in *Handbook of the Philosophical Foundations of Business Ethics*, Vol. 1, edited by Christoph Luetge, 1st edn, 3 vols, pp. 297–312, Dordrecht: Springer.

Nadelhoffer, T. and E. Nahmias (2007) 'The Past and Future of Experimental Philosophy', *Philosophical Explorations*, 10, 2, pp. 123–149.

Nickerson, R. S. (1998) 'Confirmation Bias: A Ubiquitous Phenomenon in Many Guises', *Review of General Psychology*, 2, 2, pp. 175–220.

Norcross, A. (2008) 'Off Her Trolley? Frances Kamm and the Metaphysics of Morality', *Utilitas*, 20, 1, pp. 65–80.

Nussbaum, M. C. (2003) *Upheavals of Thought: The Intelligence of Emotions* (Cambridge: Cambridge University Press).

Petrinovich, L. and P. O'Neill (1996) 'Influence of Wording and Framing Effects on Moral Intuitions', *Ethology and Sociobiology*, 17, 3, pp. 145–171.

Prinz, J. (2010) 'Ethics and Psychology', in *The Routledge Companion to Ethics*, edited by John Skorupski, pp. 384–396, Routledge Philosophy Companions, Abingdon and New York: Routledge.

Prinz, J. and S. Nichols (2012) 'Moral Emotions', in *The Moral Psychology Handbook*, edited by John M. Doris, 2nd edn, pp. 111–146, Oxford, Oxford University Press.

Rawls, J. (1971/1999) *A Theory of Justice* (Cambridge: Belknap Press of Harvard University Press).

Russell, B. (1999) 'Intuition', in *The Cambridge Dictionary of Philosophy*, edited by Robert Audi, p. 442, Cambridge: Cambridge University Press.

Schwitzgebel, E. and F. A. Cushman (2012) 'Expertise in Moral Reasoning? Order Effects on Moral Judgment in Professional Philosophers and NonPhilosophers', *Mind and Language*, 27, 2, pp. 135–153.

Searle, J. R. (1983) *Intentionality: An Essay in the Philosophy of Mind* (Cambridge: Cambridge University Press).

Sen, A. (1970) 'The Impossibility of a Paretian Liberal', *Journal of Political Economy*, 78, 1, pp. 152–157.

Sidgwick, H. (1879) 'The Establishment of Ethical First Principles', *Mind*, 4, 13, pp. 106–111.

Sidgwick, H. (1907) *The Methods of Ethics* (London: Hackett Publishing).

Singer, P. (1974) 'Sidgwick and Reflective Equilibrium', *The Monist*, 58, 3, pp. 490–517.

Singer, P. (2005) 'Ethics and Intuitions', *The Journal of Ethics*, 9, 3–4, pp. 331–352.

Sinnott-Armstrong, W. (2006) 'Moral Intuitionism', in *Metaethics after Moore*, edited by T. Horgan and M. Timmons, pp. 339–365, Oxford: Oxford University Press.

Sinnott-Armstrong, W. (2008) 'Framing Moral Intuitions', in *Moral Psychology (Volume 2): The Cognitive Science of Morality: Intuition and Diversity*, edited by Walter Sinnott-Armstrong, pp. 47–76 2, London: Bradford.

Sinnott-Armstrong, W., L. Young, and F. A. Cushman (2012) 'Moral Intuitions', in *The Moral Psychology Handbook*, edited by John M. Doris, 2nd edn, pp. 246–272, Oxford: Oxford University Press.

Sorensen, R. A. (1998) *Thought Experiments* (Oxford: Oxford University Press).

Thomson, J. J. (1976) 'Killing, Letting Die, and the Trolley Problem', *The Monist*, 59, 2, pp. 204–217.

Tobia, K., W. Buckwalter, and S. Stich (2012) 'Moral Intuitions: Are Philosophers Experts?', *Philosophical Psychology*, 26, 5, pp. 629–638.

Tolhurst, W. (1998) 'Seemings', *American Philosophical Quarterly*, 35, 3, pp. 293–302.

Tversky, A. and D. Kahneman (1971) 'Belief in the Law of Small Numbers', *Psychological Bulletin*, 76, 2, pp. 105–110.

Tversky, A. and D. Kahneman (1981) 'The Framing of Decisions and the Psychology of Choice', *Science*, 211, 4481, pp. 453–458.

Unger, P. (1996) *Living High and Letting Die* (Oxford: Oxford University Press).

Weinberg, J. M., C. Gonnerman, C. Buckner, and J. Alexander (2010) 'Are Philosophers Expert Intuiters?', *Philosophical Psychology*, 23, 3, pp. 331–355.

Williamson, T. (2011) 'Philosophical Expertise and the Burden of Proof', *Metaphilosophy*, 42, 3, pp. 215–229.

Part V
Future Perspectives

Introduction to Part V

The final part of this volume comprises two original chapters which point out possible directions which the current developments within Experimental Ethics in particular and Experimental Philosophy in general might take.

In his article, Julian Müller argues that philosophers in normative ethics could narrow down their disputes considerably if they agreed on a wider range of socio-economic facts. Further, he argues that these socio-economic facts in question can, for the most part, only be generated by deliberate large-scale social experimentation. He finally endorses the ambitious vision of so called 'Startup Cities', that is, communities of volunteers who are willing to pioneer new ways of living together, as a potential future step in empirical political and social philosophy.

On the background of historical parallels to the controversy around Experimental Philosophy, Hannes Rusch then discusses future prospects of the current developments within philosophy. In the historical debates in psychology and economics he finds astonishing similarities to today's discussions in philosophy. After a brief historical overview he then systematically reviews four central criticisms which Experimental Philosophy is subject to. He attests that three of these are not specifically philosophical. Rather, he argues, they necessarily accompany and drive every introduction of experimental methods to a discipline. Only the question if experimental methods can actually capture the objects of philosophical research, in his view, remains as a – weak – candidate for a specifically philosophical problem. This question is then discussed separately. Finally, Rusch advocates a constructively critical pluralism of methods and demands more serenity. Introducing experimental methods to philosophy, he holds, is an experiment itself. He recommends to simply wait and see if it succeeds.

The closing chapter of the volume presents a qualitative overview of the contributors' opinions on the central questions discussed at length in the individual chapters. The most pressing problems of current Experimental Ethics as perceived by the contributors are identified, and their expectations about the future of the field are unveiled.

16
Large-scale Social Experiments in Experimental Ethics
Julian F. Müller

16.1 Introduction

The move toward experimental ethics might be understood as a coun-
termovement against the overreliance on arm chair philosophy. This
trend in many ways mirrors the recent developments in economics.
For the most part, from the 60s to the 80s, economics relied almost
exclusively on the homo œconomicus model and deductive reasoning.
This was counteracted in recent years by a turn toward experimental
research. Experimental research in economics meanwhile has two broad
branches, laboratory experiments (Kahneman, 2011; Smith, 2008) and
observational studies of field experiments (Ostrom, 1995).

In this article we want to argue that experimental ethics – like experimental economics – should also concern itself with field experiments. In
particular we want to defend two claims: a) that philosophers in normative ethics could considerably narrow down their disputes if they could
agree on a wider range of socio-economic facts and that b) the socio-
economic facts that would be needed for this could only be generated
by *deliberate* large-scale social experimentation. This argument shall be
conducted in four steps. In the first part we want to give an overview
about how socio-economic facts and normative principles are connected
on different levels of ethical theory building. Since normative ethics is
a broad field, we will focus on three kinds of normative rules: *regulations*, *principles of regulation*, and *abstract moral principles*. Based on the
results of this survey, we will argue that much debate in political philosophy results from disagreement over empirical facts and thus could be
resolved if we could get a wider agreement on facts. In the third part
we will defend the claim that the facts that are needed to narrow down
dispute in political philosophy can, for the most part, only be gathered

through deliberate large-scale social experimentation. It shall be argued that although the democratic process generates new knowledge about socio-economic facts, it usually does not generate the socio-economic facts we need to narrow down our normative disagreement. Since the political process will not generate the socio-economic facts we need and large-scale socio-economic experimentation is presumably very expensive and ethically not unambiguous, further questions arise. The immediate question is whether there are other reasons besides academic curiosity that could justify social experimentation. We will answer that the modern democracies could prima facie hugely profit from large-scale social experimentation. This gives us a pro tanto justification to press further and think about which normative requirements deliberate large-scale social experimentation would need to fulfill. Part four will conclude by suggesting that Startup Cities might be a viable and ethically permissible way to implement large-scale social experiments.

16.2   How facts and principles mingle

If we want to understand why political philosophy and social philosophy can profit from a turn toward a more experimental stance, it is first important to understand how empirical facts filter into political philosophy. To get a handle on this complex question, we want to distinguish three levels of normative inquiry: *regulations*, *principles of regulation*, and *ultimate principles*. This approach of categorizing moral rules in many ways is inspired by Cohen (2003).

Regulations ask which kind of rules can solve a certain moral problem or, more generally, can enhance a certain state of affairs. Since regulations are usually concerned with actual social problems, they tend to be more sensitive to questions of feasibility and the actual social constraints and historical roots of the problem. In the philosophical division of labor, formulating regulations is usually done by philosophers and practitioners of applied ethics or by political scientists. Since what counts as a normative problem eligible for regulatory intervention is not unambiguous and every moral problem could be solved by a huge set of possible regulations, philosophers search for instruments to choose and order norms that identify normative problems and suggest solutions. One of the most attractive methods of ordering norms is to look for principles of regulation. Proponents of ultimate principles meanwhile argue that we should not stop at principles to order and choose from the set of regulations, but that regulations as well as principles of regulation are in some way derived from *ultimate principles*. Since we can understand these normative principles as nested in each other, there are good reasons to start the discussion with either regulations or ultimate principles. We decided for starting out with regulations.

16.2.1   Regulations

Applied ethics usually starts with real-world ethical problems. This is in many ways different from traditional political philosophy. Usually, political philosophy on the contrary asks more general questions; for instance: *What is justice? What principles should the institutional system of a modern nation follow?*

If we want to analyze the connection between facts and ethics, it seems appropriate to start with the *problems* to which regulations are the answer. First, it is important to note that social problems are only problems from a certain normative perspective. The income inequality in a society is not in itself a problem, but a problem from the standpoint of egalitarianism. For libertarians inequality of income for instance is not a problem and thus need not be fixed. The identification of a social problem thus already presupposes a certain regulative ideal. But the regulative ideal, for instance some egalitarian principle, not only helps us to identify a problem, it also presents us with a directive. It tells us that the normatively problematic state X should be transformed to the moral equilibrium state Y. Egalitarianism thus not only tells us that modern welfare states are lacking with regards to their distribution of income and opportunities, but also provides us with a goal that we should aspire to: A state of affairs where these discrepancies are at minimum. We could thus formalize:

> A *regulation* is a means to bring about a certain social state that lacks certain normative problematic properties or can in another way equalize them.

Since a regulation is a means to bring about a certain state of affairs, a regulation is also (from a given normative stance) only justified if it can bring about the desired state of affairs. Let us be a little more precise: A regulation X is justified iff X causes a process Y that changes the initial situation A into the equilibrium B and the process Y and the equilibrium B are both justified. What Cohen said about principles of regulation is thus also true for regulations themselves: a regulation is 'a device for having certain effects, which we adopt or not, in the light of an evaluation of its likely effects, and, therefore, in the light of an understanding of the facts' (Cohen, 2003, p. 243).

What is important here is that whenever philosophers or practitioners of applied ethics think about possible regulations that would solve a moral problem they essentially conduct a *thought experiment*. This thought experiment can be understood as a two-step process. In the first process the philosopher imagines which social process p the regulation r_i will cause and in which equilibrium this process will settle. This part of the thought experiment is purely descriptive. An example might be illuminating. Let us assume some children recently got poisoned after chewing on their dolls. It turns out that certain chemicals in the production of the dolls caused these problems. Practitioners of applied ethics now might think about how to prevent such harm in the future. Let us assume they come up with a regulation that states that all dolls need to undergo serious chemical tests before it is allowed to sell them in shops. The philosopher will then try to predict which processes these regulations will cause. He will for instance predict that many small businesses cannot afford the testing procedure of their products and will go out of business, while he conjectures that big businesses will establish their own laboratories to get the testing cheaper and quicker. In the end this transitioning period will lead to an equilibrium with safer dolls and less companies. This prediction is purely descriptive. The first part of the thought experiment consists thus of simulating the perturbed social world.

In a second step the philosopher will normatively evaluate particular salient features of the perturbed social world. Which features of the simulated world he will take into his overall normative calculation will depend on his normative outlook. Thus a libertarian will weight heavy the fact that this regulation will cause many small business to close down and will lament that in the future many people will be robbed of the opportunity to start a new business in the field of doll production. A socialist on the contrary might not weight the infringement of possibilities for small business very highly.

The result of this two-step procedure of first simulating a perturbed social world and secondly evaluating it shall be called a *normative social ontology*. The evaluation of the regulation itself is the sum of many small evaluations of the features of the perturbed social world.

What should be clear by now is that the soundness of a normative social ontology is critically dependent on the sound mental simulation of the perturbed social world. Mentally simulating the perturbed social world is in no way trivial. The literature on complex systems is full of regulations that went awry. The normative social ontology philosophers are developing in thought experiments is thus highly dependent on economic and social background theories. Let us briefly restate where we are: We said that regulations are justified only if they produce the intended result. Whether the regulations can achieve the result is dependent on two factors: A) On the correct simulation of the perturbed social world. B) On the correct normative evaluation of the social world. In the next section we want to analyze how far normative social ontologies can be deficient.

16.2.1.1   *Defunct descriptive part*

The first problem of such a social normative ontology is that the underlying empirical causal claims might be wrong. A simple example shall illuminate this idea. Many people hold, for instance, that the minimum wage is morally justified. If they are asked to give a reason for this belief, they might answer 'because it enables the poor'. The justification of minimum wage in this example thus depends on a purely empirical claim. Wrong descriptive claims thus easily infect normative claims.

In fact one might think that many debates in political philosophy are actually caused not by deep disputes about the validity of normative principles, but essentially by (concealed) disagreement about facts. William K. Frankena seems to share this view:

> Certainly, a large part of the debate about what to do about drugs, pollution, or a war arises because we are ignorant of much of what bears on these problems. [...] I stress these points because I think that moral philosophers cannot insist too much on the importance of factual knowledge and conceptual clarity for the solution of moral and social problems. (Frankena, 1973, p. 139)

The role of facts is especially important in political philosophy and maybe even more so for applied ethics. In applied ethics the goal is to solve particular social moral predicaments. Coming up with successful solutions for real-world moral problems is premised on correct simulation of the (perturbed) social world. If the philosopher makes grave mistakes in his initial simulation, there is of course a high chance that the proposed solutions will not be successful.

16.2.1.2   *Defunct evaluation*

A question which is equally important, but seldom raised, is the question of the evaluative side of the normative social ontology in thought experiments. If we conduct a thought experiment and thus imagine the perturbed world after the implementation of the regulation, we will attach moral value to certain salient features of the simulated social world. So, for instance, if we propose a rule that prohibits organ trading and instead proposes some kind of lottery for organs, we might attach a high value to the fact that everyone in need of organ transplantation now has an equal chance to receive one. The point to be made here is that the normative evaluation of the simulated social world can go wrong in several ways.

16.2.1.3   *Incomplete description*

Practitioners of applied ethics and political philosophy regularly cope with quite distinctive normative problems. The solutions to these problems are often very narrow in scope. If we view normative social ontologies as landscapes, then philosophers often just map the area close to the problem and leave the rest of the landscape uncharted. This of course leads to the problem that many proposed solutions solve one problem and create two new ones. This problem is of course not genuine to normative philosophy, but a general problem of complex systems. What shall be emphasized here is that the problem of *incomplete description* is significantly different from the problem of getting the simulation wrong. Predicting that a minimal income law will raise the average income of all employees might be a true descriptive statement. That such a regulation will lead to more unemployment and thus moral ills of a different kind is not a problem of wrong prediction, but just a problem of incomplete description from a moral point of view.

16.2.1.4   *Incomplete normative mapping*

But even if we have a complete map of all important causal mechanisms that a certain regulation will produce, we might still fail to evaluate the outcomes correctly. A reason for this might be that our normative evaluations are incomplete. This means that we do not, for instance, account for all the goods (and bads) that are realized in collective actions, single actions, or modes of production. Let us assume that a regulation outlaws mass multiplayer online role playing games (MMORPG), for the reason that people who play MMORPGs tend to spend more time online playing the game than engaging in their community activities. Regardless of what we might think of the justification of such a rule, the justification internally might be based on an incomplete normative mapping. Few of us have enough experience in such MMORPGs to understand what values the interaction between strangers in a virtual environment produces. This is mostly because very few practitioners of philosophy, or so we assume, have ever engaged in these games, and thus most do not have firsthand experience with what (moral) values are realized in such games. Experience and the discovery of value meanwhile are intimately linked. Even Gerald Cohen concurs: '[I]t is typically in and through experience that people form and adjust their principles [...]' (Cohen, 2003, p. 232).

The regulation might be thus based on an incorrect calculation of the moral goods and bads, because the advocates of the regulation just have an incomplete understanding of what moral values are produced in MMORPG. Another important point that relates to incomplete normative mapping is the following: The further reaching philosophical plans for changing the world are, the more difficult it gets to anticipate not only the descriptive accuracy of the perturbed world, but also the normative mapping of the perturbed world.

We can thus summarize that regulations are usually designed to solve a problem. The justification of a regulation is dependent on its ability to solve a social problem. We have seen that regulations can go awry because the underlying socio-economic theories are wrong, but also because the normative evaluation of the perturbed social world were defunct. Since we suffer from basic knowledge problems, we usually just have conjectures about which regulations are justified and which are not. The justification of a particular regulation is thus heavily dependent on facts.

16.2.2   Principles of regulations

As was mentioned before, one of the central problems of political philosophy is that there often are different regulations that would solve a social problem. In addition it is often not clear what counts as a social problem in need of a solution and what does not. Philosophers confronted with a host of norms to identify and solve a problem are looking for a way to sort and rank the different norms. *Principles of regulation* do exactly that, they weight and order norms 'in the light [...] of the facts' (Cohen, 2003, p. 241). For reasons of space, we cannot analyze principles of regulations in general, but need to be content with analyzing just a particular example. One of the most famous principles of regulations is without a doubt Rawls's theory of justice. Confronted with a set of possible social arrangements, the two principles of justice pick out the one institutional scheme that gives each person an 'equal right to the most extensive basic liberty compatible with a similar liberty for others' (Rawls, 1971/2005, p. 60). And furthermore they arrange social and economic inequalities 'so that they are both: (a) to the greatest benefit of the least-advantaged, consistent with the just savings principle, and (b) attached to offices and positions open to all under conditions of fair equality of opportunity' (Rawls, 1971/2005, p. 302). If we are interested in the relationship between facts and norms in Rawls's principles of regulation, it seems to be profitable to distinguish two questions. The first one is how facts and norms mingle in the creation of principles of regulation. The second question is in how far facts are important for the application of Rawls's principles.

16.2.2.1   *How facts influence the creation of principles of regulation*

In the current debate about ideal and non-ideal theory, John Rawls's theory of justice is often portrayed as being not 'adequately fact-sensitive' (Farrelly, 2007, p. 845) to give guidance for solving real-world problems. This easily lets one forget that Rawls himself saw contract theory in general and his theory of justice in particular as dependent on natural facts.

> Contract theory agrees, then, with utilitarianism in holding that the fundamental principles of justice quite properly depend upon the natural facts about men in society. This dependence is made explicit by the description of the original position: the decision of the parties is taken in the light of general knowledge. Moreover, the various elements of the original position presuppose many things about the circumstances of human life. (Rawls, 1971/2005, p. 159)

Rawls argues further that 'a problem of choice is well defined only if the alternatives are suitably restricted by natural laws and other constraints' (Rawls, 1971/2005, p. 159). Which set of options is feasible, and thus in the choice-set, is of course in the last instance not only a question that depends on natural facts, but is of course subject to change, in accordance, for instance, to technological progress. But for a choice to yield a definite result, we need not only outline a clear choice set but also, as Rawls tentatively formulates, 'certain inclinations to choose among them' (Rawls, 1971/2005, p. 159) or, to put it differently, some kind of ranking. Thus Rawls concludes: 'Indeed, one cannot avoid assumptions about general facts any more than one can do without a conception of the good on the basis of which the parties rank alternatives' (Rawls, 1971/2005, p. 160).

The conception of the good in Rawls's concept is not only needed to allow for a choice behind the veil of ignorance. It is also a necessary condition for the Rawlsian concept of justice to generate an institutional system that is stable 'for the right reasons' (Rawls, 2005, p. 459).

What is not always recognized is that a necessary condition for the two principles of justice to be justified is that they can generate their own support. If they can actually do so, that is, if they can create an overlapping consensus in a pluralist society, is of course again a purely empirical question.

16.2.2.2 Facts and selecting social worlds

The importance of social scientific facts is not only important for the selection of the 'right' principles of regulation, but also for applying the principles. In this section we thus want to ask: Which institutional scheme is selected by Rawls's two principles of justice? This, importantly, seems to be a purely empirical question. Rawls himself was of the opinion that his two principles of justice will most likely select a property-owning democracy or a certain kind of democratic socialism out of the set of all possible institutional sets (Rawls and Kelly, 2001, p. 138). Which institutional set will realize 'equal right to the most extensive basic liberty compatible with a similar liberty for others' (Rawls, 1971/2005, p. 60), while arranging social and economic inequalities so that they are to be of the 'greatest benefit of the least-advantaged' members of society (Rawls, 1971/2005, p. 60), is of course a very difficult question. Different experts in the fields of economics, sociology, and political science might come to very different answers. It might thus even be the case that a Nozickean minimal state fulfills the conditions of the two principles of justice best. Kofman seems to agree that it is a matter of socio-economic facts which institutional set will be selected by Rawls's two principles: 'Depending on how the characterization of economic, social, and psychological "reality" unravels, a standard egalitarian apprehension is that the [difference principle] could turn Rawls-the-would-be-egalitarian into a von Hayek or Milton Friedman in egalitarian clothing' (Kofman, 2012, p. 249).

Since the question which institutional set realizes the two principles best is a purely empirical question, it cannot be solved by philosophical discourse. But – and this needs to be stressed – it can neither be settled by economic theory. In the end, only continual deliberate social experimentation can do so.

We thus can summarize that empirical facts play a role for both the construction of principles of regulation as well as for their application. At the level of construction, facts are, at least in Rawls's conception, important to constrain the choice set and to delineate a realistic motivational theory that allows us to both choose behind the veil of ignorance and to check if the principles can be stable under reasonably favorable conditions (Rawls and Kelly, 2001, p.13). Secondly, we have seen that Rawls's principles of regulation cannot answer the question of which kind of institutional structure is justified without social experimentation.

16.2.3   Abstract moral principles

We have established that regulations and principles of regulations are highly fact dependent. From philosophy of science we know that the most effective way to gain knowledge about the facts of the world is experimentation. We should at least be open to the suggestion that social experimentation is necessary to make progress in normative ethics. Of course, there are some political philosophers that claim that there is a class of ethical principles that is not grounded in facts. Gerald Cohen, one of the main proponents of this thesis, calls such principles 'ultimate principles' (Cohen, 2003).

Cohen argues that every regulation and every principle of regulation – he calls them 'fact-sensitive principles' – are 'always ultimately grounded also by another principle not sensitive to facts' (Kofman, 2012, p. 251). He thus argues that 'principles that reflect facts must, in order to reflect facts, reflect principles that don't reflect facts' (Cohen, 2003, p. 214).

Cohen explains his thesis in the following words:

> Suppose that proposition F states a factual claim, and that, in the light of, on the basis of, her belief that F, a person affirms principle P. We may then ask her why she treats F as a reason for affirming P. And, if she is able to answer that question, then her answer, so we believe, will feature, or imply, an affirmation of a more ultimate principle (call it P1), a principle that would survive denial of P itself, a principle, moreover, which holds whether or not F is true, and which explains why F is a reason for affirming P: it is always a further principle that confers on a fact its principle-grounding power. (Cohen, 2003, p. 215)

Let us illustrate Cohen's argument with an example. Suppose that Anna holds the principle: *We should pay back our debt* (call that P), *because only if we pay back lent money, trust relationships can exist* (call that F). Cohen now argues that she will then surely agree that she believes that F supports P because she affirms a higher order principle P_1. In our example P_1 would be for instance *we should honor trust relationships*. Cohen explains:

> It is P_1 that makes F matter here, that makes F support P, but the subject's affirmation of P_1, as opposed to whether or not that

affirmation induces her to affirm P itself, has nothing to do, essentially, with whether or not she believes that F. She would affirm P_1 whether or not she believed the factual statement F: P_1 is not, in her belief system, sensitive to whether or not F is true (Cohen, 2003, p. 216)

We might then further press and ask why Anna affirms P_1. She might then answer, *because only if trust relationships exist, human beings can flourish* (F_2). The principle that makes F_2 matter here would be a further principle, for instance P_2, that states roughly: *We should support human flourishing.* If we ask Anna again, why this is the case, she might tell us that there is no further fact that supports P_2. We thus would have discovered the ultimate principle in Anna's system of normative beliefs. A principle that is not sensitive to facts. Cohen holds that every interrogation will not proceed forever (Cohen, 2003, pp. 217–218).

Although Cohen holds that there are ultimate fact-insensitive principles, he nevertheless does not discount the importance of facts for normative theory. His two most important reasons that could be understood as a pro tanto affirmation of social experimentation are: a) that we discover ultimate principles through experience. This does not contradict Cohen's thesis because his thesis is about the logical structure of our normative beliefs and not about the genesis of normative beliefs. Cohen furthermore sees that b) 'facts undoubtedly help to decide what principles of regulation should be adopted, that is, legislated and implemented, if only because facts constrain possibilities of implementation and determine defensible trade-offs (at the level of implementation) among competing principles' (Cohen, 2003, p. 244). This seems to be a similar point to the one made by Rawls, namely that only through the knowledge of facts we know which rules or regulations we should adopt.

We can conclude that even at the level of ultimate principles, experience is the necessary condition of forming and adjusting one's own principles. Given that there are ultimate principles, it is nevertheless true that we could not find them without experiencing and comparing different values.

16.3   Epistemic problems of social philosophy

When it comes to ethical decisions, we usually have a very clear picture of what is at stake and which decision entails what kind of repercussions. But when it comes to the question of which social rules and laws we – as ethical persons – want to live under, our intuitions are blurred. This is in part because we do not have a clear picture of what kinds of social states a new rule will produce, mainly because rule changes often show unintended consequences. While the change of single rules might be morally computable for a rational individual, computing the change of a set of rules becomes next to impossible. The ongoing discussion between liberals and utilitarian libertarians, for instance, is that fierce because both sides evaluate very different normative socio-economic ontologies when they try to imagine the social outcomes within a libertarian society. Libertarians, for instance, believe that cutting back on state action will lead people to be more virtuous in their daily life and better educated. In addition, they think that a libertarian society would produce a host of new social rules and thicker social networks, while at the same time make the society as a whole more wealthy and free. Liberals, on the contrary, envision a libertarian utopia as a society where very few people have everything while most of the people are uneducated, poor, and suffer hardship. As it should be clear, libertarians and liberals do not only disagree on ethics, but also on basic economics and sociology.

One of the underlying premises of normative discourse seems to be the belief that progress in political philosophy can only be achieved by argument and thus by convincing our philosophical rivals. This premise seems to me very dubious for many reasons. John Maynard Keynes, for instance, famously held that: '[I]n the field of economic and political philosophy there are not many who are influenced by new theories after they are twenty-five or thirty years of age' (Keynes, 2011, p. 164).

But even if one is more optimistic about the power of arguments, another objection should give one pause. If one compares predictions in engineering planes and the normative problem of engineering health care systems, one must surely admit that engineering planes is easier. As a naïve philosopher, one would think that since nature is basically law-like it should be a pretty easy deduction to create a plane. So there should be little disagreement within engineering on how to best build a plane – and thus little need for testing conjectures about planes. Interestingly enough, planes, like every machine or engines, are not built like a syllogism. Different parts of a plane will be tested for robustness, and computer models will try to simulate how the airplane as whole will behave under certain stresses. This process usually takes years. But the great success of our technological innovation is not even derived from smart engineers testing all aspects of a machine, but through the competition of teams of engineers that all try out different ideas for making planes better in some way.

The problem of social engineering of course, leaving normative problems aside for a moment, is that the subjects themselves are not soulless things, but individuals who have their own life plans and will adapt and also often sabotage the plans of the social engineer. In addition, the social life is in many ways much more interconnected than the realm of objects. It is just curious that in the realm of normative engineering where we have to deal with more variables and adaptive behavior, we are solely relying on reaching consensus by discussion, although reaching consensus by discussion is not even possible in fields which are much simpler than social engineering.

From this perspective, the pure reliance of normative philosophy on the better argument – even in normative matters that are heavily fact dependent – seems absurd. In the last part we have given an overview of the connection between facts and norms. From this it should be clear that, at least when it comes to regulations and principles of regulations, we could make huge progress just by getting the facts right. Of course this is not the same as claiming that every dispute in normative ethics could be resolved by getting the facts right; this would be equally absurd.

16.4   Large-scale social experiments

A way to narrow down the normative questions would be to get a better grip on the facts of social science. The claim that we want to defend here in this section is that the socio-economic facts that would be needed to narrow down normative disagreement *can only be generated by large-scale social experimentation.*

The question which then immediately arises is why we could not rely on our usual repertoire of qualitative and quantitative methods to get our facts right. Why is it that we need to rely at least partly on deliberate large-scale social experimentation?

It seems to me that this question introduces a false distinction. Qualitative and quantitative methods are tools that can be employed *post hoc*. This means that we can employ the methods of social science to find out what was going on in a special instance of experimentation. The methods of social science can thus tell us something about existing data. The point to be made here is that the data we would need to resolve normative conflicts often just does not exist.

A possible counterargument would be to point out that in the future the democratic process could in principle create all the data we need, and thus there is no need for deliberate social experimentation outside the normal democratic process. We think that the data in question can only be produced *outside* the normal democratic process because the usual democratic process is strongly path-dependent (Denzau and North, 1994). After a nation gives itself a certain set of institutions, an education system, a healthcare system, a social net, and so forth, it will engage in fine tuning. In general, the democratic process will opt for solutions that immediately relieve us from pains. This means that modern democracies mostly engage in fine tuning and hardly ever risk a leap, which further entails that many data which would be needed to settle normative conflicts will never be gathered.

This, of course, leads to the question if deliberate large-scale social experiments would be worth the cost. It surely is dubious whether a society would be willing to invest huge sums of money in social experiments just to satisfy philosophers' thirst for knowledge. The question thus arises if there are additional reasons for deliberate social experimentation. We think there is a clear case for deliberate large-scale social experimentation. If it is true that modern day democracies are mostly engaged in fine tuning, there is a good chance that because of path dependence modern democracies will get stuck on a poor local optimum and thus cannot find forms of social organization that are far superior to ours. It might, for instance, be the case that the Rawlsian scheme of a property owning democracy is not on the route of our democratic learning paths. That of course would entail that if the institutional scheme of a property owning democracy is better, we will never discover it. If one of these grand constitutional ideas really would produce social worlds which are far superior to ours and these worlds could be tested without creating moral bads – or insufferable economic costs – there seems few reason not to engage in testing. Of course, such testing can only be facilitated by actual ethically permissible social experimentation.

We thus can now refine our claim. What we are in need of are social experiments that usually are not on the learning path of existing social democracies. It is surely hard to know which regulations will most likely not be on the path-dependent learning routes of social democracy. But certainly far reaching social experiments with institutional schemes are most unlikely. This is also true for regulations that depend on strongly contested socio-economic theories (e.g., free market economics). On the other hand, some of these institutional schemes and outlandish regulations might prove to be a huge improvement over our current institutional situation.

16.5   Startup Cities and social experimentation

If it is accepted that deliberate large-scale social experimentation could prove beneficial for society and at the same time narrow down normative debates in philosophy, then at least two further questions arise:

- *How can deliberate social experimentation be conducted without treating individuals as objects?*
- *How can we institutionalize a way of testing outlandish but promising regulations and principles of regulation?*

The problem with testing promising principles of regulation is, of course, that they are designed for whole societies. But we already ruled out that democratic nations would elect to dare leaps (and that for good reasons). In my opinion there are some reasons that point to cities as ideal experimental spaces: i) Cities historically have often been prime locations for moral innovation. ii) The transaction costs in cities are relatively small, which is especially important when it comes to collective-action problems (Eichenberger and Funk, 2011), like the implementation of social moral rules. iii) Cities are becoming more and more interested to establish their own brand and develop their own culture (Bell and De-Shalit, 2011).

We want to close with mentioning that an especially interesting idea for implementing morally permissible social experimentation would be Startup Cities (SCI, 2013). A Startup City is essentially a newly founded city that is part of a larger entity like a modern democratic state or a Union like the EU but has considerably more freedom to test different socio-economic policy schemes, while adhering to some minimal standard of human rights and free exit. Choosing Startup Cities as experimental spaces has the clear moral advantage that only people who are willing to be part of an experiment would move to such a city. This of course would also have the benefit that the constituency of such a newly founded city would be more homogenous when it comes to moral views and risk profiles, which would make it considerably easier to test promising proposals of political philosophy.

16.6   Conclusion

In the first part of the paper we gave an overview about how facts and norms mingle on the level of simple regulations, on the level of principles of regulation, and on the level of ultimate principles. As a result of this analysis we concluded that normative theory relies much more on facts in general and in particular on socio-economic theory than is often understood. We further argued that many disputed questions in political philosophy can in principle not be resolved without looking to empirical facts. This is true for debates about regulations as well as for the discussion about and implementation of principles of regulation. In part three we argued that although modern democratic states already conduct many social experiments by legislating on diverse issues, policy making usually restricts itself to matters of fine tuning. The kind of large-scale social experiments political philosophy would need to resolve some of their debates would on the other hand represent actual leaps. This raised the question whether large-scale social experiments of this kind could be justified just by academic curiosity. We argued that such experiments would not only be interesting for purely academic reasons but also could rationalize the democratic learning process. In the final part we presented some preliminary ideas on how large-scale social experimentation could be conducted with regards to institutional implementation and normative permissibility.

According to John Rawls, one important role of political philosophy is 'probing the limits of practicable political possibility' (Rawls and Kelly, 2001, p. 4). We agree with Rawls on this point. In this article we merely added that in the end what is feasible and practicable cannot be decided by mere thought experiments alone.

References

Bell, D. and A. De-Shalit (2011) *The Spirit of Cities: Why the Identity of a City Matters in a Global Age* (Princeton, NJ: Princeton University Press).

Cohen, G. A. (2003) 'Facts and Principles', *Philosophy & Public Affairs*, 31, 3, pp. 211–245.

Denzau, A. T. and D. C. North (1994) 'Shared Mental Models: Ideologies and Institutions', *Kyklos*, 47, 1, pp. 3–31.

Eichenberger, R. and M. Funk (2011) 'Stadtstaaten: Der Schlüssel zu einer besseren Welt', in K. Hummler (ed.), *Stadtstaat – Utopie oder realistisches Modell?: Theoretiker und Praktiker in der Debatte*, Zürich: Neue Zürcher Zeitung, pp. 115–131.

Farrelly, C. (2007) 'Justice in Ideal Theory: A Refutation', *Political Studies*, 55, 4, pp. 844–864.

Frankena, W. K. (1973) *Ethics*, Prentice-Hall foundations of philosophy series, 2nd edn, (Englewood Cliffs, NJ: Prentice-Hall).

Kahneman, D. (2011) *Thinking, Fast and Slow* (New York: Farrar, Straus and Giroux).

Keynes, J. M. (2011) *The General Theory of Employment, Interest and Money* (CreateSpace Independent Publishing Platform).

Kofman, D. (2012) 'How Insensitive: Principles, Fact and Normative Grounds in Cohen's Critique of Rawls', in *Socialist Studies / Études socialistes*, 8, 1, pp. 246–266.

Ostrom, E. (1995) *Governing the Commons: The Evolution of Institutions for Collective Action* (reprint, Cambridge [u.a.]: Cambridge Univ. Press, The Political Economy of Institutions and Decisions).

Rawls, J. (1971/2005) *A Theory of Justice* (Original edn, Cambridge, MA: Belknap Press).

Rawls, J. (2005) *Political Liberalism* (expanded edn, New York: Columbia University Press, Columbia Classics in Philosophy).

Rawls, J. and E. Kelly (2001) *Justice as Fairness: A Restatement* (London, Cambridge, MA: The Belknap Press of Harvard University Press).

SCI (2013) Startup Cities Institute, http://startupcities.org/, date accessed November 21, 2013.

Smith, V. L. (2008) *Rationality in Economics: Constructivist and Ecological Forms* (Cambridge, New York: Cambridge University Press).

17
Philosophy as the Behaviorist Views It? Historical Parallels to the Discussion of the Use of Experimental Methods in Philosophy

Hannes Rusch

> *I favor any skepsis to which I may reply: 'Let us try it!' But I no longer wish to hear anything of all those things and questions that do not permit any experiment.*

(Nietzsche, *Gay Science*, Book 1, §51)

17.1 Introduction

Numerous instances of branchings of new independent disciplines from philosophy can be found in the history of science and scholarship. Standard examples include biology, physics, economics, and psychology, whose pioneers always also were influential philosophers. All of these four sciences possess methodologies of their own now, which always also include experimental methods. Some historians of science even hold that the introduction of experimental methods marks those points in time at which physics and psychology had successfully become independent disciplines of their own – at the time of Galilei in physics and at the time of Wundt in psychology. The examples of economics and biology, however, show that experimental methods can also gain importance within independent disciplines much later – at the time of Priestley and Mendel in biology and at the time of Thurstone in economics (see Roth, 1993).

The recent developments within philosophy, which this volume is dedicated to, most likely represent an instance of the latter type, as it seems unlikely that we are currently witnessing another branching of a new discipline from philosophy. Rather, it seems, experimental methods are finally being introduced to philosophy, too. We observe a noteworthy vehemence, though, with which some established philosophers oppose this young experimental philosophy movement (see, e.g., Horvath and Grundmann, 2012; Sommers, 2011). Instead of adding yet another statement to this debate, however, in this chapter I will discuss historical parallels to the current debate among philosophers and try to delineate possible future developments within philosophy on this basis – without claiming prophetic powers, of course. For pragmatic reasons I limit the discussion of historical parallels to the two most recent introductions of experimental methods within other disciplines, namely psychology and economics. As we will see, there are astonishing similarities between views in these historical debates and contributions to the current dispute in philosophy. For psychology and economics, however, we are in the fortunate historical position to also be able to trace which directions the developments within these disciplines have taken.

17.2   Historical parallels to the current debate about experimental philosophy

17.2.1   Experimental psychology and behaviorism

In his 1913 behaviorist manifesto 'Psychology as the Behaviorist Views It' John B. Watson writes:

> Due to a mistaken notion that its fields of facts are conscious phenomena and that introspection is the only direct method of ascertaining these facts, it has enmeshed itself in a series of speculative questions which, while fundamental to its present tenets, are not open to experimental treatment. In the pursuit of answers to these questions, it has become further and further divorced from contact with problems which vitally concern human interest. (Watson, 1913: 176)

Replace 'conscious phenomena' with 'expert intuitions' and let 'it' refer to 'philosophy' instead of 'psychology' and you have a sentence as it could be found in any programmatic paper by experimental philosophers of today. An opposing view was held, for example, by William

James – who was once disparagingly called an 'arm-chair professor' by Hall, although without explicit mention of James' name (see Hall, 1895; Evans, 1990). James wrote on experimental psychology:

> This method taxes patience to the utmost and could hardly have arisen in a country whose natives could be bored. Such Germans as Weber, Fechner, Vierordt, and Wundt obviously cannot; and their success has brought into the field an array of younger experimental psychologists, bent on studying the elements of the mental life, dissecting them out from the gross results in which they are embedded, and as far as possible reducing them to quantitative scales. (James, 1890/1983; Cf. Evans, 1990: 434–435)

Instead, he presents his ideal of a psychological method, based on 'introspection' by expert psychologists, like this:

> The only safeguard is in the final consensus of our farther knowledge about the thing in question, later views correcting earlier ones, until at last the harmony of a consistent system is reached. Such a system, gradually worked out, is the best guarantee the psychologist can give for the soundness of any particular psychologic observation which he may report. Such a system we ourselves must strive, as far as may be, to attain. (James, 1890/1983; Cf. Evans, 1990: 435)

James' criticism of the experimental method is aimed at denying the validity of its results, a standard objection to every form of experimentalism (see Section 17.3). If we replace 'psycholog...' with 'philosoph...', on the other hand, James' description of his ideal of a psychological research method would perfectly fit into numerous defenses of the traditional philosophical way of working against criticism from experimental philosophers.

As these passages show, there are obvious similarities between the current dispute in philosophy and the debates within psychology, that is, the debates regarding experimental psychology, starting about 1860, and later, from about 1910 onwards, regarding behaviorism. Experimental researchers criticize the lack of 'arm-chair professors'' will to ground their own discipline on exact quantitative foundations. Supporters of classical methods, in contrast, accuse the experimenters of having lost track of the actually relevant questions of their discipline because they are too entangled in the technical details of operationalization and measurement. This is a stance which was later also taken by Freud, who depicted behaviorism as 'vaunting in his naïvety that he had eliminated the psychological problem altogether' (Freud, 1925/1991, p. 79, translated by HR). It is particularly noteworthy that in both debates, the philosophical and the psychological, criticism is not limited to technical details of the experimental method or problems of interpreting specific results, but that the general value of experimenting for the disciplines' scientific progress is questioned (see Section 17.4).

However, one central difference between both debates must be mentioned, too: There is relatively little dispute on the question what the main *explanandum* of psychology is, namely the multitude of human, and sometimes non-human, behavior and thinking, be it conscious or unconscious. Such a consensus, as minimal as it may be, does not seem to be, and probably never was, within reach for philosophers (see, e.g., Golding, 2011).

With respect to the current debate in philosophy it is now particularly interesting to track the developments of the disputes in psychology. Did one of the parties prevail? The well-known answer is: 'no'. The old quarrel of the camps is still virulent within psychology. Some schools in psychology still pursue James' ideal of furthering the discipline by means of expert discourse, while others, particularly cognitive psychologist schools, apply the experimental methods of the empirical sciences and strongly rely on their results. While the latter probably play the more important role in academic psychology, today, theories based on Freudian psychoanalysis, for example, are still taught at many universities. Psychology, as a scientific discipline, was split by the dispute over methods and has not been able to overcome this separation in the last 100 years.

17.2.2 Experimental economics

The second, and most recent, historical parallel to the current debate in philosophy is the experimental branch of economics, which started to grow in the 1950s. Unlike in psychology and philosophy, the introduction of experimental methods to economics was not accompanied by much uproar or dispute (Roth, 1993; but see Section 17.4 below). Today, experiments are a standard method in economics, just like mathematical modelling and case and field studies. Prominent debates in experimental economics revolve around questions regarding the interpretation of certain results (Binmore and Shaked, 2010), the validity of experiments with students (Henrich, Heine, and Norenzayan, 2010), or the methodological soundness of certain studies (Binmore, 2007). Even very critical economists like Binmore, however, regard experimentation as a valuable addition to the tool box of economic research (Binmore, 1999; Starmer, 1999).

There is an important similarity between experimental philosophy and economics, however, although regarding another issue: Just like experimental philosophy, experimental economics began with vignette studies (Thurstone, 1931), in which participants were asked to state their preferences regarding a number of options (Roth, 1993). This method was criticized almost immediately by established economists (Wallis and Friedman, 1942) and soon replaced with decision experiments in which participants face real monetary incentives. This development was substantially facilitated by the introduction of game theory as a formal tool at about the same time (Neumann and Morgenstern, 1944/2007). Similar to the behaviorist movement in psychology, attention shifted from mere self-reported evaluations to decision behavior with actual monetary consequences for the participants also in economics. This focus on monetarily incentivized experiments has become so exclusive in economics, currently, that results from questionnaires are only rarely, and no more than briefly, reported in the economic literature.

On the background of this parallel, it can be asked, if a similar sharpening of methods will be necessary to increase the acceptance of the results of experimental philosophy, and, more importantly, if such a sharpening is possible at all. (An instructive study which shows that this seems possible in the context of the so called 'Knobe effect' was conducted recently by Utikal and Fischbacher, 2009.)

These two briefly outlined examples surely do not exhaust the available set of historical parallels to the current developments in philosophy. They are fruitful enough, however, to allow for a historically informed examination of the current situation in philosophy.

17.3   Central issues in the discussion of experimental philosophy and the historic development of similar debates in experimental psychology and economics

The gist of many current criticisms of experimental philosophy is skepticism regarding the validity of this new methodology, that is, it is doubted that experimental instruments are apt to address questions of actual philosophical relevance, let alone adding to answering them. Two forms of skepticism can be distinguished here: doubts regarding internal and doubts regarding external validity (see, e.g., Campbell and Stanley, 1963; Woolfolk, 2013).

17.3.1 Internal validity

The internal validity of a methodology is at stake when reasonable doubts can be raised that the methodology captures and measures those concepts for whose investigation it was introduced. Doubts of this kind can be raised against at least two characteristics of a research method. First, it could be that the method is completely off target, that is, not measuring what it is supposed to measure. Second, the method could be on target, but at the same time capture too many confounding irrelevant influences so that results are too noisy, making it impossible to arrive at precise statements on causal relationships in the object or system under investigation.

17.3.1.1 *Is experimental philosophy off target?*

In all of the three debates on the introduction of experimental methods, we find contributions which doubt that the new method is at all suited to capture the relevant objects of study. As we have seen above, James, for example, accused experimental psychologists of getting lost in the minutiae of measurement, thus losing track of the relevant objects of study and their complex relationships. Analogously, the beginnings of experimental economics were accompanied by the criticism that subjects' real preferences cannot be elicited by mere survey question-naires (Wallis and Friedman, 1942; Roth, 1993). Moreover, even today there are some economists who hold laboratory experiments to be completely useless for the progress of economic theory (see Oprea and Powell, 2010). In philosophy, finally, many concerns have been brought forward that surveying 'folk intuitions' and the conditions which form them can actually contribute anything useful to philosophical theory, however perfect this measurement process may be (see, e.g., Shieber, 2010; also see Section 17.4).

Experimenters in psychology and economics were able to settle much of the criticism raised against their new methodologies by continuously improving them. In both disciplines this was achieved mostly by a transition from mere questionnaire surveys to the investigation of actual behavior. This helped their acceptance to quite some extent. The doubt that experimental methods can actually capture objects of interest is thus seldom heard in psychology and economics today (but see Oprea and Powell, 2010, for economics). In the 1950s the cognitivist research program in psychology introduced a synthesis of the strictly positivistic behaviorist agenda and the notion that cognitive processes, while not being directly observable, must nevertheless be taken account of in theories of human psychology, a stance owing much of its impact to Chomsky's critique of Skinner's work (Chomsky, 1959). In economics the introduction of experiments was accompanied by the flourishing of behavioral economics on the theoretical side, which tries to reconcile the observed deviations from 'rational behavior', as a neo-classical understanding of economic rationality would predict it, by studying modified variants of the 'homo œconomicus'-model (see, e.g., Tversky and Kahneman, 1974).

Now, can we expect to see experimental philosophy countering its critics by performing a similar 'behavioral turn'? Will an improvement of its methods settle the doubts raised against its right to exist? This is probably one of the few questions which cannot fully be addressed through reference to historical parallels in other disciplines because, unlike experimental psychologists and economists, experimental philosophers and their critics do not even seem to agree what the target of philosophical investigation should be in the first place. Before we get back to this point in Section 17.4, however, let us briefly review the other doubts that can be raised about the validity of philosophical experiments.

17.3.1.2   *Is experimental philosophy too noisy?*

A good example of early criticism regarding lacking exactness of the methods used in early experimental psychology – in this case the method of 'introspection', which was an early attempt at studying psychological processes more objectively – is the following passage by Watson:

> If you fail to reproduce my findings, it is not due to some fault in your apparatus or in the control of your stimulus, but it is due to the fact that your introspection is untrained. [...] If you can't observe 3–9 states of clearness in attention, your introspection is poor. If, on the other hand, a feeling seems reasonably clear to you, your introspection is again faulty. You are seeing too much. Feelings are never clear. (Watson, 1913: 163)

In order to avoid such an arbitrariness inherent in the introspective method – a criticism which again parallels views within current philosophy – Watson suggested focusing research solely on the observation of behavior and thus became the father of behaviorism.

Similarly, critics of experiments in economics repeatedly argued that certain experimental methods were not incentive compatible, that is, subjects' decisions elicited in the lab would be confounded by influences actually irrelevant to the theoretical question in focus. A prominent example of such an influence is anonymity. It still is a matter of debate in experimental economics how much anonymity must be ensured in order to be able to observe subjects' private decisions. This question is a big issue, for example, in the dictator game, which has become a standard tool of experimental economics. It is still an open research question, if subjects' prosocial decisions in this game are caused by reputational concerns provoked by an insufficient degree of anonymity in the experiments or if they are an expression of genuine altruism (see, e.g., Franzen and Pointner, 2012).

In experimental philosophy discussions like this are known, for example, from the critique of the 'Knobe effect'. Knobe and colleagues invested much effort into showing that the main effect does not depend on the wording of the vignettes used or their situational context and into making sure that their designs actually capture the philosophical concept of intentionality. Step by step, experiment by experiment, they ruled out that their observations were confounded by irrelevant influences (Pettit and Knobe, 2009).

Thus, on the background of these historical parallels, expecting 'a solution' to the problem of potentially insufficient exactness of methods in experimental philosophy seems mistaken. Instead, the history of other disciplines, and even recent developments in experimental philosophy itself, show that improving the exactness of experimental methods is a continuous process which might never come to an end. Although experimental psychology and economics were able to agree on minimal standards of exactness and some standard procedures, it is by far not guaranteed that the results obtained in accordance with these standards are unbiased. Rather, in both disciplines it is frequently the case that seminal experimental designs produce striking new observations, which are then carefully dissected in more detailed follow-up experiments in order to allow for a correct interpretation of the initial results (see, e.g., Luetge and Rusch, 2013). It thus should not be understood as a good reason to do away with experimenting in philosophy altogether if the first experiments are criticized because of insufficient exactness. Rather, this criticism should be seen as a challenge to improve methods, as it continuously happened and still happens in psychology and economics as well.

17.3.2 External validity

A second line of criticism of the results of experimental philosophy acknowledges that the new methodology might be apt to capture interesting aspects of philosophical problems. It denies, however, that the results obtained under controlled and therefore very artificial conditions are generalizable. It is doubted that the inference from the philosophical experimental lab to the real world is permissible. Here, again, two main lines of such criticism can be distinguished.

17.3.2.1 *Generalizability with respect to subjects*

The first objection to generalizability of most experimental results, in philosophy just like in psychology and economics, usually is that university students are not representative of the population in general. It is a commonplace that the results of experimental psychology first and foremost are results on psychology students. Moreover, systematic biases of these results are almost inevitable as these students are Westerners, highly educated, and from industrialized, rich and democratic countries ('WEIRD people', Henrich, Heine, and Norenzayan, 2010). Although the practical feasibility of everyday research frequently limits studies to this subject pool, when interpreting the results obtained here, we must always be aware that this 'convenience sample' likely deviates from the world population in many respects (Henrich, Heine, and Norenzayan, 2010). Experimental economists face an additional problem: Critics raise the suspicion that business and economics students might additionally differ from students of other subjects, as self-selection into the study of business and economics and the perpetual exposition to economic theory – which allegedly raises plain egoism to the status of economic rationality – might lead to biased distributions of characteristics like fairness norms or preferences for reciprocity in this particular sample (but see, e.g., Neubaum et al., 2009).

17.3.2.2 *Generalizability with respect to situations*

The second objection to the generalizability of experimental results raises the question if observations of behavior under artificial laboratory conditions can be taken as representative of behavior in the real world. Even if we assume the representativeness of the sample of experimental subjects in the laboratory, both economics and psychology face the problem of not knowing how natural their subjects' behavior is, that is, how 'ecologically valid' the observations made in the lab actually are. Frequent problems include:

- inference from decision behavior in economic games to real-world behavior (Yamagishi et al., 2012, showed that even the inference from observed behavior in one game to behavior in other games is not warranted);

- the so-called 'experimenter demand effect' (see, e.g., Zizzo, 2010);
- oversimplified experimental designs which preclude unambiguous interpretation of results (see, e.g., Binmore, 2007); or
- insufficient levels of anonymity (see, e.g., Franzen and Pointner, 2012).

All these issues are well-known in psychology and economics and are most relevant also in experimental moral philosophy, that is, Experimental Ethics, where moral attitudes are frequently measured using self-reported preferences stated in questionnaires presenting intricate moral dilemmas.

There is no simple reply to both these lines of criticism regarding external validity. While it might be the case that for some research questions, for example, in the psychology of perception, small samples of 'WEIRD people' are enough to establish fundamental effects, usually single experiments do not yield more than a first indication that something interesting might have been found. If first tentative findings then attract enough interest from colleagues, follow-up experiments will clarify the conditions under which a potential effect can be observed, and specifically devised field studies and the analysis of archive data, not necessarily in this sequence, will explore its scope. Only if all of these efforts lead to convergent results, we can speak of a tested and well-tried empirical theory. Only few theories have reached this status in psychology today. Among the best candidates is probably Thorndike's and Skinner's theory of operant conditioning (see, e.g., Skinner, 1956). In economics, Kahneman and Tversky's 'prospect theory' may be an aspirant for a candidacy (Kahneman and Tversky, 1979).

From a historical perspective, it is also important to note that the experimental method has not become an all-purpose tool in economics or psychology. Rather it has taken its place among a number of other, complementary methods. Its application is limited to a specific range of research questions, and it has to stand perpetual intra- and interdisciplinary criticism. It is an open question if such a situation will be reached in philosophy as well. On the historical background briefly outlined here, the problems raised by critics, however, that experimental philosophy might yield results which are too noisy and do not generalize to a sufficient degree in order to be of interest with respect to philosophical issues, do not appear to be unsurmountable obstacles, but rather challenges spurring experimentalists on to improve their methods.

The only potentially fatal problem of the experimental endeavor in philosophy that remains, thus, is whether experimental philosophy can actually capture philosophical issues (see Section 17.3.1.1). The next section is dedicated to this question.

17.4   Does experimental philosophy have a specifically philosophical problem at all?

In order to be able to give an answer to the question if experimental philosophy can add to the progress of philosophy in general, we first need to answer the question of what we should regard as 'philosophical progress'. If we did not at least aim at approximating a generally acceptable answer to this question, the discussion of the relevance of experimental philosophy for philosophy in general would be vain anyway. The opposing sides of this debate should then make better use of their time and simply wait in frictionless, contact-free coexistence for the answer which the history of science and scholarship will give in the long run – which seems to be the current situation in psychology (see Section 17.2.1).

Although psychologists have reached a minimal consensus about what the central questions of their discipline are, they have been unable to agree on the methods which should be used to investigate them, impeding any further cooperation between the different schools.

Also in economics – although certainly not in the main focus of scientific attention – a debate on the question can be observed, if experiments are apt to test economic theories at all (see Oprea and Powell, 2010). In a simplified account, some economists take the stance that economic theorizing is a purely aprioristic enterprise. Experiments which show that the assumptions of economic theories are violated, in this view, cannot be taken as arguments against these theories. All that the experiments are said to show is that, in a given specific situation, the assumptions of certain economic theories do not apply. From the perspective of philosophy of science, we get a strong impression that this rationale eventually leads to an immunization strategy (also see Starmer, 1999). It shows, though, that also in economics voices can be heard which call the relevance of experimenting into question.

Do we thus have to be pessimistic about the possibility of a settlement of the current debate in philosophy? The following section tries to outline a suggestion of how an amicable agreement could be reached.

17.4.1   The systematic place of experiments in philosophy

Let us, for simplicity, assume that a consensus had been reached on what 'philosophical progress' actually means – unfortunately this likely is a counterfactual assumption (Feyerabend, 1989; Golding, 2011). What object is it then which philosophy gathers more and more information about? A look at the variety of philosophical subdisciplines immediately shows that there is no such thing as 'the object of philosophical study'. Rather, the many branches of philosophy – logic; epistemology; and philosophy of science, metaphysics, aesthetics, ethics, and more – have quite distinct fields of study. Now, most important for the question about the relevance of experimental methods for a particular field of study are the means by which philosophical research is trying to tackle its objects of study. Two categorically distinct approaches have to be distinguished here: There is, first, an analytical and normative approach. Its aim is the development of languages which allow for the consistent and exact description of objects of philosophical interest. It is mainly concerned with devising and refining definitions, for example, of the concept of 'knowledge'; developing ontologies for its fields of interest; and trying to work out criteria for the comparison of the 'goodness', or 'suitability', of languages for certain purposes. There is, second, another approach which is mainly descriptive and historical. This approach investigates and compares people's views regarding questions of philosophical relevance and tries to understand, or even explain, these views and the conditions that caused them in the terms elaborated by analytical philosophers.

The systematic place of experiments in philosophy obviously is descriptive-historical philosophy. Only here questions about factors which might exert systematic influence on philosophically relevant abilities and attitudes, or 'intuitions' – for example, logical thought, perception and cognition, religious beliefs, or moral and aesthetical judgments – can be posed. For analytical-normative philosophy, the real world only becomes relevant if it is claimed that the devised concepts and theories describe this world as it is, and not only as it could be. No analytical-normative philosopher, however, can be forced to raise this claim. Nonetheless, it is also clear that a philosophical anthropology, as, for example, Kant proposed as the aim of philosophy, is possible only when these two approaches are combined.

17.4.2 The function of experiments in philosophical enquiry

In such a philosophical anthropology, whose aim is the understanding and explanation of the factual situation of mankind in a well suited language, the experiment will then, analogously to other disciplines, take one place in a set of complementary research tools. The only difference to other disciplines will be the area of research: philosophers simply ask other questions. For all of the five core areas of philosophical research mentioned above, significant experimental results already exist: Logical thought has been found to be context sensitive (Cosmides and Tooby, 1992); knowledge might partially be represented probabilistically in our memory (Vul and Pashler, 2008); religiousness correlates with cognitive styles (Shenhav, Rand, and Greene, 2011); moral judgment interferes with the ascription of intentionality (Knobe, 2003); and disgust can change moral judgments (Pizarro, Inbar, and Helion, 2011). These experimental findings, among others, require explanation in a philosophical anthropology whose goal it is to understand current – and past – human existence. On the other hand, this also implies that in analytical-normative philosophy, which only deals with the description of possibilities and their evaluation, experiments have no function at all.

17.4.3   Excursus: Where descriptive and normative philosophy meet

However, at least from the perspective of one particular philosophical school, namely philosophical naturalism (see, e.g., Rusch, 2010), the just-mentioned distinction between the historically descriptive and the analytically normative part of philosophy can be called into question. Laying out this argument in more detail would require many intermediate steps which are all debatable, do not need to be accepted, and go beyond the scope of this chapter. I will therefore only sketch its core rationale: In a naturalistic view of the world a theory, particularly also a normative theory about moral or aesthetical judgments, cannot be true solely because it is elegant, or consistent, or morally desirable. The highest status a theory can attain is to be generally accepted, and factual acceptance is something that can be investigated in historical and descriptive enquiries. When this view of the status of theories is accepted itself, the problem of having to distinguish normative from descriptive theories disappears, and only descriptive theories remain (see, e.g., Voland, 2004). In such a philosophical anthropology, the experiment then becomes almost indispensable (Holtzman, 2013).

It should be explicitly stressed, however, than such an argument only works when backed by naturalistic metaphysics, which nobody can be forced to accept. For many other philosophical schools with alternative metaphysical views, this argument is not convincing. Here, the function of experiments remains limited to testing the descriptive contents of philosophical theories.

17.5 An example of successful experimental research on questions of philosophical relevance and the threat of a detachment of philosophy

Before we come to a summary of the historically comparative perspective on the current situation in philosophy, at least one example of current research should be mentioned. It shows how fruitful experimentation can be with regard to philosophically relevant issues and illustrates one imminent threat which academic philosophy is currently facing: detachment and increasing isolation.

In the course of the development of modern sociobiology (Wilson, 1975/2002), evolutionary psychology (Barkow, Cosmides, and Tooby, 1992), and evolutionary game theory (Smith, 1982), biologists, psychologists, and economists have devoted much effort to the problem of understanding how cooperative behavior can evolve and stabilize, or even prevail, in evolutionary processes. Countless theoretical models have been developed, field studies conducted, and laboratory experiments devised to investigate human reciprocity and fairness norms (see, e.g., Nowak and Highfield, 2011). Although the results of this field of study currently cannot be explained by one unified theory – which is partly due to the Babylonian confusion of terms and concepts which permeates this field, whose clarification would be a task worthwhile for analytical philosophers – research in this field has shed quite bright light on originally philosophical questions, namely questions regarding the human state of nature and the evolution of human sociality (Hobbes, 1651/2012; Hume, 1739/2010). By now, seminal empirical findings have been made regarding, for example:

- how fair sharing can evolve on biological markets (André and Baumard, 2011);
- how egalitarianism can become the norm in sizeable groups despite the unequal distribution of power and strength (Gavrilets, 2012);
- human willingness to incur costs in order to prevent unequal distributions (Dawes et al., 2007); or
- the existence of prosocial preferences even in our closer primate relatives (Rusch, 2013).

This short list already shows that whole fields of research can flourish as soon as the historically descriptive parts of philosophical theories have been laid out in enough precision and detail so that they can be submitted to empirical tests. However, we can also observe that, as soon as empirically working researchers start to get interested in philosophical questions, many of the respective philosophers start to withdraw. Thus, it can happen, for example, that moral philosophers do away with 'trolley research', which has become an institution of its own now (see, e.g., Appiah, 2008), by regarding it as mere 'moral psychology', not even to speak of the reflection and interpretation of results from evolutionary psychology (see, e.g., Kurzban, DeScioli, and Fein, 2012).

Projecting these patterns on a possible future development of philosophical research indicates a crucial threat: By continuing down this lane, philosophy could more and more lose touch with the other disciplines and pauperize to a mere residual category of academic research which has no longer anything to say about current developments in the empirical (social) sciences. Maybe experimental philosophy is a means to counter this threat. In order to do so, it would be desirable, however, that experimental philosophy broadened its scope to become a real intermediator between the empirical sciences and philosophy and if it improved its methodology beyond the frequently – and often rightly – criticized vignette studies.

17.6   Conclusion: 'We err up'[1]

In this chapter I have tried to argue on the grounds of a historical comparison of the current situation in philosophy with similar developments in psychology and economics that much of the criticism raised against experimental philosophy is not specifically philosophical, but rather accompanies experimental research in all disciplines. The only – weak – candidate that remained for a specifically philosophical issue was the skeptical question if experimental philosophy can capture any philosophically relevant phenomena at all. We have seen that similar concerns also were raised in the beginning of experimental psychology and economics, but experiments have nevertheless successfully made their way into the tool box of both disciplines by now, where they now complement the available research methods. Analogously, I hold that we should understand experimental philosophy as a new tool to be added to the set of available philosophical methods, not as replacement for them.

We cannot, of course, infer from the historical developments in psychology and economics to the future of experimental philosophy. The space of possibilities covers everything: the experimental movement in philosophy might soon die away, experimental philosophers might decide to switch over to other disciplines, or experiments might become a new tool in philosophy. In this last case, another multitude of developments is conceivable: experimental philosophy might peacefully coexist with other methods, could be brought into fruitful relation with them, or even replace some of them. It is an open question which of these routes will be taken by the history of science and scholarship. From the perspective of philosophy of science, however, good reasons exist to speak up for a critical but constructive pluralism of methods (Albert, 1968/1991), even though this might entail the cost of having to discuss methodology in great detail, as the contributions in this book do.

Finally, one note should not be forgotten: Following, for example, Vollmer (1988), the scientific method of 'trial and (the elimination of) error' is self-applicable. We are in the fortunate historical position to be able to witness an attempt by committed young colleagues to introduce a new scientific method to philosophy. Time will tell if this attempt will succeed – 'Until then, it may be best not to try to fit all scientists into any single mold' (Skinner, 1956).

Note

1. This phrase is borrowed from Gerhard Vollmer's obituary for Karl R. Popper titled 'Wir irren uns empor' (Vollmer, 1995).

References

Albert, H. (1968/1991) *Traktat über kritische Vernunft*, 5th edn (Tübingen: Mohr).
André, J.-B. and N. Baumard (2011) 'The Evolution of Fairness in a Biological Market', *Evolution*, 65, 5, pp. 1447–1456.
Appiah, K. A. (2008) *Experiments in Ethics* (Cambridge MA u.a.: Harvard Univ. Press).
Barkow, J. H., L. Cosmides, and J. Tooby (eds) (1992) *The Adapted Mind: Evolutionary Psychology and the Generation of Culture* (New York: Oxford University Press).
Binmore, K. (1999) 'Why Experiment in Economics?', *The Economic Journal*, 109, 453, pp. 16–24.
Binmore, K. (2007) *Economic Man—or Straw Man? A Commentary on Henrich et al.*, http://else.econ.ucl.ac.uk/papers/uploaded/262.pdf.
Binmore, K. and A. Shaked (2010) 'Experimental Economics: Where Next?', *Journal of Economic Behavior & Organization*, 73, 1, pp. 87–100.
Campbell, D. T. and J. C. Stanley (1963) *Experimental and Quasi-experimental Designs for Research* (Boston: Houghton Mifflin).
Chomsky, N. (1959) 'Review of B.F. Skinner's "Verbal Behavior"', *Language*, 35, 1, pp. 26–58.
Cosmides, L. and J. Tooby (1992) 'Cognitive Adaptions for Social Exchange', in J. H. Barkow, L. Cosmides, and J. Tooby (eds) *The Adapted Mind: Evolutionary*

Psychology and the Generation of Culture (New York: Oxford University Press) pp. 163–228.

Dawes, C. T., J. H. Fowler, T. Johnson, R. McElreath, and O. Smirnov (2007) 'Egalitarian Motives in Humans', *Nature*, 446, 7137, pp. 794–796.

Evans, R. B. (1990) 'William James, "The Principles of Psychology," and Experimental Psychology', *The American Journal of Psychology*, 103, 4, p. 433.

Feyerabend, P. (1989) *Irrwege der Vernunft*, 1st edn (Frankfurt am Main: Suhrkamp).

Franzen, A. and S. Pointner (2012) 'Anonymity in the Dictator Game Revisited', *Journal of Economic Behavior & Organization*, 81, 1, pp. 74–81.

Freud, S. (1925/1991) 'Selbstdarstellung', in S. Freud (ed.) *Gesammelte Werke. Chronologisch geordnet* (Frankfurt am Main: Fischer).

Gavrilets, S. (2012) 'On the Evolutionary Origins of the Egalitarian Syndrome', *Proceedings of the National Academy of Sciences*, 109, 35, pp. 14069–14074.

Golding, C. (2011) 'A Conception of Philosophical Progress', *Essays in Philosophy*, 12, 2, pp. 200–223.

Hall, G. S. (1895) 'Editorial', *American Journal of Psychology*, 7, pp. 3–8.

Henrich, J., S. J. Heine, and A. Norenzayan (2010) 'The Weirdest People in the World?', *Behavioral and Brain Sciences*, 33, 2–3, pp. 61–83.

Hobbes, T. (1651/2012) *Leviathan* (Oxford: Clarendon Press).

Holtzman, G. (2013) 'Do Personality Effects Mean Philosophy Is Intrinsically Subjective?', *Journal of Consciousness Studies*, 20, 5–6, pp. 27–42.

Horvath, J. and T. Grundmann (eds) (2012) *Experimental Philosophy and Its Critics* (London, New York: Routledge).

Hume, D. (1739/2010) *A Treatise of Human Nature* (Oxford: Oxford University Press).

James, W. (1890/1983) *The Principles of Psychology* (Cambridge, MA: Harvard University Press).

Kahneman, D. and A. Tversky (1979) 'Prospect Theory: An Analysis of Decision under Risk', *Econometrica*, 47, 2, p. 263.

Knobe, J. (2003) 'Intentional Action and Side Effects in Ordinary Language', *Analysis*, 63, 279, pp. 190–194.

Kurzban, R., P. DeScioli, and D. Fein (2012) 'Hamilton vs. Kant: Pitting Adaptations for Altruism Against Adaptations for Moral Judgment', *Evolution and Human Behavior*, 33, 4, pp. 323–333.

Luetge, C. and H. Rusch (2013) 'The Systematic Place of Morals in Markets', *Science*, 341, 6147, p. 714.

Neubaum, D. O., M. Pagell, J. A. Drexler, F. M. McKee-Ryan, and E. Larson (2009) 'Business Education and Its Relationship to Student Personal Moral Philosophies and Attitudes Toward Profits: An Empirical Response to Critics', *Academy of Management Learning & Education*, 8, 1, pp. 9–24.

Neumann, J. von and O. Morgenstern (1944/2007) *Theory of Games and Economic Behavior*, 60th anniversary edn (Princeton: Princeton University Press).

Nowak, M. A. and R. Highfield (2011) *Supercooperators: Evolution, Altruism and Human Behaviour or Why We Need Each Other to Succeed*, 1st edn (Edinburgh u.a.: Canongate).

Oprea, R. and B. Powell (2010) 'Why Austrians Should Quit Worrying and Learn to Love the Lab', in R. Koppl, S. Horwitz, and P. Desrochers (eds) *Advances in Austrian Economics* (Bingley, UK: Emerald) pp. 145–163.

Pettit, D. and J. Knobe (2009) 'The Pervasive Impact of Moral Judgment', *Mind & Language*, 24, 5, pp. 586–604.

Pizarro, D., Y. Inbar, and C. Helion (2011) 'On Disgust and Moral Judgment', *Emotion Review*, 3, 3, pp. 267–268.

Roth, A. E. (1993) 'The Early History of Experimental Economics', *Journal of the History of Economic Thought*, 15, 2, pp. 184–209.

Rusch, H. (2010) 'Naturalistic Impositions', in U. J. Frey (ed.) *The Nature of God – Evolution and Religion* (Marburg: Tectum) pp. 129–157.

Rusch, H., (2013) 'What Niche Did Human Cooperativeness Evolve In?', *Ethics and Politics*, 15, 2, pp. 82–100.

Shenhav, A., D. G. Rand, and J. D. Greene (2011) 'Divine Intuition: Cognitive Style Influences Belief in God', *Journal of Experimental Psychology: General*, 141, 3, Aug 2012, 423–428. doi: 10.1037/a0025391.

Shieber, J. (2010) 'On the Nature of Thought Experiments and a Core Motivation of Experimental Philosophy', *Philosophical Psychology*, 23, 4, pp. 547–564.

Skinner, B. F. (1956) 'A Case History in Scientific Method', *American Psychologist*, 11, 5, pp. 221–233.

Smith, J. M. (1982) *Evolution and the Theory of Games*, 11th edn (Cambridge: Cambridge University Press).

Sommers, T. (2011) 'In Memoriam: The X-phi Debate', *The Philosopher's Magazine*, 52, 1, pp. 89–93.

Starmer, C. (1999) 'Experiments in Economics: Should We Trust the Dismal Scientists in White Coats?', *Journal of Economic Methodology*, 6, 1, pp. 1–30.

Thurstone, L. L. (1931) 'The Indifference Function', *The Journal of Social Psychology*, 2, 2, pp. 139–167.

Tversky, A. and D. Kahneman (1974) 'Judgment under Uncertainty: Heuristics and Biases', *Science*, 185, 4157, pp. 1124–1131.

Utikal, V. and U. Fischbacher (2009) *On the Attribution of Externalities*, http://www.twi-kreuzlingen.ch/uploads/tx_cal/media/TWI-RPS-046-Utikal-Fischbacher-2009-09.pdf.

Voland, E. (2004) 'Genese und Geltung. Das Legitimationsproblem der Evolutionären Ethik und ein Vorschlag zu seiner Überwindung', *Philosophia Naturalis*, 41, pp. 139–153.

Vollmer, G. (1988) 'Mehr oder weniger Vernunft. Kritisierbarkeit, Selbstanwendbarkeit und andere Rationalitätskriterien', in G. Vollmer (ed.), 1993, *Wissenschaftstheorie im Einsatz. Beiträge zu einer selbstkritischen Wissenschaftsphilosophie* (Stuttgart: Hirzel).

Vollmer, G. (1995) 'Wir irren uns empor. Zum Tode des Philosophen Karl Raimund Popper', *Skeptiker*, 8, 1, pp. 4–6.

Vul, E. and H. Pashler (2008) 'Measuring the Crowd Within: Probabilistic Representations Within Individuals', *Psychological Science*, 19, 7, pp. 645–647.

Wallis, W. A. and M. Friedman (1942) 'The Empirical Derivation of Indifference Functions', in O. Lange, F. McIntyre, and T. Yntema (eds) *Studies in Mathematical Economics and Econometrics* (University of Chicago Press) pp.175–189.

Watson, J. B. (1913) 'Psychology as the Behaviorist Views It', *Psychological Review*, 20, pp. 158–177.

Wilson, E. O. (1975/2002) *Sociobiology: The New Synthesis*, 2nd edn (Cambridge, MA: Belknap Press of Harvard University Press).

Woolfolk, R. L. (2013) 'Experimental Philosophy: A Methodological Critique', *Metaphilosophy*, 44, 1–2, pp. 79–87.

Yamagishi, T., Y. Horita, N. Mifune, H. Hashimoto, Y. Li, M. Shinada, A. Miura, K. Inukai, H. Takagishi, and D. Simunovic (2012) 'Rejection of Unfair Offers in the Ultimatum Game Is No Evidence of Strong Reciprocity', *Proceedings of the National Academy of Sciences*, 109, 50, pp. 20364–20368.

Zizzo, D. J. (2010) 'Experimenter Demand Effects in Economic Experiments', *Experimental Economics*, 13, 1, pp. 75–98.

18
Outlook: Current Problems and Future Perspectives of Experimental Ethics

Christoph Luetge, Matthias Uhl and Hannes Rusch

The chapters assembled in this volume, we think, show that Experimental Ethics is well on its way. We have seen that Experimental Ethics has quite a clear mission, that is, the empirical research of human moral reasoning in its relationship to classical philosophical ethics, and a historical foundation to build on (Part I of this volume). It is concerned with important current issues in moral philosophy (Part II) and able to reflect on and progressively improve its methods (Part III). Finally, it can speak up for itself in response to its critics (Part IV).

With this short chapter we would like to close this volume by presenting an overview of today's most pressing problems of Experimental Ethics and an outlook on future directions which this new branch within Experimental Philosophy might take. Instead of stating our own, partisan, views on these questions, however, we chose to leave the final words to a (non-representative) sample of expert philosophers, that is, our volume's contributors. To this end, we asked them to state their qualified opinions on a number of questions regarding the current state of affairs in Experimental Ethics in a short questionnaire – anonymity was guaranteed. As sample size is limited, prohibiting elaborate statistical analyses, we will review their responses qualitatively in the following.

18.1   Views on the demarcation problem of Experimental Ethics

We asked our contributors to state their opinion on two questions regarding the scope of Experimental Ethics: (a) within Experimental

Philosophy, and (b) in contrast to moral psychology. Their answers show that particularly the second delimitation is taxing. Most of our contributors agree that Experimental Ethics is that part of Experimental Philosophy which is primarily concerned with the study of moral reasoning – including justification and metaethical stances – moral intuitions, and the usage and implications of ethical concepts in real life, as opposed to arm-chair thought experiments. Regarding the question if there is a specific difference between moral psychology and Experimental Ethics, however, our contributors are much less decided. The following answer can be seen as representative:

> I don't see much of difference between these [Experimental Ethics and moral psychology]. Those who identify themselves as psychologists will speak of 'moral psychology' those who lean toward the philosophical side may speak of 'experimental ethics'. Maybe, the experimental ethicist will put more emphasis on the theoretical background and on conceptual clearness, while the moral psychologist will be more concerned with the experimental part. Anyway, I think that both terms are largely interchangeable. Why shouldn't there be an overlapping research field to which both philosophers and psychologists can contribute?

18.2   Most important contributions to Experimental Ethics so far

We also asked our contributors to point out which of the recent contributions to the empirical study of morality they hold to be most seminal. Interestingly, and revealing of the fact that the scope of Experimental Ethics is quite broad already, not too many works were mentioned repeatedly. Nonetheless, the works by Joshua Knobe and Joshua D. Greene were most frequently elected by our contributors. In addition, the works on folk intuitions about free will and compatibilism by Eddy Nahmias and colleagues also received multiple nominations. Further mentions include the results obtained on prosocial preferences by experimental economists. Finally, as the most important philosophical contribution by Experimental Ethics itself, our contributors repeatedly identified its challenge to traditional ideas of the possibility of grounding normative claims by recourse to folk morality.

18.3   The most pressing problems of contemporary Experimental Ethics

In our short survey we asked our contributors to name the three most pressing problems they observe in current Experimental Ethics and point out which improvements they hold to be most urgently needed in the further development of the field. The following list presents the tenor of their answers in order of perceived importance: most to least important.

1. *Methodological rigor needs to be increased.*
   Our contributors unanimously agree that Experimental Ethics needs to develop more methodological rigor. Apart from the standard problem of overreliance on small convenience samples, our contributors addressed a lack of thoroughness in the presentation of experimental designs, procedures, and results which they hold to be quite common in the current literature. Moreover, they see an urgent need for better statistical training of philosophers and for better control for biasing effects in philosophical experiments. Some of our authors suggested that more detailed process models of moral decision making could help overcoming some of these issues, as having a theory on the cognitive processes in focus would force experimenters to operationalize their concepts quite sharply. Notably, our contributors also repeatedly demanded more self-criticism by Experimental Ethicists. Although they might attract short-run attention in the philosophical community, far-reaching conclusions drawn from very limited samples, these authors remind us, impede the long-term acceptance of experimental methods in philosophy rather than foster it.

2. *The relation of Experimental Philosophy and traditional philosophy needs to be clarified.*
   The next big issue identified by our contributors is the current lack of a consistent theoretical framework for Experimental Ethics – as for Experimental Philosophy in general. Very interestingly, thus, although most of our contributors are active Experimental Ethicists, they feel that a sound theoretical foundation which integrates the young experimental branches of philosophy with its more traditional roots is a requirement for sustainable growth in this field. Apart from the increase in self-criticism and theoretical discretion demanded from their colleague experimentalists by some of our authors, another measure proposed is more awareness of the history of philosophy. 'In a

more romantic vein', one of our contributors stated, 'I think that some big thinkers – David Hume and Adam Smith are clear examples – are still a wonderful source of inspiration for Experimental Philosophy. They are still marking new paths to think about core concepts, cases, customs, etc. So it would be nice to explore further this legacy.'

3. *The acceptance of experimental methods in philosophy needs to be improved.*

   Apart from being urgent desiderata from a theoretical point of view, the just mentioned current problems of Experimental Ethics are also perceived by our authors as hindering the acceptance of this young field within philosophy. This lack of acceptance, though, also poses a problem itself: young philosophers, some of our contributors attest, although favorable of the experimental approach to philosophy, shy away from fully engaging in the field, as prospects of publication and thus career options in academic philosophy seem less promising for experimentalists than for more traditionally oriented philosophers.

4. *Experimental Ethics needs to expand its methodological tool-box.*

   Most of our contributors, furthermore, hold current experimental work in philosophy to be too limited methodologically. The heavy use of surveys, although understandable from a practical perspective, is deemed too unaspiring. Many of our colleagues stated that Experimental Ethics should: (1) import methodological expertise from other disciplines, like economics, psychology, and sociology; (2) focus more on the investigation of actual behavior, ideally in natural environments, instead of relying on hypothetical self-reports; (3) use more elaborate content analyses of answers stated in free form instead of presenting subjects with preformatted answer options; and (4) adjust itself closer to the methodological rigor and standard procedures of other sciences in general.

5. *Experimental Ethics needs closer integration with other disciplines.*

   Finally, another point was repeatedly raised by our respondents: many of them wish for a closer integration of the experimental strands in philosophy with other empirical disciplines. While our contributors see this as a suitable way of importing methodological knowledge into philosophy, they also highlight that experimentalists in philosophy are currently inclined to 'reinvent wheels' which are well tested and smoothly turning in neighboring disciplines already. By working together more closely with experts from these established disciplines, our authors hold, Experimental Ethicists could thus safe time and more easily link up with the state of the art in empirical social science.

18.4   Views on the future of Experimental Ethics

Finally, we asked our contributors to state where they see Experimental Philosophy in ten and twenty years from now and in the farther future and whether they anticipate that it will be eventually accepted by more traditional philosophers as a coequal branch of the discipline. While most of our authors do anticipate further growth of the experimental field within philosophy and are optimistic that philosophy departments will begin to devote chairs to Experimental Philosophy, they are less confident that the divide between the traditional and the experimental school will be successfully bridged. Some of our authors suspect that a change in opinion within philosophy will not be attainable through sophisticated arguments, though, but only by the continual retirement of traditional philosophers. Others are less pessimistic, but none of our contributors prophesied the dawning of a golden age for experimental approaches to philosophical questions. Nevertheless, many of our contributors revealed an adventurous attitude in response to the current situation. As one of our authors put it: 'Personally, I don't care that much about whether my work is categorized as philosophical or psychological. The only thing that matters is that the method – be it philosophical or psychological – fits to the research question.'

Name Index

289

Subject Index

Printed and bound in the United States of America